SHAW 4

---

continuing

The Shaw Review

Stanley Weintraub, *General Editor*

John R. Pfeiffer
Bibliographer

Rodelle Weintraub
Assistant Editor

Suzanne Wills
Editorial Assistant

Editorial Board: Elsie B. Adams, California State University, San Diego; Sidney P. Albert, California State University, Los Angeles (Emeritus); Charles A. Berst, University of California at Los Angeles; Bernard F. Dukore, University of Hawaii; Robert Chapman, Harvard University; Louis Crompton, University of Nebraska; Frederick P. W. McDowell, University of Iowa; Michael J. Mendelsohn, University of Tampa; Ann Saddlemyer, Graduate Center for Study of Drama, University of Toronto; Warren S. Smith, Pennsylvania State University (Emeritus); Barbara Bellow Watson, City University of New York; Jonathan L. Wisenthal, University of British Columbia.

SHAW

The Annual of Bernard Shaw Studies
Volume Four

Edited by

Stanley Weintraub

The Pennsylvania State University Press
University Park and London

ISBN 0-271-00366-9   ISSN 0741-5842

Note to contributors and subscribers. *SHAW*'s perspective is Bernard Shaw and his milieu—its personalities, works, relevance to his age and ours. As "his life, work, and friends"—the subtitle to a biography of G.B.S.—indicates, it is impossible to study the life, thought and work of a major literary figure in a vacuum. Issues and men, economics, politics, religion, theatre and literature and journalism—the entirety of the two half-centuries the life of G.B.S. spanned—was his assumed province. *SHAW*, published annually, welcomes articles that either explicitly or implicitly add to or alter our understanding of Shaw and his milieu. Address all communications concerning manuscript contributions (in 2 copies) to S234 Burrowes Building South, University Park, Pa. Unsolicited manuscripts are welcomed but will be returned only if return postage is provided. In matters of style *SHAW* recommends the *MLA Style Sheet*.

Contents

Ray Bradbury

SHAW/CHESTERTON:
TWO POEMS HARDLY LONGER
THAN THEIR TITLES

O' What I'd Give to Hear and See
Wry G.B.S., Spry G.K.C.

It isn't right, it isn't fair,
I never spoke with Shaw,
Or spent the day with old G.K.
To see what that man saw.
He glanced at Shaw and dubbed him Bosh,
As Bosh said Shaw to him;
So Chesterton and Shaw were pals
Who wrestled at a whim.

O, Lord, I'd love to have been there
When both took off and flew
From pulpit here to podium there,
Full arguing, those two,
With Shaw all Life-Force lecturing
From start to end of day.

"How can you love a vacuum, sir,"
Said wise fat old G.K.

"Attention, Chesterton," cried Shaw,
"Wake up, for here Shaw speaks!"

"Oh, Lord," said Chesterton, dismayed,
"This may drone on for weeks."

"No, months," barked Shaw, and tossed a laugh,
"Those angels on your pin

Are dancing multifold in mobs
Because you flew them in."

"Not I," puffed Chesterton, "not I;
God made those fairie things,
To celebrate the joys of life
When every churchbell rings."

"Your God," said Shaw, "is impotent,
Imprisoned in your laws;
I far prefer my Life-Force Beast
Who springs from Primal Cause."

"Drat Primal Cause," cried Chesterton,
"Go curb that Messy Pup;
He only barks in primal dark
Because God wound him up—
The cause *after* the Cause he is,
There's nothing more to speak!"

"A few more hours of argument,"
Cried Shaw, "will save my week!"

And so it goes, and so it went
G.B. and rare G.K.
We will not find their like again
Until the Judgment Day.
I fret on that, can hardly wait;
It's worth their game to die,
To sit with Shaw and Chesterton
A-bicker in the sky,
The thin one winning points at noon,
The fat one just at tea,
And no one dares to join their fight:
Not God, sweet Christ, nor me.

Behold the Beast: Shaw/Chesterton

Behold the beast: Shaw/Chesterton
Where is its head, its tail?
Does it have two brains, one a spare?
The answer makes God quail.

For when great God created them
And sent them forth with shout
He could not guess that they might guess
At what God seemed about.
Their arguments flashed round the world:
Some souls fled them to Hell,
While others found at Heaven's Gate
Sweet silence for a spell.

Yet on Shaw raved, and G.K., too,
No one could shut them up,
They argued back to Time's commence,
When Prime Cause was a Pup.
They charged down bloody centuries,
Left Christ at Galilee
Aflounder with their questionings
Of what His life might be.

So loudly rang their battle cries,
That Moses dashed his Laws,
And cried to skies, "Dear God above,
Quick, find some *Final* Cause.
Or sink them in the sumps of Hell
In ordure to their jaws!"

"No use!" cried God, "No use, no use!
For God to judge or speak,
No matter how I thunder-cried
They'd not pipe down all week!
They gunfire off my brightest Texts,
Tart Shaw, glib G.K.C.,
I'd gladly re-baptize the both,
And sink their souls at sea!
But that would me the Devil make;
I'll let them prattle on.
Perhaps in listening I'll find
Just what I meant that Dawn
When I said 'Light!' and all *was* Light
When I said: 'Firmament!'
What fancy shaped my birthing Words?
Shaw'll tell me what I meant.
And if Shaw silences himself
For even half one day,
I'll tune my ear to Chesterton
And lean on old G.K.

It's fascinating thus to hear—
I often stand in awe—
To hear his estimate of me
As he decants my Law.
There surely is no harm in it,
To eavesdrop on the roar
As Shaw and G.K. total Me,
And show God what He's for?
I may learn something in their fight,
Their mix of joy and pain;
If Shaw and Chesterton shout, 'Go!'
I just might start again.
But this time, using Primal Bang
To advertise my Laws,
No roustabouting Chestertons,
No sly, rambunctious Shaws!"

SHAW'S DRAMATIC CRITICISM IN
OUR CORNER, 1885–1886

From June 1885 through September 1886, Shaw received a few pounds a month from Annie Besant for a monthly "Art Corner" review of the concert halls, theaters, and galleries for her Socialist organ, Our Corner. *His fifteen reviews were sometimes miscellanies, sometimes considered and lengthy essays for which he did substantial preliminary homework. Nine contributions were either entirely or largely about drama or the theater. These are here reprinted, for the first time, complete.*

Not all of the dramatic reviews are inspired, and one is even a bit incoherent, perhaps a reflection of the quality of the work under review. Shaw found it difficult to rise to the occasion in reporting on a cheap melodrama, Human Nature, *that was intended as an audience pleaser. The November 1885 piece is as poor a job of writing as he ever permitted in print.*

Earlier, Shaw had reviewed Henry Arthur Jones's Hoodman Blind *(actually written by Jones in collaboration with Wilson Barrett, actor-manager at the Princess's Theatre), which had opened on 18 August 1885. It had succeeded a brief revival of the popular Jones melodrama* The Silver King, *which had a long run in 1882–83. In Shaw's diary he notes that he is writing a review of "*Hoodman Blind *and* Othello*"; as the review makes clear however, what he meant was that he was using the comparison to* Othello, *which some critics had made, as a lens by which to examine the far inferior new work. As tailpiece Shaw added his observations on G. W. Wills's* Olivia, *the latest vehicle for Henry Irving and his theater, the Lyceum. A decade later, Shaw the playwright would swallow his pride as theatrical craftsman and attempt to get his plays staged by writing one for each of the male principals in* Olivia, *Henry Irving and William Terriss. Irving, however, found his role in* The Man of Destiny *uncongenial, and Terriss was murdered by a disappointed job-seeker before he could appropriate* The Devil's Disciple.

Two additional plays by Jones would be noticed in the April 1886 Our Corner, *as the prolific pioneer of the New Drama interspersed courageous original writing with romantic claptrap that was easier to write and easier to sell. As usual, one was a collaboration with Wilson Barrett; without Barrett's name on the bill, it was difficult to use his theater.*

Additional melodrama—that staple of late-Victorian theater—would be reviewed by Shaw, grudgingly, in the August 1885 "Art Corner." One can see just how reluctant Shaw was to give such works any notice by the scant space devoted to them. His notice of Pinero's Money-Spinner *and even lesser fare takes up less than half the space he usually utilized.*

Yet Shaw was not totally down on Arthur Wing Pinero. When Pinero's Mayfair, *a competent adaptation from the French of Sardou, was taken off and his more original* Impulse *substituted, Shaw observed in the January 1886* Our Corner *that* Mayfair *was "thirty times better" than its successor—still, perhaps, not much of an accolade. But he went on to cite chapter and verse to make his point.*

Equal space was given that month to a non-commercial performance—one of Browning's verse drama Colombe's Birthday, *an ambitious effort of the Browning Society, of which Shaw was a stalwart. Yet his notice is not a puff: there is some useful analysis of the theatrical qualities of the work in print and in performance. As a Shelley Society member he would do the same for a Shelley closet-drama, noting in the June 1886 issue that the work had best remain henceforth in the closet.*

In another "Art Corner" essay Shaw describes the occasion for the production of Shelley's proscribed play The Cenci *and details the technicalities by which the Lord Chamberlain's censorship was legally evaded. As publicity director for the Shelley Society production, Shaw had an easy task of it. The notoriety of the work caused it to sell itself, and the demand for tickets exceeded the supply. However, at a Shelley Society meeting after the production, Shaw declared that aside from the historic element, the values of staging the work were minimal. In his opinion, according to the meeting transcript, "*The Cenci *was a play unworthy of the genius of Shelley. It was simply an abomination, an accumulation of horrors partaking of the nature of a* tour de force, *and probably written by Shelley merely to satisfy his ambition of producing something for the stage. He considered it as bad a piece of work as a man of Shelley's genius could be capable of, so bad indeed that it was hardly worth discussion. In his opinion excision would not remedy the fault of the play after the third act. . . . As a whole he thought the* Cenci *performance could not have been improved upon by the company of any London theatre."*

Before Shaw went to see W. G. Wills's adaptation of Goethe's Faust *(part one) "to Mr. Henry Irving's purposes" (for the March 1886 issue), he returned to the original text and read it through. Few dramatic critics have prepared so fully— especially for a stint of writing which would earn three or four pounds at best, as part of an omnibus essay which might also include mention of several art exhibitions and musical performances.* The real Faust, Shaw discovered, had been left out, and his substitute insured that the Wills Faust *"will sooner or later go the way of Garrick's and Cibber's adaptations of Shakspere's plays, or Kalkbrenner's version of* Don Giovanni. *The scenery partly compensates the spectator, though it by no means wholly indemnifies him, for the task of following the lines."*

The review of a student production of Love's Labour's Lost *(the consistent misspelling of the title in the essay is Shaw's, as he proofread his own piece) is one of Shaw's earliest considerations of Shakespeare (for whom he used an idiosyncratic spelling adopted by many in his day). It is also one of his least admiring glances at Shakespeare. But there was not much new art to notice nor music or theater to review in July, and Shaw's unenthusiastic reaction accurately reflected the performance.*

Shaw's review of the physically illustrated lecture on Delsartism by husband-and-wife disciples of the great man from America is tongue-in-cheek, yet Shaw recognized that there was real value in such formulas by which man, through his body, gives form to feeling. François Delsarte (1811–1871) never wrote a word (other than in letters) to preach his philosophy, but as singer and actor, and later as voice teacher, he set into motion a "Delsarte craze" that affected late-Victorian Aestheticism and altered, for decades, the way singing, acting, dance, and speech would be taught. His principles, which in his own lectures, he had called "a course in applied aesthetics," attracted a large group of admirers, Hector Berlioz and King Louis Phillipe among them. His last public appearances, at the Amphitheatre of Medicine in the Sorbonne in 1867, were packed, and press reports raised his "science of expression" to a near-religion. In America, actor-director Steele Mackaye, father of the playwright Percy Mackaye, had become Delsarte's chief missionary, resulting in the lecture tours of yet other Americans to propagate the gospel, which Mackaye termed "Harmonic Gymnastics." But Shaw, a disciple of Vandeleur Lee, was more interested in voice than in gesture.

The essay on Delsartism in the September 1886 issue was Shaw's last in the "Art Corner" series. He was actively reviewing art and literature elsewhere; he was busy lecturing to, and participating in, meetings both cultural and political; besides, his relations with Mrs. Besant were becoming strained as she wanted their affairs put on a more romantic footing than Shaw's other flirtations and involvements would allow. The regular appearances in Our Corner ended, but they would represent Shaw's most sustained trial run as a theater reviewer. Nine years later, as G.B.S. in Frank Harris's Saturday Review, he would become the leading dramatic critic of his generation. Here and there in these essays are explosions of wit and insight which foreshadow that future.

S.W.

Miss Hading and Mrs Kendal

At the theatres nothing very remarkable has occurred except the revival
of "Olivia," which has been dealt with at great length by the daily papers,
and the appearance of Madame Sarah Bernhardt here in Sardou's
"Théodora." She was preceded by the Gymnase Company, whose performance of Ohnet's "Maître de Forges" was made interesting by the
acting of Madame Jane Hading in a part that has been played in London
by Miss Ada Cavendish and Mrs Kendal. "Le Maître de Forges" is not a
good play—not to be compared with Mr Robert Buchanan's version entitled "Lady Claire." Claire, the heroine, married Philippe Derblay to
spite the Duc de Bligny, who had jilted her. When Philippe discovers
that his wife loathes him instead of loving him, he tells her that some
day he will see her at his feet, imploring his pardon, and longing vainly
for a word of pity for him. This settles his pretensions to be a hero as
far as the audience is concerned; but Claire admires him for it; falls in
love with him; and enables him to fulfill his spiteful threat to his heart's
content. There is little scope for genuine acting in the piece; but it presents many opportunities for emotional display. The impression left by
the whole performance was that Madame Jane Hading is an interesting
and attractive woman, and that one would like to see her in a good play,
in order to ascertain whether she can really act or not. M. Damala, who
impersonated the sham hero Philippe, is an actor of considerable natural force and dignity; and the skill with which he moves and speaks only
needs to have the evidences of study worn off it to entitle him to be
considered an adept in his own line. The remaining parts were all well
played; M. Saint Germain achieving the feat of amusing an English audience by a vocal peculiarity which prevented most of them from understanding what he was saying.

Mrs Kendal has been playing with consummate skill in Mr Pinero's
"Money Spinner," a clever comedy which interests the audience until the
curtain descends, when they go away rather disagreeably affected by the
glimpse they have had of the household of a dishonest clerk married to
a gambler's decoy, watched by a detective who is the most respectable
character in the play, and visited by his father-in-law, an old gambling
saloon keeper, who has retired from his profession in order to marry his
remaining daughter to a foolish Scotch lord, who avowedly accepts her
only because she occasionally reminds him of her married sister, his real
love. Baron Croodle, with his brandy flask, and his opinion that "to eat
without drinking is a dog-like and revolting habit," is the only tolerable
person introduced, because he is the only one that does not claim more

sympathy than he deserves. After acting such a detestable character as Millicent Boycott, Mrs Kendal cannot again be accused of prudery as to the morals of the heroines she represents. An afterpiece entitled "Castaways," by Theyre Smith, the author of "Uncle's Will," serves only to waste the time of the audience and the talent of Mrs Kendal.

August 1885

Hoodman Blind and *Othello*

"Hoodman Blind," the new play by Mr Henry A. Jones, which has succeeded the "Silver King" at the Princess's Theatre, is inferior to it in interest; and the illusion produced by the performance is much weaker. The story, which has been compared with that of "Othello," but which is at least as like that of the "Comedy of Errors," is of the jealousy of a young farmer who, misled by a strong personal resemblance, mistakes what is called in the playbill "a waif" for his wife, and is confirmed in his error by a villain. Unlike "Othello," however, "Hoodman Blind" has not only a story, but also that dramatic cancer, a plot. There is no plot in "Othello." As we cannot know a man's character until we have seen him tried by circumstances, a set of circumstances are provided for the exhibition of the characters in Shakspere's tragedy. But Desdemona does not in the last act turn out to be Bianca's half-sister, and heiress to a large fortune left by Brabantio. Emilia does not interrupt her death-speech to inform Iago that Roderigo was their child, stolen in infancy by gipsies under circumstances known only to Cassio under seal of an oath of secrecy. Nor do the Cypriote police arrest Iago on a charge of having strangled Brabantio in order to obtain possession of a bond for forty thousand pounds, payable by the Turkish tourist at whose expense Othello so officiously displayed his mercenary patriotism at Aleppo. "Hoodman Blind" is full of this kind of childish make-believe, to make room for which the action of the drama is distorted, irrelevant and disagreeable incidents are introduced, and the spectators are pestered by suppressed wills, long lost relatives, documents hidden in safes, and other matters of no interest to them. As Mr Jones's name is coupled, as usual, with that of a collaborator, he may not be wholly responsible for the ill-judged plot-machinery; but the dialogue is evidently his; and this leaves him responsible for some "sentiments" which have been deliberately written down to the silliest level of British cant in order to please the gallery,

and which are the most reprehensible feature of the drama. In spite of
these blemishes, there is enough power shown in the play to sustain the
reputation which Mr Jones founded by the "Silver King." Like that play,
"Hoodman Blind" contains many minor parts which are easy to act well,
and effective when well acted. The leading parts are far less happily
contrived. Mr Jones has not done his best for either Mr Willard or Mr
Wilson Barrett; and they have revenged themselves by ill-treating their
opportunities. Mr Wilson Barrett's acting is shallow and monotonous
throughout. There is no reticence in his manner, and no variety in his
elocution. Before the play is half over his presence on the stage becomes
an affliction; and the scenes in which he does not appear assert themselves as the redeeming points in the play. It is but fair to add that this
is partly the author's fault. Jack Yeulett, the hero, was evidently not intended to appear anything worse than a very hotheaded young farmer—
a manly fellow in the main. But he is so ill-tempered, so vindictive, and
so atrociously inconsiderate even when he is not in a rage, that he only
needs to have the offensive side of his character accentuated to become
intolerably disagreeable. This accentuation is the only effect produced
by Mr Wilson Barrett's acting. Mr Willard's failure is more extraordinary. If his part were that of a righteous man in sore trouble, his acting
would be a little triumph in its way. But Mark Lezzard, as created by Mr
Jones, is a most sordid scoundrel. Consequently Mr Willard's grief-stricken
face, and his voice softened and saddened by emotion, are beside the
mark: they only suggest that he fancies himself the Silver King, and that
he would make a capital substitute for Mr Wilson Barrett in that part.
One result of this has been that the retribution which overtakes Mark in
the last act so revolted the audience on the first night that the scene had
to be modified at the subsequent representations. Fortunately for Mr
Willard, his acting, inappropriate as it is, is so clever and effective that
his performance has been greatly admired and praised; and his share
of the incongruity of the last act has been visited upon Mr Jones. The
best part in the play, and one of the best acted, is Chibbles the black-
smith, by Mr George Barrett. His speech at his wedding supper, where,
in a desperate attempt to make light of his marriage, he blunders into
assuring the company that he has no particular affection for his bride,
is the best stroke of comedy the piece contains; and it is the more keenly
relished for occurring in the only scene in which there is a momentary
relief from that pervading nuisance, the plot. Artistic honors, as far as
the male characters are concerned, are divided between Mr George Barrett and Mr Charles Hudson, who plays the small part of the gipsy. It is
interesting to see Miss Eastlake, as Nance the farmer's wife and Jess the
waif, alternately playing at two different levels of habit and education.
Both parts are easily within her powers. Her greatest effect is made in a

scene in a public house, where Jess, worn out by illness, finds her lover with his arms about the neck of another woman, and makes a heartbroken effort to eclipse her rival's gaiety by attempting to dance.

The performances of Mr G. W. Wills's "Olivia" were resumed at the Lyceum Theatre on the 3rd September. The redecoration of the house during the recess by Mr Phipps seems to indicate a reaction against the prevailing system of excluding the draughtsman from the auditorium, and merely setting the upholsterer and the paint-pot man to tint the lines of the building. The change is only partly successful. The ceiling, covered with a design of medallions and arabesques in the manner of the famous decoration of the Vatican *loggie* by Raffaello and Giovanni da Udine, is admirable, as is the design after Baldassare Peruzzi on the panels of the dress circle. But the other circles are colored too garishly; the ceiling is marred by the chandelier and the centre piece from which it descends; and there is an excess of detail on too small a scale for the size of the theatre. The alteration is nevertheless in the right direction. The very worst ceiling that can result from the exercise of an artist's intelligence is likely to be better than a roof which seems like an ottoman upholstered in old gold brocade, and turned upside down over the British public.

The acting at the Lyceum unfortunately needs looking after more than the house did. Taking into account the representative position of the theatre, it is not too much to say that the playing of the minor parts in "Olivia" is deplorable. Moses is unnatural without being in the least amusing: Messrs Howe and Wenman, as Flamborough and Burchell, are perfunctory to an inexcusable degree. Mrs Primrose, as represented by Miss L. Payne, is an undignified shrew who occasionally becomes ridiculous. Miss Winifred Emery, as Sophia, does her best, and her best is very fair; but her pains are heavily discounted by Mr Winman's mannerism, which seems to have even less thought than usual behind it, and by the burlesque of Mr Norman Forbes and Miss L. Payne. Judged even as burlesque, Mr Norman Forbes's Moses would appear crude even at the Gaiety or Toole's. "Olivia" is no longer the play that charmed London years ago at the Court Theatre. Mr Irving's make-up as the Vicar is capital; and his playing in the second act is not only remarkable—Mr Irving's acting is always that—but excellently to the purpose of acting. Nevertheless, he elsewhere sets the example of burlesque which some of his colleagues have followed: and the total effect of his impersonation is less than that made by Mr Hermann Vezin in the same part. Miss Ellen Terry tries very hard to reproduce her old Olivia; but the very effort does away with the apparent spontaneity that was once so fascinating. It is inevitable that her representation of the dawn of womanhood should be a little more artificial than it was; but there is no valid reason why such memorable points in the old Court performance as the glimpse of Olivia's face as she passes the window in her flight should be replaced by the monstrous improbability of her opening the lattice widely and kissing her hand several times to her father. Playgoers who have never seen Miss Terry in this part should not lose the opportunity of doing so; but those who have tender recollections of the original Olivia will do well to keep away from the Lyceum. The spectacle of Miss Terry imitating herself, and overdoing it, would not compensate them for the disappointments which they would suffer in the course of the play. Mr Terriss alone repeats his first success without abatement. His appearance and manner suit the part so happily that he has only to be his external self (the only part for which Mr Terriss has yet shown any marked aptitude) to be Squire Thornhill to the life. At the conclusion of the performance Mr Irving made a brief speech. He did not say that his company were doing what they could to bring the run of "Olivia" to an end; but he promised that it should be succeeded by Mr Wills's "Faust," with Mrs Stirling in the cast.

October 1885

Human Nature and Excelsior

A new drama by Henry Pettitt and Augustus Harris was produced at Drury Lane Theatre on the 12th September. It is entitled "Human Nature," of which, in its [their?] willingness to applaud plays in which it [human nature] has no part, the authors have taken considerable advantage. A fiendish Frenchman, whom the audience succeeded in identifying with the late M. Olivier Pain,* succeeds by plot and perjury in wrecking an English officer's home, and divorcing [him from] his wife. An equally diabolical lawyer has been left £20,000 by somebody on condi-

---

*Olivier Pain, journalist, was born Olivier Troyes in 1845. After participating in the 1870 Commune in Paris he was deported to a penal colony on New Caledonia, from which he made a dramatic escape, with the Marquis de Rochefort, in a small boat. He became *persona grata* in France again after the 1880 amnesty, his flight from Nouméa even being painted by Edouard Manet. As a war correspondent he flamboyantly covered the Russian-Turkish conflict and British operations in Egypt and in the Sudan against the Mahdi. He died in the Sudan in 1885.

tion that the officer's little son does not grow to manhood. The play shows us on the one hand the officer out in the Soudan capturing a city in the desert—popularly supposed to be Khartoum—and finding there the perfidious Frenchman, who dies confessing his guilt; and on the other, the despairing mother flying through England with her child [while fleeing] from the ogreish lawyer. Eventually all the disagreeable people are removed in custody, and husband and wife are reunited. The story is pleasantly diversified by a lady who calls herself Cora, lives in a villa, and smokes cigarettes. She is therefore reprobated in Drury Lane as a person patently abandoned, and when her husband turns up in the last act and fusillades her with a revolver, it is felt that the highest claims of poetic justice have been satisfied. Miss Isabel Bateman, as the hunted mother, surprised the audience with a performance no less striking than the famous Leah of her sister Mrs Crowe. Mr Fred Thorne's Lambkin the baby farmer is a capital study of brutal ruffianism in a dull, middle aged phase. Mr Harry Nicholls is very funny as Horatio Spofkins, a lawyer's clerk with a taste for rhyming. Miss Lizzie Claremont's Mrs Lambkin is a repulsive piece of realism. The talent of no less than thirteen gentlemen and nine ladies finds employment in the play; but only the four already mentioned can be said to distinguish themselves. The other leading parts are played by Miss Ormsby, Miss Illington, Miss Katie Barry, Miss Amy McNeil, Messrs Henry Neville, [Leo] Leather, J. G. Grahame, and J. H. Clynds.

A determined attempt is being made at Her Majesty's Theatre to accustom the British public to the Italian three-act *ballet d'action*. "Excelsior" has now been played nearly a hundred and thirty times, and it certainly does not disappoint those who are curious enough to see it. The music is, of its kind, excellent; and the dancing, in which a considerable body of men and children are employed, is graceful and spirited. The action, which illustrates the progress of steam, electricity, and engineering enterprise, is interesting and amusing; and there is not a single dance, group, or scene, in which the personal attractions of the female performers are relied on to please the audience. A bishop might, in pursuance of Mr Stewart Headlam's advice, witness "Excelsior" without a misgiving as to the perfect good faith both of the performers and the spectators in the purely artistic character of the entertainment. The ample stage room at Her Majesty's, and the combinations of bright positive colors, thoroughly Italian in taste, produced an effect which is very cheerful and almost classic in its refinement and simplicity. Under Mr [Charles] Hawtrey's management the ballet has been supplemented by Planche's "Secret Service," in which Mr Herman Vezin is supported by Mr Frank Archer and Mr Arthur Dacre. Miss Kate Vaughan now appears in the second act of "Excelsior," and gains what her Italian colleagues must think rather cheap applause by her dancing of a feeble waltz by Signor Tosti.

November 1885

Pinero and Browning

The managers of the St James's Theatre have withdrawn Mr Pinero's "Mayfair," and substituted "Impulse." This indicates a pretty state of things. "Mayfair," an adaptation of Sardou's *Maison Neuve*, is about thirty times as good a play as "Impulse," and provides a correspondingly greater scope for the highest powers of the St James's company. The morality of "Impulse" is the morality of Mr Pecksniff. In one scene, an elderly British husband, catching his wife in the act of eloping with a Frenchman, gives her a sermon on her duties to her lord and master, which is a stronger indirect incitement to revolt against the institution of the family than a dozen *Palais Royal* farces. The play became popular because the spectacle of Mr Kendal following his wife about the stage, and idiotically repeating the formula "You *are*: you really *are*," somehow tickled the public. The play, on the whole, was rather amusing. It contained nothing deep enough to puzzle even a downright fool; and it did not disparage the West End. Now Mr Pinero, in "Mayfair," not only disparaged the West End, but attacked it directly and bitterly by exhibiting society as a tedious fraud. Society accordingly fled from the stalls; and to lure it back again Mr Kendal has had to suppress Mr Pinero, and to resume his assurances to Mrs Kendal that she is—she really is. The hero of "Mayfair" is a prosperous elderly stockbroker, who lives in an old fashioned house in Bloomsbury, and declines to do speculative business. He proposes to take into partnership his nephew, a young stockbroker with a pretty and ambitious wife. The nephew, in a hurry to be rich, hankers after speculative business; is ashamed of living so far East as Bloomsbury; and secretly considers his uncle an old stick-in-the-mud (a compound epithet much used at present to describe a conscientious person). His wife is equally base in her aspirations, and is delighted when he tells her that he has secretly taken and furnished a house in Mayfair. But they are afraid to tell Uncle Nicholas; and the selfishness and cowardice with which, impatient to be in their new house, and not daring to face the unpleasantness of an explanation, they slip away from the Bloomsbury mansion at a moment when their desertion most wounds and disappoints the old man, are mercilessly emphasized. Mr Pinero has been blamed for not softening this point; but he could not have done so without spoiling the first act, and stultifying himself as a translator of M. Sardou. It is to be feared that the complainants saw nothing vile in the aspirations of Jeff and Agnes, and were therefore unable to see the consistency of their stupid cruelty. The rest of the play deals with the attainment of the paltry ambition of the young couple; the sort of friends they gain by their lavish expenditure; the entanglement of the weak husband in an intrigue with an adventuress who blackmails him; his wife's discovery of his faithlessness, and her characteristic revenge by inviting another man to degrade her; the collapse of Jeff's speculative stockbroking; and the rescue of the pair from the consequences of their folly by honest Uncle Nick. All this is as much to the point in London to-day as *Maison Neuve* was in 1867 in Paris under the *régime* of Napoleon III and Hausmann. Mr Pinero might perhaps have made the social contrast clearer by substituting for Bloomsbury one of the northern or eastern suburbs in which our old-fashioned city people dwell; for Russell Square is hardly so outlandish as a foreigner might infer it to be from witnessing a performance of "Mayfair." But this does not seriously interfere with the effect of the play, which is interesting and witty all through its five acts. Mrs Kendal has acquired a few tricks lately which occasionally betray the unreality of her impersonations in the lighter scenes; but when she is thoroughly in earnest she displays a surer command than she has ever before attained of the varied resources she has developed so highly. Mr Brookfield's counterfeit of a broken man-about-town could not be bettered. Mr Hare, as the old stockbroker, divides with Mr Brookfield the artistic honors that fall to the men. Miss Linda Dietz, as a French maid, is relieved for a while from the sentimental aspect in which she is usually condemned to appear; and she makes the most of the opportunity. The other parts are satisfactorily played with the important exception of Lord Sulgrave, who, as enacted by Mr Cartwright, does not fit into his place. Mr Cartwright does his best; but the part does not suit him, and the third and fourth acts suffer in consequence.

A very remarkable performance of one of Robert Browning's plays, "Colombe's Birthday," took place at St George's Hall on the 19th November. It was announced as "the fifth annual entertainment of the Browning Society." When it is proposed to put a work of Mr Browning's on the stage, doubts arise not so much as to the quality of the play as to the quality of the audience. The safe and usual course in theatres is to present the public with nothing above the mental capacity of children, although the incidents may be beyond childish experience. The result of this is that serious people, as a class, do not go to the theatre. When the manager declares that "the public" will not have this, that, or the other, he means that frivolous people will not have them. Point out to him that earnest people will have them, and prefer them, and he can reply that earnest people never think of coming to his theatre; and that, if they did, there are not enough of them to keep a play running sufficiently long to pay for the initial expenditure on dresses and scenery. Much of that expenditure is, however, in itself a concession to frivolity. Again, the ordinary play has its run of so many hundred nights, after which it dies, and its dresses and scenery are of no further use. But "Hamlet" has enjoyed an intermittent run of nearly three hundred years: it wears out its wardrobes and its scenery. And it does not wear out its audiences. The same man will go again and again to see "Hamlet"; but no reasonable man goes twice to a "popular" piece unless he happens to fall in love with one of the actresses, in which case he is, for the time, unreasonable. Earnest people—earnest enough, at least, to prefer "Colombe's Birthday" to a Gaiety burlesque—are not so scarce as the managers suppose. Enough of them could easily be lured back into the habit of playgoing to support at least one theatre, which would raise the standard of dramatic art to be a school for actors as well. It pays to issue shilling reprints of deep and weighty classics, enormous numbers of which are sold in London alone. At lectures and public meetings crowds of citizens sit out appallingly tedious orations in the hope of improving their minds. Yet the managers tell us that the public will not stand long speeches. That is all the managers know about it. If they can persuade the public that theatregoing is not a waste of valuable time, and that as much can be learned by listening to a play as by reading a book, they will find that they have hitherto been taking a great deal of trouble to please the wrong people and to keep away the right people. The masterpieces of English dramatic poetry are surely not less likely to be appreciated than the masterpieces of classical music. Mr Browning's "In a Balcony" would not recommend itself to Mr Charles Wyndham for the subject of his next enterprise at the Criterion Theatre; but it is much more popular than one of Beethoven's posthumous quartets. Yet these draw to St James's Hall people who are as unmistakeably the intelligent public, as the majority of the frequenters of our theatres are unmistakeably the silly or half-educated public. Let the managers go to the Monday Popular Concerts; consider their ways; and be wise.

"Colombe's Birthday" proved more interesting in action than even Browning enthusiasts expected. The truth of the study of courtier nature in the group of envious timeservers who constitute the Duchess's court is amply verified by the numerous court memoirs with which retired palace lackeys from time to time favor us. It supplies just the necessary background to Guibert, the marshal, who cynically professes himself a Machiavellian scoundrel, but who invariably acts, when put to the proof, upon honorable and generous impulses. The position of the Duchess between the ambitious prince who courts her from political motives, but will not simulate a passion he does not feel, and the poor advocate who has failed somewhat ignominiously to conceal his apparently desperate love for her, is more interesting as Browning has treated it than any conventional dramatist could have made it. The relief given to the ear of the jaded theatre-goer by the pregnant and pointed verse was beyond description. The acting proved that we have still material for a company of players capable of restoring dramatic poetry to the stage. Miss Alma Murray played Colombe quite satisfactorily, which is equivalent to saying that she achieved an arduous feat in the highest department of her profession. Mr Leonard Outram did very well as Valence. The other gentlemen only require more practice in the class of work required, to qualify them thoroughly for it. The impression made by the performance was so favorable that the Browning Society was greatly pleased with itself; and Dr Furnivall, in a speech between the first and second acts, promised a representation of "Strafford" for next year, possibly at the Lyceum Theatre.

January 1886

The Lyceum *Faust*

"The Lyceum Faust," as Mr W. G. Wills's "adaptation" of the first part of Goethe's tragedy to Mr Henry Irving's purposes is now commonly called, is very unsatisfactory. To save it from intolerable tediousness, the dialogue has been pared to the slenderest possible thread. Although the curtain is up for only two hours and eighteen minutes, there are eleven scenes; so that there is, on an average, something new to look at every eleven-and-a-half minutes, without counting the changes of light, the eruptions of subterranean fire, the visions, the apotheosis, the flights of witches on broomsticks, the incandescent rain on the red-hot mountain at the sabbat, and the magic wreaths of mist that proceed from a copper of boiling water beneath the stage near the right upper entrance. Of the illusion thus laboriously produced, about nine-tenths is destroyed by the acting and dialogue. Goethe's tragedy requires two actors of the highest class, the better of the pair to play Faust, and the other to play the easier part of Mephistopheles. Faust and Mephistopheles are a dual present-ment of one character: the play is a one-part play; but the one person-ality has been decomposed by the author into what is popularly called its own good and evil angel, and so it has to be impersonated by two men. And unless there be a certain equation of power in these men, and a certain reflection of the one in the other, there can be no credible Faust. When a popular actor selects Mephistopheles as a show part, and engages a walking gentleman to speak as many of Faust's lines as cannot well be left out, he courts failure and shows that he is not the man to grapple with Goethe. Mr Irving is not the first actor-manager who has been seduced into this error by the fascination of the scarlet coat and cock's feather of the fiend, in spite of the verdict on such attempts hav-ing always been that Goethe's masterpiece is not interesting on the stage. That verdict will never be set aside by any attempt to present "Faust" with the part of Faust left out. In the Lyceum version, the philosopher is our old friend of Gounod's opera, a senile pedant changed into a sentimental fop: his age overdone in the first phase, his youth in the second. As he sneaks irresolutely after the fiend, who bullies him, and threatens to tear him to pieces, and scatter his blood like rain on the blast, there is not a gleam in him of the Faust of whom Mephistopheles speaks as "*der mir so kräftig widerstand.*" The relations of Faust and Mar-garet are absurdly reversed. Instead of the philosopher and the maiden, we have a refined and sensible woman, and an unripe youth whose pas-sion for her is developing him into a dissolute young spark. The Mephistopheles is little more than the operatic Mephistopheles, a gro-tesque person posing in red limelight, and collapsing when a cross is flourished in his face. Mr Irving presents him as a malicious sorcerer with certain monstrous mental deficiencies, walking the earth with the awkward strut of a creature made only to perch and fly. He inspires disgust rather than interest and awe, as if he were obviously and contin-ually the "abortion of fire and filth" that Faust sees in him in a moment of revulsion against his pessimism. Mr Irving seems to have forgotten that the same Mephistopheles who terrified and repelled poor Margaret because he was proof against the limited scale of simple emotions which was to her the whole of human feeling, was yet so genial in his inter-course with higher intelligences that Faust never became quite con-vinced that his companionship was an unmixed evil. God Omniscient himself confessed to enjoying an occasional chat with him, and declared that without him human virtue would stagnate. Mephistopheles, as an eternal spirit, is incapable of temporal compromises, and absolutely in-different to the death or the particular form of suffering endured by any mortal individual. To ordinary intelligences he therefore appears in emergencies as a monster devoid of pity, love, or fear. But he has interests and even passions to serve: they are the motive for his activity among men. He takes care to make himself agreeable, padding his cloven hoof with a false calf, and dressing himself sprucely. The Prince of Darkness becomes thus an interesting and accomplished gentleman in his intercourse with human society. Mr Irving's devil is an unpresentable person, slow, deadly, sour, and sardonic in his graver moments, but dropping at other times into the manner of the eminent tragedian's impersonation of Alfred Jingle. We get occasional glimpses of the mediaeval Satan; but they are few and far between. The scenes of purely mundane comedy with Martha are the best in the play, thanks to Mrs Stirling, whose acting is better than that of any of her colleagues, male or female. Miss Terry's Margaret is in no way memorable or remarkable, though one or two points in it suggest that with a thoroughly congenial opportunity she may, when freed from the unfavorable artistic conditions of the Lyceum Theatre, again do something to justify her great reputation. Mr Wills's part of the business has been badly done. He has flattened out the animated rhythms and rhymed endings of Goethe's pregnant lines into blank verse that is poor in ideas and commonplace in expression. As may be imagined, the altered verse-form spoils the utterances of Margaret, Mephistopheles, and Valentine. The extensive omissions may not be Mr Wills's fault, as the pruning-knife has been freely used since the manager discovered that the audience could not possibly have too little dialogue to please them. But the dilution of what is retained, and the changes and additions, are clearly the work of the "adapter and arranger." Even the prison scene, a page of dramatic literature which even Ducis would have refrained from meddling with, has been hacked and cooked in such a fashion that the interest declines steadily from the first line to the last. Though the alterations, measured by a compositor's rule, are small, they are, as Mercutio says of his wound, "enough." Mr Wills's "arrangement" will sooner or later go the way of Garrick's and Cibber's adaptations of Shakspere's plays, or Kalkbrenner's version of "Don Giovanni." The scenery partly compensates the spectator, though it by no means wholly indemnifies him, for the task of following the lines. The music presents no novelty (except that Mr Irving actually sings the serenade); and the orchestra is of fair quality, though feeble. Lindpaintner's old-fashioned overture is played before the rising of the curtain. It might be replaced with advantage by Gounod's beautiful prelude, which is better suited to a small orchestra than any of the works to which Mr Meredith Ball's choice is limited by the subject.

March 1886

Two by Henry Arthur Jones

Two new plays by Mr H. A. Jones have been produced lately, and are still running. One, a comedietta entitled "Bed of Roses," serves as "curtain raiser" at the St James's Theatre. The other is "The Lord Harry," described in the playbill as "an entirely New and Original Romantic Play in Five Acts, by Henry Arthur Jones and Wilson Barrett." It is not, however, either new or original enough to bring anything more serious in question than the curious law of collaboration imposed upon dramatic authors at the Princess's Theatre. Apparently no play is accepted there unless somebody officially connected with the establishment has favored the dramatist with enough more or less judicious advice and more or less skilled assistance, to justify the insertion of his name in the programme as joint author. If this law may not be abrogated, it should be furnished with a clause excluding actors from collaboration. The temptation to insist as much as possible on their own parts is too likely to corrupt them as playwrights, forced as they are into perpetual self-assertion by the struggle for existence. Stage managers and scene painters should also be forbidden to bear on the play during its artistic growth. Not even the call boy or the check taker should be trusted; for the first might be tempted to arrange the exits and entrances with a view to saving himself trouble rather than to perfecting the balance of the scenes; and the second might too easily make his post a sinecure by damaging the play to such an extent that no one could be induced to witness its performance. If someone connected with the theatre must collaborate, let him be the fireman, whose duties are invariable whether the play be good or bad. "The Lord Harry" is a flimsy play in comparison with "Hoodman Blind"; but it is much more agreeable. "Upon the tented field, and where castles mounted stand," we spend the hours more pleasantly than we did among the sanctimonious rustics of Abbots Creslow, and the waterside refuse of London. Mr Wilson Barrett swaggers for God and King Charles. Mr Willard, the sticking-plaster gaps in whose front teeth gave a horrible jaggedness to his malicious smiles, is for the Parliament; though it soon appears that he is merely backing the winner, and is quite ready to change sides as the fortunes of war fluctuate. Miss Eastlake is the daughter of a Roundhead colonel; and of course she and Mr Wilson Barrett fall in love with one another. Duels, threats of the rack, sentences of death, the condemned in prison visited by his beloved, escapes, treacheries, faithful servants, alarums, and excursions, relieve the wordiness of the persons concerned: the Lord Harry having a turn for description, and the colonel and his daughter being adepts at extemporaneous prayer. In the thrilling scene of the rising flood, Miss Eastlake all but raises a laugh by beginning, as she clings to a chimney stack, and looks in vain for a boat, "Oh thou, that walkedst on the waters," etc. The sole superiority of "The Lord Harry" to Mr Jones's previous works consists in its almost complete freedom from the incubus of a plot. Signs are not wanting in it that to be collaborated with by Mr Wilson Barrett means, in effect, to be crippled and stultified by the limited aims and personal interest of an actor-manager, who can act better than he can write, and who can manage much better than he can act. Perhaps the fact that "The Lord Harry" has had a narrow escape from failure, may induce Mr Wilson Barrett to allow dramatic authors the same independence in their own department as he doubtless claims for himself in his. Of the acting little need be said. Mr Charles Coote's Shekeniah Pank, a minor comic part, is the most thorough feat of impersonation in the performance. Miss Eastlake plays very well: so do Miss Lottie Venne and Mr Willard. Mr Clynds applies his academic method to the part of Col. Breane with his usual steadiness, and emphasizes by contrast the want of method in Mr Wilson Barrett's more imaginative, but unconvincing attempt to play the dashing cavalier. A stage battle, a flood, and a coast scene, at the ends of the third, fourth, and fifth acts respectively, are important factors in the success of the drama.

At the St James's Theatre, "Antoinette Rigaud," translated by Ernest Warren from the French of M. Deslandes, is preceded nightly by "A Bed of Roses." In this little play, Mr Jones, not having had to provide Mr Wilson Barrett with a part, acquits himself far more featly than in his vast works for the Princess's. The plan of the piece is slight and familiar. A couple of pairs of sweethearts are crossed in love for a while by a crusty old stage father, who soon winds up the business with the customary "Take her, Charles," which has superseded the old fashioned "Bless you, my children. May you be happy." Miss Webster, who is thrown away as a "walking lady" in "Antoinette Rigaud," finds some worthier employment in the part of Dora Vallacott. Her recent exploit as the Maiden Queen in the performance by the Dramatic Students of Dryden's "Secret Love," has drawn due attention to her development from a stiff, joyless, laborious apprentice, into an accomplished actress of serious parts. Only in representing lightheartedness are any traces of the heaviness of her novitiate now perceptible. In the pathetic passages of Mr Jones's comedietta, her acting was remarkably truthful and in the nicest taste.

"Antoinette Rigaud" is a string of tolerably interesting scenes, brought about on impossible pretexts. Mr Warren, the translator, has a bad ear for dialogue: he makes his characters converse, even at emotional crises, in the artificial periods of essayists and historians. "Filled with vague alarm, I hastened to her room," says General de Préfond. "Trembling and breathless I lay, not daring to stir," says his daughter Marie. Mr Warren may consider, like the novelists of last century, that these inversions impart style to the remarks of his characters; but none—not even a professed pedant—ever did or ever will talk so in real life under the influence of emotion. Antoinette Rigaud is married to a jolly but jealous man of business. An artist, to whom she has written some compromising letters, meets her at General de Préfond's. She asks him to give up the letters; and he does so with such scrupulous haste that instead of waiting until morning to hand them to her safely at the railway station on her departure, he breaks into the general's house at night, and presents himself in Antoinette's room. Whilst he is there, her husband unexpectedly arrives, making nothing of paying a midnight visit at the house of his friend the General. There is a terrible to-do to hide Sannoy (the artist) and get him off the premises unknown to Rigaud. At last he manages to slip out of Antoinette's chamber, but only to blunder into the bedroom of the General's daughter, and scare her almost out of her senses. He then gets through the window; tears away the roses from the wall; tramples the flower bed beneath; drops a medallion portrait of Antoinette; and makes off, leaving behind him much circumstantial evidence of his escapade. Next morning Antoinette's brother is accused of having broken into the room of Marie de Préfond, with whom he is admittedly in love; and he, suspecting the truth, saves Antoinette's honor by pleading guilty. The exasperated General is about to eject him from the premises when Antoinette confesses her folly. The General promptly produces his daughter and says, "Take her, Henri." The jealous husband is apparently satisfied without receiving any explanation of this change of front; and the curtain descends on domestic bliss. The play requires for its acceptance rather more make-believe than a Briton of average incredulity can afford; but it is saved from failure by the acting of Mrs Kendal as Antoinette, Mr Hare as General de Préfond, and Mr Barnes as Rigaud. Mr Kendal as Henri, the scapegoat, plays so much more in sorrow than in anger—which is just the reverse of what might be expected—that he becomes too lachrymose for robust tastes. Miss Linda Dietz's impersonation of Marie, the *ingénue*, is clever; and Mr Hendrie hits off the maritally disposed stockbroker very happily. But the weight of the play falls on Mrs Kendal, who begins badly by depending on a few effective mannerisms for the lighter phases of her part, but who addresses herself to the subsequent serious business with extraordinary variety and subtlety, reading whole chapters of psychology into the play between the lines. Her powers are deplorably wasted on the repertory of the St James's Theatre.

April 1886

Shelley's *The Cenci*

The most remarkable event of last month with which I have any concern in this Corner is the performance of Shelley's tragedy, "The Cenci," for the first time during the sixty-seven years which have elapsed since it was published in 1819. The Censor forbade the representation; and the Shelley Society could therefore do no more than engage a large theatre—the Grand at Islington—and have their play in strict technical privacy, which in this case meant in the presence of a crowded audience who were only distinguished from other audiences by the fact that they had not paid for their seats at the doors in the usual way. That tickets may, nevertheless, have changed hands for money is quite possible: I am myself a member of the Shelley Society; I received applications from people desirous of purchasing my tickets; and it was certainly not any sentiment of loyalty to the Lord Chamberlain that restrained me from meeting their wishes. The official license was withheld on the ground that the performance of such a play would deprave the public. Yet the play has been performed; its attractions have been supplemented by the presence of a number of celebrated persons in the auditorium; and as many people as the theatre could hold have been not only admitted for nothing, but invited and personally welcomed. So far, the anticipated depravation of the public seems not to have come off; for the conduct of the nation has not perceptibly altered for the worse since the afternoon of Friday, the 7th of May, 1886; whilst the attempt to drive theatregoers from the performance of the Shelley Society to such licensed alternatives as the Criterion Theatre, for example, has so accentuated the anomaly, folly, and hypocrisy of the censorship as to strengthen the hope that the institution may soon be as extinct as the Star Chamber, to which, in point of obnoxiousness to all accredited political principle, it is exactly similar.

A performance of "The Cenci" must have come sooner or later, because Shelley, although he rushed into print before he was ripe for it, and often disgraced himself by doing very ordinary literary jobs in an unworkmanlike way, is yet, with the exception—under certain limitations—of Shakspere, the greatest of English poets; and "The Cenci" is the only work which he wrote with a view to actual representation on the stage. In indulging his whim to produce something in the obsolete and absurd form which Shakspere had done so much with, Shelley no doubt believed that he was engaged upon a solid and permanent composition. In reality he was only experimenting to find a suitable form for his efforts to "teach the human heart, through its sympathies and antipathies, the knowledge that every human being is wise, just, sincere, tolerant, and kind." This, he says, is the purpose of "the highest species of drama"; and it seems to me that such purpose makes all the difference between the writer of fiction and the ordinary imaginative liar. However that may be, Shelley, groping for the scientific drama which is yet in the future, and which alone could have reconciled his philosophic craving for truth to the unrealities of the stage, certainly got hold of the wrong vehicle when he chose the five-act tragedy in blank verse which had sufficed for [Thomas] Otway and Nicholas Rowe. The obligations imposed on him by this form and its traditions were that he should imitate Shakspere in an un-Shaksperean fashion by attempting to write constantly as Shakspere only wrote at the extreme emotional crises in his plays; that his hero should have a dash of Richard III in him; that the tragedy should be raised to "the dignity of history" by the arbitrary introduction of incidents (mostly fictitious) mentioned in recondite historical manuscripts; and that the whole should be made sufficiently stagey to appear natural and suitable to actors and frequenters of the theatre, and outrageous and impossible to everyone else. Shelley, with the modesty of a novice, complied with these conditions. He produced a villain worse than Richard III, Macbeth, Iago, Antiochus, and Ireland's Vortigern all rolled into one. He expanded Othello's "Put out the light; and then put out the light" into a whole scene. He wrote a father's curse compared to which Lear's on Goneril appears a mere petulance. He put Lady Macbeth's famous "Give me the daggers" into the mouth of a heroine urging her father's murder. He gave her a sad song to sing before her death, like Desdemona. Long tirades, thunder and lightening, a banquet, a castle, murders, tortures, and executions were not spared. The inevitable historical document was duly translated from the Italian original. And he wrote a preface in which he scrupulously stated that an idea in one of the speeches was suggested by a passage in Calderon's "El Purgatorio de San Patricio." This, he said, was the only plagiarism he had intentionally committed in the whole piece; a declaration which proves how unconsciously he had been guilty of all the second-hand Shakspere. The result furnishes an artistic parallel to Wagner's "Rienzi." It is a strenuous but futile and never-to-be-repeated attempt to bottle the new wine in the old skins.

"The Cenci," then, is a failure in the sense in which we call an experiment with a negative result a failure. But the powers called forth by it were so extraordinary that many generations of audiences will probably submit to have the experiment repeated on them, in spite of the incidental tedium. And if the play be ever adequately acted, the experiment will not be even temporarily fatiguing to witness, though it perhaps may prove at one or two points unendurably horrible. For Count Cenci, mere stage puppet, striking figure in Italian history, tragedy villain and so forth, as he is supposed to be, is really a personification of the Almighty Fiend of "Queen Mab," the God whose attributes convicted the average evangelical Briton in Shelley's eyes of being a devil worshipper. Cenci is ruthless, powerful, and malignant; and, above all, there is no appeal and no relief from his injustice. He identifies his cause with that of his God by the appalling preface to his valediction against Beatrice:

> "The world's Father
> Must grant a parent's prayer against his child."

Beatrice too, banishes all mere stage heroinism from our minds when she absolutely despairs, and, without losing her self-possession, dies in her despair. She withstands physical torture; but she succumbs, as she tells her torturer

> "——with considering all the wretched life
> Which I have lived, and its now wretched end,
> And the small justice shown by Heaven and Earth
> To me or mine; and what a tyrant thou art,
> And what slaves these; and what a world we make,
> The oppressor and the oppressed."

Those who have witnessed the agony and death of any innocent creature upon whom Nature has wantonly fastened a dreadful malady, will recognize here a tragedy truer and deeper than that of any conventional heroine whose lover dies in the fifth act. Shelley and Shakspere are the only dramatists who have dealt in despair of this quality; and Shelley alone has shown it driven into the heart of a girl. The devil-god, incarnate in a wicked human tyrant, is characteristically Shelleyan. He is of course as pure a superstition as the benevolent *deus ex machina* of optimistic religious playwrights; but both represent a real aspect of nature; and the one is therefore as terribly real and effective as the other is delightfully pleasant and useful.

The performance could not have been materially improved upon at any other theatre in London. Miss Alma Murray played with remarkable power—quite startlingly at some points—whilst her strength lasted. When it began to fail (which occurred, it seemed to me, after the third act), she husbanded it so skilfully, and managed her part with so much tact, that her inability to give full breadth and intensity to the more formidable passages in the last act only won additional sympathy for her from the very few who felt the shortcoming. Shelley does not seem to have thought of the limits to human endurance, and the possibility of contriving intervals of rest and relief during the player's task, which he made about as arduous as three successive performances of Juliet or

Pauline Deschappelles on the same day would be. Not a line of the play was cut; only a few were forgotten. Mr Herman[n] Vezin did what he could with the part of Cenci, and did it very well considering the impossibility of such an impersonation to an actor who happily cannot make a monster of himself. Mr Leonard Outram had the most important of the really feasible parts—that of Orsino; and his treatment of it confirmed the high estimate of his ability which his performance as Valence, in "Colombe's Birthday," caused the Browning Society and their guests to form last year at St George's Hall. Miss Maude Brennan's appearance was surprisingly in accordance with the description of Lucretia in Shelley's historical document; but the effect was not quite satisfactory from the artistic point of view. Mr de Cordova and Mr Foss came off with credit as Giacomo and Marzio; and Mr Mark Ambient's earnestness helped him through the self-sacrifice of playing the tragic boy Bernard Cenci. A prologue by Mr John Todhunter, in which Mr Browning, who was present, was pointedly apostrophized, was recited by Mr Outram. A rough-and-ready orchestra played the most sublime pieces in their repertory—the overture to "Masaniello," "The Lost Chord," the march from "The Prophet," selections from "Lucrezia Borgia," and the like, with the best intentions.

June 1886

A Sort of Shakspere Entertainment

A performance of "Love's Labor Lost" is a sort of entertainment to be valued rather for Shakspere's sake than for its own. The Dramatic Students did not tempt many people into the St James's Theatre on the sultry afternoon of the 2nd July by the experiment, and it is perhaps as well that they did not, for their efforts bore much the same relation to fine acting as the play does to "Antony and Cleopatra." They failed not only in skill and finish, but in intelligence. Having gathered from their study of the play that they must all be very amusing and in desperately high spirits, they set to work to produce that effect by being obstreperous in action, and in speech full of the unnatural archness by which people with no sense of humor betray their deficiency when they desire to appear jocund. Though they devoutly believed the play a funny one, they did not see the joke themselves, and so, ill at ease in their merriment, forgot that dignity and grace may be presumed to have tempered the wit of the gentlemen of the Court of Navarre, and the vivacity of the ladies of the Court of France. In some scenes, consequently, the performance was like an Elizabethan version of "High Life Below Stairs." I shall say nothing of the feminine parts, except that they were all unfortunately cast. The men were better. Mr G. R. Foss as Boyet and Mr Frank Evans as Holofernes were quite efficient; and Mr Lugg as Costard, though as yet a raw actor and prone to overdo his business, enlivened the performance considerably by his fun and mimetic turn. He sang "When Icicles Hang by the Wall" with commendable spirit, and with the recklessness of a man who had got the tune on his ear and considers that it is the conductor's business to keep the band with the singer, which poor Herr Schoening tried gallantly to do, with more or less success. Mr Bernard Gould and Mr de Cordova, as Berowne and Armado, were next best; but they made very little of their large share of the best opportunities of the afternoon. Mr Gould's gaiety lacked dignity and variety: he swaggered restlessly, and frittered away all the music of his lines. His colleague looked [like] Armado, but did not act him. Mr de Cordova is always picturesque; but his elocution, correct as far as it goes, is monotonous; and the adaptability and subtlety which go to constitute that impersonative power which is the distinctive faculty of the actor are not at present apparent in him. His qualifications, so far, are those of an artist's model: he has yet to make himself an actor.

The play itself showed more vitality than might have been expected. Three hundred years ago, its would-be wits, with their forced smartness, and their indecent waggeries, their snobbish sneers at poverty, and their ill-bred and ill-natured mockery of age and natural infirmity, passed more easily as ideal compounds of soldier, courtier, and scholar than they can nowadays. Among people of moderate culture in this century they would be ostracized as insufferable cads. Something of their taste survives in the puns and chaff in such plays as those of the late H. J. Byron, and even in the productions of so able a writer as Mr Gilbert, who seems to consider a comic opera incomplete without a middle-aged woman in it to be ridiculed because she is no longer young and pretty. Most of us, it is to be hoped, have grace enough to regard Ruth, Lady Jane, Kitisha and the rest as detestable blemishes on Mr Gilbert's works. Much of "Love's Labor Lost" is as objectionable and more tedious. Nothing, it seems to me, but a perverse hero-worship can see much to admire in the badinage of Berowne and Rosaline. Benedick and Beatrice are better; and Orlando and Rosalind much better. Still, they repeatedly annoy us by repartees of which the trivial ingenuity by no means compensates the silliness, coarseness, or malice. It is not until Shakspere's great period began with the seventeenth century that, in "Measure for Measure," we find this sort of thing shown in its proper light and put in its proper place in the person of Lucio, whose embryonic stages may be

traced in Mercutio and Berowne. Fortunately for "Love's Labor Lost,"
Berowne is not quite so bad as Mercutio: you never absolutely long to
kick him off the stage as you long to kick Mercutio when he makes game
of the Nurse. And Shakspere, though a very feeble beginner then in
comparison to the master he subsequently became, was already too far
on the way to his greatness to fail completely when he set himself to
write a sunny, joyous, and delightful play. Much of the verse is charming: even when it is rhymed doggrell it is full of that bewitching Shak-
sperean music which tempts the susceptible critic to sugar his ink and
declare that Shakspere can do no wrong. The construction of the play
is simple and effective. The only absolutely impossible situation was that
of Berowne hiding in the tree to overlook the king, who presently hides
to watch Longaville, who in turn spies upon Dumain; as the result of
which we had three out of the four gentlemen shouting "asides" through
the sylvan stillness, No. 1 being inaudible to 2, 3, and 4; No. 2 audible
to No. 1 but not to 3 and 4; No. 3 audible to 1 and 2, but not to No. 4;
and No. 4 audible to all the rest, but himself temporarily stone deaf.
Shakspere has certainly succeeded in making this arrangement intelli-
gible; but the Dramatic Students' stage manager did not succeed in making it credible. For Shakspere's sake one can make-believe a good deal;
but here the illusion was too thin. Matters might have been mended had
Berowne climbed among the foliage of the tree instead of affixing himself to the trunk in an attitude so precarious and so extraordinarily
prominent that Dumain (or perhaps it was Longaville), though supposed to be unconscious of his presence, could not refrain from staring
at him as if fascinated for several seconds. On the whole, I am not sure
that "Love's Labor Lost" is worth reviving at this time of day; but I am
bound to add that if it were announced tomorrow with an adequate cast,
I should make a point of seeing it.

July 1886

Mr and Mrs Edmund Russell's Lecture on del Sarte

On Saturday afternoon, the 31st July, Mr and Mrs Edmund Russell gave
a lecture on what has been dubbed (though not by the lecturers) "del
Sartism." Mrs Russell, a clever and interesting lady, had made her mark
during the season in London society; and Mr Russell had played up to

her, more or less intentionally, by wearing a colored silk neckcloth instead of the usual white tie, and taking himself and everyone else so seriously that he was soon described in newspaper paragraphs as "beautiful Edmund Russell,"—and compared to Mr Oscar Wilde—not the staid and responsible Mr Oscar Wilde of to-day, but the youth whose favorite freak it was to encourage foolish people to identify him with the imaginary "aesthete" invented by Mr [George] du Maurier. Mr Russell was pointed out to me one evening as an American who had brought us over a new religion, or philosophy, or aesthetic doctrine, or (the manner of my informant implied) some such tomfoolery. I had the pleasure of a brief conversation with him later on, and found him, apart from a certain not too oppressive gravity, as of a man with a mission of some sort, an unexceptionable young American gentleman, still full of the novelty of being in London, well-mannered, with a characteristic Transatlantic touch of formality occasionally recollected and put on with a certain degree of artistic method in Mr Russell's case, and that pleasant readiness to give and anxiety to get information which makes an American a conversational godsend in an English social gathering to well-to-do people. Subsequently I learned from a newspaper paragraph that Mr Russell was a professor of del Sartism. That probably conveyed no definite idea to more than two or three score people in London; but I was by chance one of the two or three score. The oddest acquaintance I ever formed was with an ex-opera singer, who, in searching throughout Europe for that phoenix, a perfect singing master, had fallen into the hands of del Sarte, and had recognised in him an artist of extraordinarily subtle perception and noble taste; a faultless teacher of elocution, deportment, and gesture; and a philosophic student as well [as] a practical master of his profession. Whether del Sarte was actually all this or not, I of course cannot say; but it does not overstate the impression he produced upon my poor friend D—,* who was a trustworthy judge, having previously tried nearly every famous master in Europe. D—'s ambition, in fact, was to become an improved del Sarte himself, and he might perhaps have succeeded but for extreme thinskinnedness and an incorrigible infirmity of will, which left him, in spite of his considerable artistic gifts, his fine voice, lofty aspirations, and imposing person, a mere builder of castles in the air. Thus, although a knowledge of the English language

---

*Richard Deck, who died in London in 1882, was an Alsatian singing master who, in 1881–82, taught Shaw some French in return for Shaw's teaching him some English. Shaw would go to him three times a week at his single room in a Camden Town lodging-house. At the time Shaw was beginning his novel *Love Among the Artists*, and it is likely that the character of the Welsh singing master Owen Jack in that novel owes much—even the ring of the surname—to Deck.

would have been of the utmost value to him, he contrived to spend twelve
years in London without learning to carry on a conversation in it. Indeed, properly speaking, he knew no language at all; for he had forgotten his native Alsatian dialect of German, and he had adopted an un-
academic French, which, though appallingly fluent, was seldom free from
quaint Italian locutions and scraps of slang from all the countries in
which he had sojourned. He told me a good deal about del Sarte; though
to this day I do not exactly know how much of his theory of artistic
training was del Sarte's, and how much D—'s. On one point he was quite
clear. Del Sarte's knowledge of singing (in the restricted sense of producing the voice) was limited to a shrewd suspicion of his own ignorance. He had broken his voice by sheer ill-usage long before D— knew
him; but his skill in declamation, and his command of facial expression,
enabled him nevertheless to sing certain airs with striking effect. Mr
Russell admits that del Sarte's voice had failed, but ascribes the failure
to extreme privation in early life. D—, who knew better, no longer lives
to dispute the point. He died in a London hospital of a complaint which
to a man rich enough to command careful treatment and nursing in his
own house would have been a trifle, leaving implanted in me sufficient
interest in del Sarte to induce me to pay a couple of shillings for admis-
sion in the pit of Drury Lane Theatre on the 31st July.

My impression of the lecture was that its delivery would not have satisfied del Sarte except at a few points, whilst its style was ill-adapted to
engage the faith of a British audience. Mr Russell told anecdotes of del
Sarte which neither I nor, I suspect, any one else present, believed. The
story about his being jocularly challenged by a manager to whom he
applied for an engagement, to go before the public dressed in rags as
he was, and sing to them; his acceptance of the challenge; and his immediate and immense success, is probably just as true as the romance of
his refusing to interrupt a train of thought in order to appear before an
audience of three thousand people then waiting to hear him lecture. No
doubt Mr Russell thinks these tales true; but he was wrong to repeat
them without giving sufficient dates, authorities and circumstances to
convince skeptics that truth is sometimes stranger than fiction. Even when
fortified in this way, the story would be impolitic, as the only effective
way of persuading the British public that del Sarte was a hero of romance will be to convince it that he was an unpractical man. Mr Russell's
delivery lacks spontaneity. He is preoccupied with his method; betrays
that he is repeating by rote a prepared address; and adopts as his normal facial expression a sort of tragic mask which may have been appropriate enough to del Sarte in the act of declaiming a recitative by Gluck,
but which was extremely ill-chosen by a strange lecturer with a suspicious British audience to win over. A still greater error, and one into

which Mrs Russell subsequently plunged, was that of acting the lecture
as if it were a dramatic monologue, and even accompanying it with im-
itative gestures. Imagine a temperance lecturer quaffing imaginary gob-
lets and reeling about the platform; or a Socialist orator enforcing the
moral of the factory acts by imitating the motion of a power loom! How
the people would laugh! How del Sarte's ghost, if present and capable
of utterance, would unravel the confusion between representation and
persuasion, concentration and irrelevance, which had led the speaker
astray! Mrs Russell did even worse than this form of del Sartean point
of view. Her normal attitude, instead of being one of perfect equilibrium, was not even upright. She constantly swayed and stooped, sometimes with a lateral movement which was distressing and unmeaning;
and she held her arms downwards, with the forearms turned outward
at an ungraceful oblique angle which was exactly equal at both sides (a
curiously elementary blunder). Further, she was draped and made up
to so little advantage that I hardly recognised the remarkably interesting
and attractive young lady who had been pointed out to me in private as
Mr Russell's wife. I give, with some remorse, these unfavorable impressions for what they are worth, hoping that they may be at least as helpful
as the no-criticism which the lecture has so far elicited. Now for the
pleasanter duty of pointing out the qualities which convinced the little
audience that there was something in del Sartism in spite of the mistakes
of its exponents.

First, there was Mr Russell's excellent enunciation, unforced and perfectly clear. A few obscure vowels were suppressed, as a galry for gallery; a final r introduced, as in arenar; and an occasional American-
ism—jahschoor for gesture, for example—let slip. But these are not
defects of method. Del Sarte taught verbal enunciation with rigorous
thoroughness; and Mr Russell fully justified his school by affording us
the rare treat of publicly hearing without effort a gentleman speaking
without effort. Mrs Russell, being constitutionally restless, neither speaks
nor stands so del Sarteanly as her husband; but she, too, makes herself
audible without the least effort. Perhaps the most striking proof of the
soundness of her master's method was the magic change in her appearance when she left off her set speech and came to the real business of
her lecture. The set speech was not only—to be quite frank—three parts
bosh, but it was, as I have already complained, treated as drama instead
of as rhetoric. But when Mrs Russell proceeded to practical illustration,
she at once became graceful and expressive; and the audience became
interested and friendly.

If Mr Russell intends to settle in London as a teacher of artistic speech
and motion, he will at least find plenty of clumsy people to teach, on
and off the stage. Everyone who has compared Signor Salvini's Hamlet

with Mr Irving's or Mr Wilson Barrett's knows that the techniques of
these English actors is, in comparison with that of the great Italian, violent, wasteful, and futile. Even Mrs Kendal, accomplished as she is,
sometimes wavers and proceeds tentatively in passages such as Madame
Ristori treats with firmness and certainty. It is true that there must always be bad actors—men and women who honestly see nothing in classical acting, and rant because they think ranting fine: but there will also
be a large body of players without sufficient insight to discover the laws
of good acting for themselves, but quite well able to appreciate them
when they are revealed by a subtle and intelligent teacher such as del
Sarte was. Acting and stage business are based on the sciences of expression and aesthetics: our knowledge of them grows and gives us trustworthy rules just as our knowledge of arithmetic does. There are certain
conditions of graceful motion which are as much past debate, and as
binding on the most original genius, as that two and two make four; and
these conditions should, without any reference to acting, be taught to
every child by its dancing master, who ought, by and bye, to be a highly
educated artist with the social standing of a university professor. If Mr
and Mrs Russell will make a start in transforming a nation of bad speakers, bad walkers, vile singers, and prematurely stale athletes into healthy,
lasting, and graceful creatures, I, for one, am quite ready to take their
mission seriously, believing, as I do, that what del Sarte taught had an
important bearing on moral, as popularly distinguished from physical,
welfare. But I hope they will not be tempted to make a mystery of their
profession; or to deny that del Sarte's conclusions have been arrived at
independently before, during, and since his time in various places by
men who never heard of him; or in any way to claim a monopoly of
acute reasoning and cultivated taste in the arts of speech and gesture.
Finally, I will place on record (perhaps it may prove useful to Mrs Russell) the polyglot precept which my unfortunate friend D— used to address to his sturdy British pupils when they set their teech and clenched
their fists in the face of a difficulty. "*Ma non*," he would explain: "*il faut
que tout cela vient al-so-lument sans effort. Soyez* sheepish, *mon enfant: soyez*
sheepish."

September 1886

Bernard F. Dukore

SHAW'S "BIG THREE"

Trilogies are as old as recorded western drama, though only one from ancient Greece survives in its entirety, *The Oresteia*. While Shaw's first three volumes of plays—*Pleasant, Unpleasant,* and *for Puritans*—each cluster around a clearly stated theme, they are trilogies or (the second) a tetralogy only in this loose sense. Unlike the Greek work just cited, they do not trace characters or families and they do not represent the introduction, development, and (particularly important) culmination of a theme. In the latter respect—but only, I must caution, in that respect—one can consider *Man and Superman, John Bull's Other Island,* and *Major Barbara*—completed in three successive years beginning 1903—to constitute a trilogy. Urging his German translator to publish them in one volume, Shaw called them "the big three."[1] Although several critics have related one of them to another to the others, none has exhausted the subject. I lack sufficient hubris to expect this essay to do so; still, I should like to examine them as a trilogy. Inevitably I will repeat what others, including myself, have said on the subject.[2] Also inevitably I will take issue with some views. Nevertheless, I hope this treatment of Shaw's "big three" will both tie together ideas already presented and advance somewhat new or different ways of regarding these plays.

While Shaw probably did not intend to follow *Man and Superman* with developments of its thematic implications, much less a culmination, he did so partly because of his writing practice (the preface of one play, written after it, points to the next play) and partly because of the Vedrenne-Barker seasons, which plunged him into play production activities that absorbed his attention to the exclusion of other matters. Significantly, it was when "the big three" did so at more or less the same time that he complained he was "too busy rehearsing and producing to attend any publishing business for the moment."[3]

Consider the chronology. He completed *Man and Superman* in June 1903, then wrote its preface and published them the same year. On 26 April 1904, at the Court Theatre, J. E. Vedrenne and Granville Barker

presented *Candida*, whose success emboldened them to plan a full season in the fall. Shaw began to write *John Bull's Other Island* on 17 June
1904, completed it on 23 August, and directed its first production there
on 1 November, its revival on 7 February 1905. On 22 March 1905, only
a month and a half later, he began the composition of *Major Barbara*,
finished Act I on 4 April, and stopped writing Act II at the point that
Undershaft arrives at the Salvation Army shelter. Although Shaw does
not date the break-off, it might have been in mid-April. His 9 May letter,
just cited, suggests this, as does English rehearsal practice at the time:
four weeks was usual, a mere three sometimes necessary. When he stopped
work on *Barbara* he was directing a revival of *John Bull*, which opened
on 1 May 1905. Near the end of these rehearsals or immediately there-
after, he rehearsed *Superman*, which opened on 23 May. During rehearsals of *John Bull*, therefore, he probably prepared the blocking of *Superman*.[4] When he returned to *Barbara* on 8 July, his head must have
resonated with the two earlier plays' dialogue, which he had heard many
times during rehearsals and at one or more performances. After a major revision of Act III, he completed *Barbara* on 15 October. Under his
direction, its first performance took place on 28 November. He himself
was aware of the relationship of *Barbara* to the two earlier plays. He
likened it to the last scene in John Bull "spun out for three hours and a
half"[5] and he compared Tanner (the protagonist of *Superman*) to Euripides (Cusins's nickname in *Barbara*).[6]

According to Louis Crompton, each of these plays is a "'philosophical
comedy'" that "begins as a Molièresque satire on a liberal reformer and
then develops into a full-fledged Platonic dialogue."[7] Although Shaw's
dialectical dramatic dialogue differs from Plato's nondramatic Socratic
dialogue, each play does develop into dramatically philosophical dis-
course (in the penultimate act of *Superman* and the last scenes of the
others) and each begins as a satire on liberalism. In *Superman*, Roebuck
Ramsden is the liberal; in *John Bull*, Broadbent; in *Barbara*, Lady Britomart (her family are Whigs, from which the liberals derive) and Stephen, who moments after *Barbara* begins "*takes up a Liberal weekly called
The Speaker*" (III,68).

Although time has passed such people by and more progressive ideas
have replaced theirs, they consider themselves in the vanguard of modern thought. "I was an advanced man before you were born," Ramsden
tells Tanner, who retorts, "I knew it was a long time ago" (II,547). Like
Ramsden, Ann cannot understand why Jack considers her views old-
fashioned: "You know we have all been brought up to have advanced
opinions. Why do you persist in thinking me so narrow minded?" (II,575).
Whereas Ramsden argues with Jack, Ann pigeonholes his ideas in a respectable niche: a possible seat in Parliament. Broadbent's mind, says

Larry Doyle, has "all its ideas in watertight compartments and all the compartments warranted impervious to anything it doesnt suit you to understand" (II,913). With convenient incomprehension, Broadbent places Keegan's scathing indictments into an impervious compartment: "They improved my mind: they raised my tone enormously" (II,1021). As Wisenthal recognizes,[8] this type of response—invulnerability to intellectual opposition—has an autobiographical ring; and he quotes Shaw's Epistle Dedicatory to *Superman*, "I . . . find all the force of my onslaught destroyed by a simple policy of nonresistance." Shaw also points out, more clearly anticipating Broadbent and Keegan, that "the ordinary citizen, knowing that an author who is well spoken of by a respectable newspaper must be all right, reads me . . . with undisturbed edification from his own point of view" (II,525–6). In *Barbara*, Lady Britomart's and Stephen's minds have compartments as watertight as Broadbent's. When Stephen is bewildered that people can differ about morality, for "Right is right; and wrong is wrong; and if a man cannot distinguish them properly, he is either a fool or a rascal: thats all," his mother aptly responds, "Thats my own boy (*she pats his cheek*)!" (III,76). Outraged by the heterodox views of Undershaft, Cusins, and Barbara, she denounces them as "a vulgar tradesman," "a Jesuit," and "a lunatic." Calmly, Undershaft characterizes her as "the incarnation of morality. . . . Your conscience is clear and your duty done when you have called everybody names" (III,176). Whereas she resembles Ramsden in this respect, Stephen resembles Ann and Broadbent. Impervious to unorthodox ideas, he ignores them: "I have satisfied myself that the business is one of the highest character and a credit to our country" (III,180).

In important matters *Barbara* more fully elucidates and in minor matters it picks up themes and threads of its two predecessors. Introducing the Sierra brigands in *Superman*, Shaw's stage direction enunciates two prominent themes of *Barbara*, the Kantian test and the virtue of money: "*We misuse our laborers horribly; and when a man refuses to be misused, we have no right to say that he is refusing honest work.*" If four-fifths of us applied for relief, we would "*knock the whole social system to pieces with beneficial reconstructive results.*" When a man, "*applying the Kantian test,*" declares that "*If everybody did as I do, the world would be compelled to reform itself industrially, and abolish slavery and squalor, which exist only because everybody does as you do, let us honor that man and seriously consider the advisability of following his example. Such a man is the ablebodied, ableminded pauper.*" With the alternatives of "*living mainly at the expense of the community and allowing the community to live mainly at his, it would be folly to accept what is to him personally the greater of the two evils*" (II,615). In *Barbara*, Shaw goes further. "The sensible course," he says in its preface, is "to give every man enough to live well on, so as to guarantee the community against the possibility of the malignant disease of poverty, and then (necessarily) to see that he earned it." In the next sentence he calls poverty a crime and in the play Undershaft echoes him. Elaborating on his earlier stage direction, Shaw calls the millionaire armaments maker

> a man who, having grasped the fact that poverty is a crime, knows that when society offered him the alternative of poverty or a lucrative trade in death and destruction, it offered him, not a choice between opulent villainy and humble virtue, but between energetic enterprise and cowardly infamy. His conduct stands the Kantian test, which Peter Shirley's does not. Peter Shirley is what we call the honest poor man. Undershaft is what we call the wicked rich one. . . .

If most people behaved as Undershaft does, not as Shirley does, the immediate result "would be a revolution of incalculable beneficence" (III,26–27). Since the common man's high regard of money "is the one hopeful fact in our civilization," everyone's first duty is to insist on having it on reasonable terms, which do not include making most people drudge ten or twelve hours for a few shillings while a few receive thousands for doing nothing. The "evil to be attacked is . . . simply poverty" (III,30–31).

Superman and *Barbara* have self-made capitalists, Hector Malone, Sr. and Undershaft, and in *John Bull* Larry, having *"fought his way up through . . . poverty"* (II,810), has shares in a capitalist enterprise. The parents, Malone and Undershaft, display a horror of poverty, from which they would save their children. When the younger Malone rejects his father's remittances, the parent pleads with him: "you dont know what poverty is. . . . I'd rather you quarrelled and took the money than made friends and starved. You dont know what the world is: I do" (II,710). Upon learning that Cusins and Barbara are "in love with the common people," Undershaft turns *"cold and sardonic,"* for he knows that because poverty brings dirt, disease, and suffering, such love "may please an earl's granddaughter and a university professor; but I have been a common man and a poor man; and it has no romance for me" (III,121). The money of each parent has saved his child from the ravages of poverty.

"Unashamed," Undershaft's motto and one of the first things we learn about him (III,73), is anticipated by Jack, who attributes his appearance of impudence to his lack of shame. The name of Undershaft's partner, Lazarus, echoes *Superman*, in which Mendoza remarks that Louisa Straker recommended he marry Rebecca Lazarus. Before Shaw completed *Superman*, General William Booth and the Salvation Army were on his mind. One of his letters refers to Booth, another to Max Beerbohm's caricature of Shaw in a Salvation Army uniform.[9]

John Bull, too, anticipates *Barbara*. Hodson's chastisement of Matt Haffigan forecasts the later play's second act, including Bill Walker's thrice-stated taunt, "Wot prawce selvytion nah?" (III,132,137–38): "Well, wot prawce maw grenfawther, Oi should lawk to knaow, that fitted ap a fust clawss shop and built up a fust clawss dripery business in London by sixty years work, and then was chacked aht of it on is ed at the end of is lease withaht a penny for his goodwill." Whereas an Irish farmer cannot be evicted for nonpayment of rent for eighteen months, Hodson was evicted, in winter, after four weeks. "They took the door off its seshes on me, and gev maw wawf pnoomownia. Oi'm a widower nah" (II,975). Whereas in *John Bull* William Morris's phrase "no man is good enough to be another man's master" appears in the preface (II,870), in *Barbara* it is in the play, a report that it stands "in mosaic letters ten feet high round the dome" of the William Morris Labor Church (III,162).

In all three plays wealthy, powerful classes of England confront beings alien to them: the Americans in *Superman*, the Irish in *John Bull*, the poor in *Barbara*. Even the aliens in *Superman* and *Barbara* link to Ireland: the senior Malone was born there and Snobby Price was named for an Irish Chartist, Bronterre O'Brien. In all three, marriage and practical business matters interweave. "You can be as romantic as you please about love, Hector," says Violet; "but you mustnt be romantic about money" (II,607). Ann aptly calls her "hard as nails . . . and businesslike" (II,717). Whereas Violet marries an heir, Broadbent becomes engaged to Rosscullen's "only heiress" (II,1010), whom he will put to work on his political campaign. Barbara is engaged to a man who becomes an heir and Lady Britomart determines that before her daughters marry, her estranged husband will settle substantial sums of money on them.

Capitalism is clearly a major theme of all three plays, though each treats it differently. In *Barbara* an ultra-capitalist transcends the usual turn-of-the-century capitalism, laying the groundwork for its supersession. "Property, says Proudhon, is theft," cites Tanner in *The Revolutionist's Handbook*, and he calls the phrase a "perfect truism" (II,787). In this handbook, though not always in the play, Tanner speaks for Shaw, who declares that "our property is organized robbery" (III,51) and explicitly, "Proudhon was right when he defined property as theft."[10] The brigand Mendoza, whose "principles are thoroughly commercial," has syndicated himself as "Mendoza, Limited," i.e., since capitalism is theft, Shaw makes a thief a capitalist. Driving the point home, he has the capitalist Malone purchase shares in Mendoza, Ltd. and has Jack call them "the two brigands" (II,627,712–13,719). Malone regards everything, marriage included, in terms of profit. If his son marries an English aristocrat, he will buy any historic house, castle, or abbey for him and give him the money to maintain it. He will do the same if his son marries a woman as poor as his grandmother. "Let him raise himself socially with my money or raise somebody else: so long as there is a social profit somewhere, I'll regard my expenditure as justified" (II,703).

This link between capitalism and marriage is significant because the play's chief exemplar of capitalism is a woman, Ann. As E. Strauss observes, Shaw "uses love-relations almost regularly as an illustration and as a small-scale model of social relations." Ann "stands for . . . capitalist society."[11] In the sphere of marriage she does what the capitalist does in the marketplace. In a letter composed while Shaw neared the completion of *Superman*, he couples imperialistic capitalism with Ann: "What is the use of being bright, subtle, witty, genial, if these qualities lead to the subjection and poverty of India and Ireland, and to the political anarchy and corruption of the United States? What says my beautiful, vital, victorious, odious-to-all-good-Americans Miss Ann Whitefield? 'The only really simple thing is to go straight for what you want and grab it.'"[12] As Strauss perceives, "Ann is the perfection of the possessive or acquisitive woman."[13]

John Bull personifies capitalism as Broadbent, who Sean O'Casey says would "take away even the green flag round Ireland's middle and turn it into a gilt-edged security."[14] Politically, and more important economically, this acquisitive man grabs Ireland—symbolized by the poverty-stricken village of Rosscullen—as a potentially profitable commodity. As Maurice Valency notes, Rosscullen also represents "the brutalizing effects of a long tradition of oppression and exploitation, a tradition the residents secretly respect and hope to emulate when they are sufficiently advanced themselves."[15] Rather than overthrow capitalism, its agrarian victims—like their urban counterparts, such as Lickcheese in Shaw's first play, *Widowers' Houses*—would become capitalists themselves. As Larry knows, those farmers who own little acreage are as greedy and oppressive "to them that have no land at all" as the former landlord was (II,962).

Once Broadbent's syndicate, in which Larry has shares, controls Rosscullen, matters will worsen. Broadbent visits Ireland not for sentimentality but for business: to develop an estate for the syndicate and to examine property it acquired when it foreclosed a mortgage. Larry admits he was taken aback by the foreclosure since when he was a boy he liked the mortgagee, but Broadbent's explanation of failure to pay interest stops any argument from Larry, who is truly his partner. In the original manuscript, Shaw is more explicit that the Garden City Broadbent claims he would make of Rosscullen is for capitalist exploitation: he calls the Garden City plan a dodge, refutes the notion that the idea has turned him into a socialist, and says that his method will require no outlay of capital since the enthusiastic voluntarism of warmhearted Irishmen, not labor for decent wages, would do the job.[16]

The play's final scene clarifies the syndicate's plans. Broadbent would create a hotel and golf course in Rosscullen and sell weekend excursion packages. He reveals that "to all intents and purposes the syndicate I represent already owns half Rosscullen" and within a month will hold mortgages to the other half (II,1011–12). He will lend landowners so much more than their property is worth that the syndicate will foreclose the mortgages when they cannot pay the interest. Through Broadbent, the syndicate will exploit Rosscullen for more profit than its present landowners do. The people will be jailed, bought, tamed, and used to help the syndicate plunder. Larry proposes a humane solution for people like Haffigan: "we'll employ him in some capacity or other, and probably pay him more than he makes for himself now." When Broadbent disagrees—"No no: Haffigan's too old. It really doesnt pay now to take on men over forty even for unskilled labor, which I suppose is all Haffigan would be good for. . . . He's worked out, you know"—Larry instantly submits: "Haffigan doesnt matter much. He'll die presently. . . . I say let him die, and let us have no more of his like." So much for Haffigan, whose fate Shaw will show in *Barbara* in the person of Peter Shirley. So much too for Larry's high-sounding hopes for Ireland, eloquently expressed in an earlier scene, and for his good will, no more than phrasemaking. "Well," he admits, with telling use of the possessive plural, "our syndicate has no conscience" (II,1013–14). Keegan predicts it will squeeze all it can from the community, engineer all phases of Rosscullen's rise and decline, and make its wretchedness more orderly. After the hotel becomes insolvent and liquidated, he continues, the syndicate will ruin its stockholders by acquiring it for a few shillings to the pound, foreclose mortgages, drive Rossculleners worthless to it to America or death, and employ some who remain to bully others who remain.

Like Ann and Broadbent, Undershaft is an acquisitive type who goes straight for what he wants and grabs it. Some of his most effective arguments are demonstrations by action. After explaining how the Salvation Army helps capitalists, he clinches the argument by acting according to Ann's precept: he "buys" the Army. Although he tells Cusins he can do so, he presents no verbal argument to support his assertion; he simply does it. If your religion fails to fit the facts, he pragmatically advises Barbara, scrap it and grab one that does. He challenges her to bring Bill Walker to him so that he can save him not by preaching but by action: giving him a well-paying, permanent job.

An exchange between Rummy Mitchens and Snobby Price recalls Tanner's paraphrase of Proudhon: "You know what ladies and gentlemen are." "Thievin swine!" (III,97). Cusins explains Lomax's remark about Undershaft, "a bit thick," by a reference in Homer's *Iliad* to a burglar who enters a thickly or strongly built house (III,81). Shaw may have recalled these references, and the Mendoza-Malone enterprise, in the preface to *Barbara*: "The faults of the burglar are the qualities of the financier" (III,47). The statement anticipates *Heartbreak House*, where a burglar and a capitalist are called "the two burglars" and "the two practical men of business" (V,181).[17] Although Undershaft is not and does not call himself a gentleman, he is, as capitalist, a "thievin swine." Among other things, Perivale St Andrews represents what Stephen calls "colossal capital" (III,159). Every aspect, however much it may benefit workers, Undershaft boasts, results in "a colossal profit, which comes to me" (III,155). Moreover, "the spectacle of his successes in making money [gives] great satisfaction to the huge majority who have rather less chance of achieving it themselves than of winning the Calcutta Sweep" (III,200). He can afford to flout William Morris's egalitarian maxim since his employees "take no more notice of it than of the ten commandments in church" (III,162–63). In his screenplay, Shaw expands this point. Seditious speeches in the Labor Church are "the Undershaft safety valve. Our people can talk here; and as long as men can talk politics they will never do anything else except work for their daily bread."[18]

Shaw takes pains to remind spectators and readers of what Undershaft represents. "*I am the government of your country*," he tells his son "*with a touch of brutality*," and Parliament and people will do what profits his firm. Parliament will wage war when it suits him and keep peace when it does not. Only after he decides on measures necessary for business will it learn of them. When he wants to raise his firm's profits, the country will find that his want is a national need. When others want to lower them, the country will call out the military and constabulary. In return, his newspapers will support, applaud, and make politicians imagine they are great statesmen. He scornfully derides political parties and newspaper articles as "toys" and emphatically concludes that because he pays the piper he calls the tunes (III,151–52).

Shaw has Undershaft display this "touch of brutality" elsewhere, both verbally and visually. Giving Mrs. Baines his check, he brutally reminds Cusins and Barbara, who listen, that his largesse comes from widows and orphans, mutilated and dead soldiers, and oceans of blood. Visually, Shaw displays it in Act III: "*Several dummy soldiers more or less mutilated, with straw protruding from their gashes, have been shoved out of the way under the landing. A few others are nearly upright against the shed; and one has fallen forward and lies, like a grotesque corpse, on the emplacement.*" He reports that his latest weapon has demolished a fort with three hundred soldiers in it. "Dummy soldiers?" asks Cusins, alluding to those lying on stage— life-size, the reader should remember and the spectator would see. Undershaft responds, "(*striding across to Stephen and kicking the prostrate dummy brutally out of his way*) No: the real thing" (III,157–59).[19]

For all three exemplars of acquisitiveness, Shaw uses diabolonian imagery. Jack calls Ann "Lady Mephistopheles" and says she has "a devilish charm" (II,578). Doran says that Broadbent "has the divil's own luck" and Keegan calls him "an efficient devil" (II,983,1015), which may be one reason that he rather than Keegan feels at home in a world Keegan regards as hell. Ann tempts Jack; the Devil is widely known as the tempter. While Broadbent tempts the villagers, Keegan sees through his temptations. Like Keegan, Cusins explicitly labels the capitalist "clever, clever devil" and "tempter, cunning tempter"; and Cusins frequently calls Undershaft such names as "Mephistopheles" and "the Prince of Darkness" (III,156,178,124,142). But when Barbara describes his factory town as a "Works Department of Hell," he is *scandalized* (III,154) and points to the presence of chapels, churches, and an ethical society. This tempter is a devil with a difference.

Perhaps to hint at the irony of such titles in this play, Shaw in the preface calls him "St Andrew Undershaft" (III,23). In the last play of this trilogy, the exemplar of acquisitiveness transcends the capitalism that results in the poverty of Rosscullen and West Ham. So far, I have emphasized his affinities to that capitalism because some critics neglect them and, following Shaw's unfortunate allusion to him as "the hero of Major Barbara" (III,27), consider him its raisonneur—which he is only to an extent, since Cusins and Barbara also speak for Shaw. The foregoing should demonstrate the incompleteness of such views. What follows should demonstrate that while they are partly correct, the part is less than the whole.

"What is the matter with the poor is Poverty," says Tanner's *Handbook* (II,794). Undershaft gives his workers well-paying jobs that adequately feed, clothe, and house them. Conscious that "the greatest of our evils, and the worst of our crimes is poverty" (III,23), he has removed "the matter." Shaw would have people "'liquidate' the underfed either by feeding them or killing them" (III,63). "Poverty blights whole cities," says Undershaft, "spreads horrible pestilences," and poisons the nonpoor, who "organize unnatural cruelties for fear [the poor] should rise against us and drag us down into their abyss" (III,172). He speaks for Shaw, who similarly declares that "Let Him Be Poor" means let him be weak, ignorant, a nucleus of disease, an exhibition of dirt, and a parent of rickety children. It means "Let his habitations turn our cities into poisonous congeries of slums. Let his daughters infect our young men with the diseases of the streets, and his sons revenge him by turning the nation's manhood into scrofula, cowardice, cruelty, hypocrisy, political imbecility, and all the other fruits of oppression and malnutrition." Appealing to our selfish as well as our unselfish instincts, he concludes that it is unwise for those not poor to permit poverty (III,25). Because one can destroy it under capitalism, why delay? Partly to emphasize his argument, he makes the killer of poverty a weapons maker.

Undershaft is a benevolent capitalist, with equal emphasis on adjective and noun. He has organized his microcosmic society to eliminate poverty—an example to the nation. There, he transcends capitalism by creating social conditions that permit his workers to do more than drudge for their daily bread. "The virtues of Broadbent," says Shaw, "are not less real because they are the virtues of the money that coal and iron have produced" (II,810). Mutatis mutandis, the virtues of Undershaft are not less real because they are products of capitalism and armaments. From the mouths of fools, truth sometimes emerges. As Lomax says, "there is a certain amount of tosh about this notion of wickedness. It doesnt work. You must look at facts" (III,175–76). The most prominent fact is what Undershaft has done.

Except for him, and perhaps old Malone, these acquisitive types are hypocrites. Ann, says Jack, has "absolutely no conscience—only hypocrisy" (II, 567). Keegan indicts Broadbent: "I know you are quite sincere." Deliberately, he misquotes Scripture to characterize Broadbent's hypocrisy: "Let not the right side of your brain know what the left side doeth" (II,989). While Broadbent denounces "the windbags, the carpetbaggers, the charlatans, the . . . fools and ignoramuses," he never dreams he denounces himself; rather, he considers himself a man "with no humbug about him, who will . . . take his stand on the solid ground of principle and public duty" (II,988). Yet his talk is humbug, his principles and sense of public duty are for corporate gain, and his promise of prosperity will economically shackle the younger workers and exile or starve the older. In developing an estate in Rosscullen for the syndicate, he claims he would "take a little money out of England and spend it in Ireland" (II,899). Not quite: he will invest money in Ireland to take more money from it. His partner, too, is a hypocrite. Although Larry declares, "I wish I could find a country to live in where the facts were not brutal and the dreams not unreal," he does nothing to alter the brutalized facts or realize the dreams. He condemns avaricious landowners whom society does not call to account but fails to condemn the syndicate, which society also does not call to account. This Irish émigré to England and his partner, the English émigré to Ireland, proclaim high motives while they work for self-interest. By contrast, the "unashamed" Undershaft admits he is "a profiteer in mutilation and murder" and unlike Broadbent is not "one of those men who keep their morals and their business in water-tight compartments" (III,89).

Despite Undershaft's benevolence, his elimination of poverty, and the possibility that his actions may one day result in the supersession of capitalism, he does not in Shaw's view represent the ultimate in social well-being. As indicated earlier, Shaw takes pains to emphasize how he is detrimental to the general welfare—for example, the passage that explains his firm to be the real government of England. "I am, and have always been, and shall now always be, a revolutionary writer," Shaw affirms in the same preface in which he calls Undershaft a saint and the play's hero, thereby suggesting his approval of the capitalist is limited to the reasons he gives, "because our laws make law impossible; our liberties destroy all freedom; our property is organized robbery; our morality is an impudent hypocrisy; our wisdom is administered by inexperienced or malexperienced dupes, our power wielded by cowards and weaklings, and our honor false in all its points. I am an enemy of the existing order" (III,59). As Lenin's famous pamphlet asks, what is to be done? Shaw's response is not that of a character of his countryman Samuel Beckett, the first line of *Waiting for Godot*, that nothing is to be done (a phrase with chiefly metaphysical resonances but also recalling Lenin's question). Very likely, Keegan's view, "when we cease to do, we cease to live" (II,1018), is Shaw's.

One might do as Tanner does, write a pamphlet to influence people. Its disposition on stage (Ramsden vehemently throws it into a waste paper basket) may be seen to represent its general reception. Although Shaw wrote pamphlets and books on socialism, he did not delude himself as to their effectiveness. Rather, "hard words, even when uttered by eloquent essayists and lecturers, or carried unanimously at enthusiastic public meetings on the motion of eminent reformers"—and he was all three—"break no bones." Disputing the idea that Voltaire, Rousseau, and the Encyclopedists created the French Revolution (which in pre-Soviet 1907, when *Barbara* was published, exemplified revolution), he calls it "the work of men who had observed that virtuous indignation, caustic criticism, conclusive argument and instructive pamphleteering, even when done by the most earnest and witty literary geniuses, were as useless as praying. . . ." Although Shaw himself is this type of genius, he is too intellectually honest to spare himself: "I, who have preached and pamphleteered like any Encyclopedist, have to confess that my methods are no use," for they succeed "only in giving cowards all the sensations of heroes" while they submit to oppression (III,37–39). And journalism, which reaches more people than pamphlets and books, is a profession for people like Stephen.

What of practical politics in a democracy? Shaw was ambivalent: while it might accomplish some good, it is ineffective as the sole means to create socialism. Fabian policy derives from an 1887 manifesto that says, "Socialism may be most quickly and most surely realized by utilizing the political power already possessed by the people . . . and to bring it to bear upon Parliament, municipalities, and other representative bodies. . . ."[20] Although Shaw increasingly considered Parliament as less and less effective, he increasingly respected municipal organizations, which worked on local levels, as more and more effective. From May 1897 to November 1900, Shaw was a St. Pancras vestryman, and a borough councillor there until October 1903. But he recognized that piecemeal reforms, though necessary, did not substitute for complete social restructure. While working at St. Pancras and writing *Superman*, he realized how fundamentally useless parliamentary methods were: "at no moment during the whole boom of Socialism was it possible to infer from the fact of a man being a Socialist how he would vote in any Parliamentary division." Socialists in Parliament even failed to impress the public of any new element there. To call a man a socialist "conveys just as much information about him . . . [as] the statement that he is a Christian."[21]

In *Superman*, when Ann proposes that Jack enter Parliament, "*He collapses like a pricked bladder*" (II,575). This does not mean he will adopt her proposal. In fact, he provokes it by declaring that since mobs of voters are worse educated than statesmen, public men who must win their votes are unlikely to create a better world. His *Handbook* maintains, "Democracy substitutes election by the incompetent many for appointment by the corrupt few" (II,782). Whereas politicians once had to flatter kings, they now must "fascinate, amuse, coax, humbug, frighten, or otherwise strike the fancy of the electorate"—skills that differ from those required to legislate for its best interests. Because "the demagogue . . . professes (and fails) to readjust matters in the interests of the majority of the electors" and fails to learn how to manage a county parish, let alone international affairs, "the whole political business goes to smash" (II,754–55). Anticipating *Barbara*, the Devil indicts a parliamentary system that caters to mass ignorance: "Over . . . battles the people run about the streets yelling with delight, and egg their Governments on to spend hundreds of millions of money in the slaughter, whilst the strongest Ministers dare not spend an extra penny in the pound against the poverty and pestilence through which they themselves daily walk" (II,655–56).

As I said, Shaw was ambivalent about practical politics. After *Superman*, he became a candidate not for the ineffective Parliament but for the effective London County Council for the borough of St. Pancras. In the election of 5 March 1904, he was third among four candidates, with fewer than fifty votes separating him from the fourth.

Three months later he began to write *John Bull*, whose subjects include the type of person who wins elections and the type who should avoid them. The latter is Larry Doyle—like Shaw an anglicized Irishman, a man with "ideas . . . not . . . popular enough" for the electorate or for those who provide financial backing, "not a Liberal," and impatient with those Irish who are "duped by Acts of Parliament that change nothing but the necktie of the man that picks [their] pocket" (II,957,964–65). By contrast, the liberal Broadbent, who stands for Home Rule (changing to green the necktie of the pickpocket), is the successful type of candidate. The Rosscullen landowners want an M.P. who will support them and "doesnt care a snap of his fingers for the shoutn o the riff-raff in the towns, or for the foolishness of the laborers" (II,959). Broadbent is for retrenchment, defined as reduction of property taxes, and reform, defined as "maintaining those reforms which have already been conferred . . . and trusting for future developments to the free activity of a free people on the basis of those reforms." Doran understands the meaning of this doubletalk: "No more meddlin" (II,967–68). Shrewdly, Keegan appraises Broadbent's chances of victory as "excellent. . . . You will get into parliament because you want to get into it enough to be prepared to take the necessary steps to induce the people to vote for you" (II,988). Among the steps is to put his fiancée to work for him by calling on voters' wives: "theyll be flattered no end by your calling, especially as youve never cheapened yourself by speaking to them before—have you?" (II,1006). Father Dempsey observes, "he hasn't much sense" (II,970), but even a sensible politician must behave as he does. As Shaw says in the preface to *John Bull*, "Every English statesman has to maintain his popularity by pretending to be ruder, more ignorant, more sentimental, more superstitious, more stupid than any man who has lived behind the scenes of public life for ten minutes can possibly be" (II,818–19).

In *Barbara*, he dismisses politics as fit for someone like Stephen, who "knows nothing and thinks he knows everything" (III,151). The final scene shows contempt for Parliament as an instrument of significant social change:

> UNDERSHAFT. . . . Your pious mob fills up ballot papers and imagines it is governing its masters; but the ballot paper that really governs is the paper that has a bullet wrapped in it.
> CUSINS. That is perhaps why, like most intelligent people, I never vote.
> UNDERSHAFT. Vote! Bah! When you vote, you only change the names of the cabinet. When you shoot, you pull down governments, inaugurate new epochs, abolish old orders and set up new.

Cusins concedes, "It is historically true" (III,174). But let us remember Shaw's ambivalence, which is practical. As Eric Bentley perceives, Shaw "operates on two time-tables: the short and the long range."[22] On the short range, unlike *most* intelligent people Cusins knows, Shaw votes for the least objectionable candidate; on the longer, he works toward socialist revolution.

To Shaw, people will revolt only when they have been educated to want socialism, and he believes revolution to be essential. Thus, in the preface to *Barbara*: "it is for the poor to repudiate poverty when they have had enough of it" (III,28). He felt "when" had not arrived. *The Revolutionist's Handbook* says that the Fabian Society's peaceful, constitutional policy of socialism is favorably regarded because of the belief "that the Fabians, by eliminating the element of intimidation from the Socialist agitation, have . . . saved the existing order from the only method of attack it fears" (II,760). I disagree with Turco that Shaw uses Tanner "to sidestep the suggestion that these sentiments were his own" and that it was not until he wrote *Barbara* that "the gist of 'Tanner's' argument must have struck root in his mind. . . ."[23] As early as 1890, Shaw expressed himself similarly: some of the Fabians' "recently acquired middle class vogue is due to an impression that we have found a way of making socialism an excuse for exhorting the working class not to do anything rash." But Parliament will pass measures favorable to workers "only when they are convinced that otherwise a worse thing will befall them; and nothing can convince them of that except the determination of the workers to resort to force if Parliament fails."[24] Constitutionalism and violence, Shaw believed, are not mutually exclusive. The former is the first stage of the long process to prepare English workers to overthrow capitalism by force. Thus, Tanner's question: "of what use is it to substitute the way of the reckless and bloodyminded for the way of the cautious and humane?" (II,762). At that time, it would have been useless, since too few English workers were ready to storm the barricades.

What, then, are we to make of Shaw-Tanner's assertion that both Fabian and barricades methods "are fundamentally futile" (II,761)? The explanation involves the Life Force and the Superman. As Eric Bentley says, these ideas provide

> the main link between Bernard Shaw's politics and his religion. Shaw had begun with socialist ethics, according to which you must change society in order to change man. The trouble was that unless you changed man he refused to change society. Shaw's way out was . . . [to ask] for change from within, *not instead but as well*. Shaw said, moreover, that you could not have democracy until everyone is a Superman. He did not say you could not have *socialism* till then.[25]

In 1896, Shaw had insisted on socialism's limitations: "The Fabian Society does not put Socialism forward as a panacea for the ills of human society, but only for those produced by defective organization of industry and by a radically bad distribution of wealth."[26] On the short range Shaw votes as a Fabian does; on the longer range he plans socialist revolution; but he has a still longer range: to help the Life Force work toward Superman. On this range peaceful Fabianism and warlike barricadism are futile. Further progress requires a new type of human being, the Superman. In *Superman* Shaw presents the theory, in *John Bull* the status quo to be fought, and in *Barbara* a recapitulation of both plus the culminating, anticipated fusion of change from without as well as within.

Shaw's politics are religious, his religion political. As the *Handbook* states, "The need for the Superman is, in its most imperative aspect, a political one" and "The only fundamental and possible Socialism is the socialization of the selective breeding of Man: in other terms, of humane evolution. We must eliminate the Yahoo, or his vote will wreck the commonwealth" (II,753,776). Like Tanner, who calls for "a Democracy of Supermen" (II,755), Shaw asserts, "We must either breed political capacity or be ruined by Democracy, which was forced on us by the failure of the older alternatives" (II,514–15). While political, the play is religious, "for the vision of hell in the third act . . . is expressly intended to be a revelation of the modern religion of evolution" (II,531). This socialist preaches with such religious fervor that his Epistle Dedicatory to *Superman* points toward Keegan and Barbara: "my conscience is the genuine pulpit article: it annoys me to see people comfortable when they ought to be uncomfortable; and I insist on making them think in order to bring them to conviction of sin" (II,495).

To Shaw, life is an underlying force—unfinished, experimenting and blundering, struggling for perfection by trial and error, not the product of an anthropomorphic being. Life aims to create "higher and higher individuals" in order to "attain not only self-consciousness but self-understanding" (II,662–63). Mind permits choice of "the line of greatest advantage instead of yielding in the direction of least resistance" (II,685), as Juan puts it, and he has learned to say not only "I am; therefore I think" but also "I would think more; therefore I must be more" (II,667). Thus, he chooses the line toward Superman.

Politics and religion link with sex, where "the initiative . . . remains with Woman" (II,512), who is irresistible. Echoing Juan's perception, "When the lady's instinct was set on me, there was nothing for it but lifelong servitude or flight" (II,678), Jack ironically remarks that he will marry Ann whether he likes it or not. Since a woman's purpose is not her own, personally, "but that of the whole universe, a man is nothing to [her] but an instrument of that purpose," which enables her to sacrifice him to it (II,556). As Juan says, "Sexually, Woman is Nature's contrivance for perpetuating its highest achievement. Sexually, Man is Woman's contrivance for fulfilling Nature's behest in the most economical way." But note: "I said nothing about a woman's whole mind. I spoke of her view of Man as a separate sex" (II,659).

In terms other than sex, both superior man and superior woman— such as Barbara and Cusins—can be artist-philosophers (II,509–10), who

Shaw says "are the only sort of artists I take quite seriously" (II,519). Such people are as unscrupulous as the mother-woman and would sacrifice spouse, children, and parents "if only the sacrifice of them enable [these people] to act Hamlet better, to paint a finer picture, to write a deeper poem, a greater play, a profounder philosophy!" (II,557). Thus, Cusins accepts the inheritance though it might mean losing Barbara; and if he had not accepted it she would have given him up in favor of the man who had. The goal of these artists "is to shew us ourselves as we really are. Our minds are nothing but this knowledge of ourselves; and he who adds a jot to such knowledge creates new mind as surely as any woman creates new men" (II,558). But this creator need not be an artist in a literal sense. More aptly, Juan calls him "the philosophic man: he who seeks in contemplation to discover the inner will of the world, in invention to discover the means of fulfilling that will, and in action to do that will by the so discovered means" (II,664). This is possible in the heaven that Juan seeks and to which not only artists like Rembrandt go but also philosophers like Nietzsche. The philosophic man may work at political science, which "means nothing else than the devizing of the best ways of fulfilling the will of the world" (III,480). As Shaw told students at the London School of Economics and Political Science shortly after *Barbara* had opened, "Intelligence and providence are what the Life Force drives at above all things at present." These students "have in hand the pressing business of conquering for the Life Force a larger, higher, more intelligent, more comprehensive consciousness of the race; and in contributing anything new . . . [they] are adding to that consciousness." As a philosopher, you cannot isolate political science as a limited aspect of the Life Force. "Every economic problem will be found to rest on a moral problem: you cannot get away from it. The moment you touch life at any point you raise numbers of moral problems of all kinds. . . . As Major Barbara says, 'Life is all one.'"[27]

Juan is a higher personification than Jack of the philosophic man through which the Life Force works. But what he is to Jack, Jack is to Ramsden, Keegan to Broadbent and Doyle, they to the Rossculleners, Undershaft to those at Wilton Crescent and West Ham, and Cusins and Barbara to him. Undershaft is more powerful than Broadbent and Doyle, who are more powerful than the capitalists of *Superman*. Furthermore, even the acquisitive Undershaft is an agent of the Life Force. Like Cusins and Barbara, he conforms to Juan's description of the philosophic man: contemplating the will of the world, trying to discover how to fulfill it, and then doing it. But the union of Cusins and Barbara promises to supersede him in greater understanding, or in Juan's terms thinking more, thereby being more, thereby doing more.

Writing about himself in the third person, Shaw says that the final scene of *Superman* "in which the hero revolts from marriage and struggles against it without any hope of escape is a poignantly sincere utterance which must have come from personal experience. . . . Tanner, with all his extravagances, is first hand: Shaw would probably not deny it and would not be believed if he did."[28] The extent to which this is accurate relates to how one considers Jack's fate. If inaccurate, note that when Shaw wrote *Superman* he lacked political and theatrical success in his adopted country. Perhaps he displaced his own professional failure into Jack's personal failure. With either interpretation, he may have disguised a cry from the heart as a laugh from the heart. Like Shaw, Jack enjoys talking and he often echoes Shaw. Like Jack, whom Ramsden reproaches, Shaw lacks shame or modesty, for which his critics reproach him. Anticipating Tanner, he repudiates "mock-modesty" in his preface to *Three Plays for Puritans*. "I am ashamed neither of my work nor of the way it is done. I like explaining its merits to the huge majority who dont know good work from bad" (II,30). "A little moderation," Straker implores his employer (II,588). Shaw too can be immoderate. On the same page of the preface to *Puritans*, he cries, "I am a natural-born mountebank. . . . The cart and trumpet for me."

But how different they are. Ann calls Jack "headstrong" (II,561), not really an apt description of Shaw. In the Epistle Dedicatory to *Superman*, possibly to hint at dissimilarities to Jack, he describes himself (apparently accurately) as "a reasonable, patient, consistent, apologetic, laborious person, with the temperament of a schoolmaster and the pursuits of a vestryman" (II,494). Jack calls marriage "apostasy, profanation of the sanctuary of my soul, violation of my manhood, sale of my birthright, shameful surrender, ignominious capitulation, acceptance of defeat" (II,726). By contrast, Shaw writes to Charlotte before their marriage: "Keep me advised of your address; keep me deep in your heart; write me two lines whenever you love me" and "I will try to find out when your train is due on Sunday night; and if the hour is not absolutely scandalous I shall present myself at the Terrace & crush you in all your ribs with an embrace that has been accumulating for 2 months."[29] While Shaw has Jack say that marriage would mean the end of his social purposefulness, it meant no such thing for Shaw. If it had, he would not have gone to the effort of composing the two-plays-in-one *Superman* together with a prefatory epistle and the hero's book as appendix. Consider too Shaw's activities while he wrote it: a member of the St. Pancras Borough Council, he spent his afternoons and evenings at committee meetings arguing such issues as drainage, paving, and salaries; he began to write *The Common Sense of Municipal Trading*; and he spoke at political rallies. The play presents no evidence that Jack similarly occupies himself with practical politics. As Charles Berst accurately states, it blends "caricature, abstraction, and playwright . . . first on a level of self-parody and fun in Jack Tanner and second on a level of personal moral and spiritual analysis in Don Juan," who like Shaw extols "contemplation and work above thoughtlessness and play." Parody and serious commentary balance each other.[30]

Shaw describes Ann in terms of the Life Force: "Vitality is as common as humanity; but, like humanity, it sometimes rises to genius; and Ann is one of the vital geniuses" (II,549). Exemplifying mother-woman, she instinctively chooses a particular man "to enable her to carry on Nature's most urgent work" and claims him for a purpose beyond her personal purpose (II,507). With the Hell scene, she more clearly does so. Because, she learns, the Superman is not yet created, she cries "*to the universe*" for "a father for the Superman!" (II,689). Directly, the play returns to the Sierras, where the search party, led by Ann (the actress who plays Ana) finds Jack (the actor of Juan). The party's first words are Ann's, "It's Jack!" to which he responds, "Caught!" Shaw underscores the point: "The Life Force! I am lost" (II,692). During the final scene, as he capitulates to her, he explains, "I am in the grip of the Life Force." As for her: "I dont understand in the least" (II,726). Nor does she have to. It suffices that she embodies the Life Force. Their union is hopeful because the embodiment of the Life Force weds the explicator of it.

Shaw calls Jack a Don Juan because he is "in mortal conflict with existing institutions" (II,497). According to Bentley, the play about Jack is considerably less grand than the paragraphs in the preface. He calls him "an ineffectual chatterbox" involved in the story of "the snapping-up of a clever young man by a shrewd young woman" and "the traditional fool of comedy in highly sophisticated disguise."[31] One might not so readily accept Jack as an ineffectual talker if the sensible Straker had not done so: "Never you mind him, Mr Robinson. He likes to talk. We know him, dont we?" (II,589). Numerous critics note that Jack understands the theory of the Life Force but is ignorant of his role in it and is wrong about the people he judges: Ann, Octavius, and Violet. Yet he may recognize that Octavius is not the artist he eulogizes, for he calls him a "maudlin idiot" about love (II,590), which the true artist is not. Although Ramsden may suggest what Jack will become, what of it? Because the Life Force strives for improvement, the advances of one generation, if it advances, are of course outmoded by those of the next.

However, these views are not the entire picture. The worst Shaw says of Jack is that he has "*impetuous credulity and enthusiasm*" with "*a touch of . . . modern plutocratic vulgarity*" (II,632). Shaw also says that, unlike anyone else in the comedy, Jack aims "at the formulation of a philosophy of life"[32]—which makes him a true counterpart of Juan. Why should we believe that Ann will tame him? Unlike the artist Jack hypothesizes, he will not have to drudge for a living to support his wife: he is rich. Only his limitations and the obstacles he faces will prevent him from fulfilling his aims. According to Shaw, his marriage will help him: "When Ann is married she will look after Tanner exactly as Candida looks after Morell. But when Candida was capturing Morell, and had not yet become his housekeeper and his nurserymistress, she was Ann."[33] Jack's statement "I am neither the slave of love nor its dupe" (II,593) may be truer for him than his remark about woman-mother using man-husband. Although he says he will be Ann's slave, her mother disagrees: "No: she's afraid of you" (II,721). One should attend to her, since she knows Ann better than anyone else in the play.

The very nature of *Superman*—preface, play, inner play, appendix—defies easy analysis. "I have only made my Don Juan a political pamphleteer," says Shaw, "and given you his pamphlet in full by way of appendix" (II,516). If one sees only the frame play, one misses an ample explanation not only of the Life Force but also of the title. As Arthur Nethercot observes, the word Superman appears in the Hell scene but not in the frame play.[34] If one fails to read the pamphlet, much of Jack's socialism may be problematical. *Superman* consists of all.

The Hell scene brings a different perspective to the comedy, from which it differs. In the comedy, love conquers. In the Hell scene, thought surmounts Hell, the home of romantic love. Without the Hell scene, the Don Juan figure may seem to subordinate his will to the woman's. By contrast, the Hell scene has him go to Heaven to do his own work for the Life Force—thereby providing an alternative fate for him. Without the Hell scene, bourgeois audiences of Ramsdens can feel superior to Jack, who may return respectably to the fold and be as Bentley says the traditional fool of comedy. With it, such audiences cannot feel so superior and the Juan figure is not merely the conventional comic fool. Without the Hell scene, Jack is a present soon to become a past, as Ramsden has; with it, he represents the future. While the Hell scene is the mutual dream of Tanner and Mendoza, it is—given the play's perspective—essentially that of Tanner, who dreams of himself as a success. Without the third act, he is disparaged; with it, he is made much of. In the frame play, the Juan figure's arguments are usually demolished; in the dream, they are not, for unlike Jack, Juan is not contradicted by facts of which he is ignorant (such as Violet's marriage). Whereas Jack, misunderstanding the others, talks but fails to face things as they are, Juan does. Jack drifts with Ann's will; Juan goes to heaven to steer. In brief, Juan is more advanced than Jack.

Note, in addition, how Shaw's preface to *Puritans* points to *Superman*: "when I see that the nineteenth century has crowned the idolatry of Art with the deification of Love . . . I feel that Art was safer in the hands of the most fanatical of Cromwell's major generals than it will be if ever it gets into mine. The pleasures of the senses I can sympathize with and share; but the substitution of sensuous ecstasy for intellectual activity and honesty is the very devil" (II,28). Without the Hell scene, the play may seem to deify love and sensuous ecstasy. With it, intellectual activity and honesty defeat "the very devil," who may be more of a tempter than any other in literature. Whereas others demand eternal damnation, Shaw's offers eternal, unthinking pleasure—for those who like that sort of thing, and as he says, they are legion. With the Hell scene, the devil recognizes "*gloomily*" that Juan's "going is a political defeat" (II,687) for the love and sensuous ecstasy he represents.

Unlike *Superman*, *John Bull* dramatizes the defeat of intellectual activity and honesty. For making Ireland suffer, Broadbent denounces English politicians as more unscrupulous than Bobrikoff (a dictatorial Russian general who subjected Finland to Russian rule) and Abdul the Damned (a bloodthirsty ruler of the Ottoman Empire who committed widespread atrocities in Armenia). But as Tanner's *Handbook* states, "What a man believes may be ascertained, not from his creed, but from the assumptions on which he habitually acts" (II,788). Broadbent's actions show that his assumptions differ from his rhetoric. Economically he will, like Bobrikoff, maintain English dominion of Ireland and by capitalistic methods will, like Abdul, commit damnable legal atrocities. Politically, economically, and romantically, his anglicized Irish partner assists him: he declines the seat in parliament, has shares in Broadbent's syndicate, and gives up the woman, who far from being an incarnation of vitality, like the women in *Superman*, is nutritionally feeble and has a will feebler than that of Broadbent, who is set on having her.

Is Larry Doyle a viable alternative to Broadbent? He likes Broadbent, is his friend, and helps him. Compare Shaw: "I am persuaded that a modern nation that is satisfied with Broadbent is in a dream. Much as I like him, I object to be governed by him, or entangled in his political destiny" (II,811). Despite Larry's high-flown rhetoric, which he fervently believes as much as Broadbent does his own, the assumptions on which Larry habitually acts reveal his true partnership with Broadbent, both ironically "civil engineers" (II,893): they will engineer (contrive, plan, guide the development) civil matters (the relationship of citizens to each other and the state). Unlike Juan, he does not dissociate himself from the person who does or will soon rule the local establishment, and he fails to work for the Life Force.[35]

Nor is Keegan a viable alternative. Without him, Larry might have more stature than he does, but Keegan only talks, not acts. While every dream may be a prophecy, as he says, he does not act to fulfill it—unlike Juan, the philosophic man who both contemplates and acts (goes to heaven). In contrast to Juan who steers, Keegan drifts to the Round Tower to break his heart uselessly, as he admits. Perhaps for this reason Shaw makes him a defrocked priest, that is, powerless. As Shaw says in his preface to *Barbara*, wherein a religious person seizes power, "it becomes the duty of the Churches to evoke all the powers of destruction against the existing order" as it is "capitalistically organized. . . . Nor can they merely endure the State passively, washing their hands of sin" (III,50–51). The passive Keegan does no better than endure and may do worse: vote for Broadbent.

Jubilation marks *Superman*, where the vital geniuses Juan and Ann win; it holds hope for the future. *John Bull* dramatizes the defeat of the Life Force: one of the two men who might work for it serves Mammon, the other abnegates his social and spiritual responsibilities. Beatrice Webb's comments on *Barbara* apply more to *John Bull*: "the triumph of the unmoral purpose," "hell tossed on the stage—with no hope of heaven."[36] In *Barbara*, moral not unmoral purpose triumphs in an arena that holds the hope of heaven.

In *Superman*, Juan refers to "honor, duty, justice, and the rest of the seven deadly virtues" (II,636). Tanner's *Handbook* calls them "trumpery ideals" and names three more: right, religion, and decency (II,752). The fact-facing agent of the Life Force should reject them. "I wouldnt have your conscience, not for all your income," says Peter Shirley. Undershaft, who faces facts, cannily inverts this platitude: "I wouldnt have your income, not for all your conscience" (III,111). According to Keegan, "every jest is an earnest in the womb of time" (II,1021). Conscience, perhaps the seventh deadly virtue, makes cowards of us all, as Hamlet says, for in terms of the Life Force it demands adherence to the others. Whereas *Superman* transvaluates conventional values in citing deadly virtues, *Barbara* does so in citing deadly sins: "Food, clothing, firing, rent, taxes, respectability, and children" (III,171–72). Money provides salvation from these sins, of which one, respectability, must be denied, ignored, or transcended, as it is by Jack and Juan in *Superman*, if one serves the Life Force. Perhaps in defiance of respectability, the Undershaft tradition demands bastardy as a condition of succession. In *Barbara*, the three principal characters aid the Life Force. All have what Shaw says in the Epistle Dedicatory to *Superman*: "the true joy in life, the being used for a purpose recognized by yourself as a mighty one . . . the being a force of Nature" rather than a "beauty monger"—rejected by Cusins as empty aestheticism—or a "sentimentalizer"—rejected by Barbara when she throws aside "feverish selfish little . . . ailments and grievances" and revitalizes herself (II,523).

As Shaw writes in his preface to *Barbara*, Undershaft has a "constant sense that he is only the instrument of a Will or Life Force which uses him for purposes wider than his own" (III,31). In the play, he reveals it. Charged by Cusins that he has no power, he replies not that Cusins is right but "None of my own, certainly," which is different. The power that drives the armaments factory is "A will of which I am a part." In other words, he is an instrument of the Life Force, used for purposes he recognizes to be greater than his own. While Cusins dismisses the statement as metaphysics, claiming instead that he is enslaved by "the most rascally part of society," Undershaft's answer is neither assent nor dissent but "Not necessarily." It is the world's will he serves, to use Tanner's phrase, and if "the rascals," he says, adopting Cusins's term, are shrewder than the good people, he is not to blame. He challenges Cusins to leave off "preaching and shirking" in favor of "fighting the rascals," but he cannot compel Cusins or any good person to do so: "I can make cannons: I cannot make courage and conviction" (III,169).

"This marvellous force of life of which you boast," the Devil tells Juan, "is a force of Death: Man measures his strength by his destructiveness" (II,653–54). Yet as Undershaft demonstrates, the force of death may serve that of life. The maxims summarize his arguments to convert Cusins and also reveal his relationship to the Life Force. Since man should not withhold the sword from the hand given by God, the use of weapons is part of a divine force. The right to fight belongs to all, the right to judge to none; therefore Undershaft provides weapons to all, without moral judgment; it is up to the good people to select this means of power and place an order. Man may have the weapon but the victory is heaven's, or the Life Force's. Whoever holds power does not own it but is an instrument of it. The weapons are for man to use; their employment is part of the Life Force's continual struggle by trial and error.

Although Undershaft is a conscious agent of the Life Force, he does not represent the ultimate in social or spiritual organization. To Shaw, no one person or principle does. A hint at Undershaft's deficiencies may be his statement that after his immediate predecessor's maxim nothing remained for him to say. To the contrary, much remains to be said—and done. Other hints abound. Money and gunpowder, says Undershaft, are necessary to salvation; no one says they are sufficient for it. When he tells his wife that Stephen does not interest him, she responds that he is their son. His comment, "I see nothing of myself in him, and less of you" (III,145), indicates myopia, for there is much of her in the boy. Furthermore, a socialist like Shaw, or even unlike him, would hardly consider a capitalist, however benevolent or farsighted, to represent the final word in social evolution.

These comments on Undershaft's shortcomings should not diminish his importance in regard to the Life Force. Apart from what has been said, the steps he takes to find the right sort of successor are those that

Juan says the philosophic man takes to help life fulfill itself. Clearly, Undershaft wants someone who will go further than he—or one*s* who will do so, since in Act III Cusins and Barbara alternate as Undershaft's antagonist, suggestive that they constitute a single entity. While they later define what they hope their separate roles will be, Shaw pits both in dialectical argument with Undershaft, thereby fusing the social-intellectual and the spiritual.

They join in marriage as well. Does this forecast the subordination of one vitalist's purpose to the other's? No, since the fulfillment of one demands the fulfillment of the other. Note one of Shaw's frequently overlooked statements: "When it comes to sex relations, the man of genius does not share the common man's danger of capture, nor the woman of genius the common woman's overwhelming specialization" (II,511). Cusins is that man of genius, Barbara that woman.

Symbolic of the Life Force's union of religion and sex is the Salvation Army's conversion of Donizetti's wedding chorus to the West Ham Salvation March. But the wedding of Barbara and Cusins unites both with social advance. Juan's discussion of sex relations fits these characters:

> In the sex relation the universal creative energy, of which the parties are both the helpless agents, overrides and sweeps away all personal considerations, and dispenses with all personal relations. The pair may be utter strangers to one another, speaking different languages, differing in race and color, in age and disposition, with no bond between them but a possibility of that fecundity for the sake of which the Life Force throws them into one another's arms at the exchange of a glance. (II,675)

In stage directions and dialogue, Cusins's desire to marry Barbara, who offers no resistance, reflects this energy. *"By the operation of some instinct which is not merciful enough to blind him with the illusions of love,"* says Shaw, *"he is obstinately bent on marrying Barbara"* (III,80). In the screen version, Shaw has him virtually paraphrase Juan when he declares to Barbara, within minutes of first seeing her:

> I have impulses that I cannot explain. They come very seldom. But when they come, nothing can stop me. There is an end of my conscience, of my prudence, of my reason. Such an impulse seized me the moment I saw you. You are poor; you are ignorant; our table manners are different; our relatives will not mix; everything is against our association with oneanother. No matter: to be with you I will join the Army: I will put on the uniform and beat the drum: in short, I am hopelessly and for ever in love with you and will follow you to the end of the world until you marry me.

Were Barbara averse to his advances, she would reject them. Instead, *"calm and greatly amused,"* she asks him to see her home and meet her family, adding only, "God has some little surprises for you, my friend."[37] Cusins has an inkling that this union transcends the personal and links to godhead: "Dionysos and all the others are in herself. I adored what was divine in her, and was therefore a true worshipper" (III,164). Unlike Tanner, who is pursued rather than pursues, Cusins is also unlike him in that he realistically regards his future as unknown: "I dont like marriage: I feel intensely afraid of it; and I dont know what I shall do with Barbara or what she will do with me. But I feel that I and nobody else must marry her" (III,118). At the end of the play, when Barbara renews her vocation, she pointedly includes Cusins and marriage. She will have him still, she says, imploring her mother to help her select a house for her and Dolly (his nickname). With children or not, their home will be no dolly's house for her, only a place, as she says, for them to live in. Whatever biological work she may do there, she is not a specialist but has other work outside.

"The law for father and son and mother and daughter is not the law of love," says Tanner: "it is the law of revolution, of emancipation, of final supersession of the old and worn-out by the young and capable" (II,599). His *Handbook* defines a revolutionist as "one who desires to discard the existing social order and try another" (II,737). *Barbara* dramatizes both ideas. As Undershaft's adoptive son, Cusins, challenged to blow up existing society, will supersede him; Barbara, marrying Cusins, will become not only Mrs. Andrew Undershaft—which connects all three characters—but also Mrs. Andrew Undershaft *VIII*, which emphasizes her union with her father's revolutionary superseder.

Tanner talks and writes pamphlets; Ann suggests that he enter Parliament. Doyle talks but serves the plutocracy; Keegan preaches but does nothing. With Shaw, Cusins recognizes that pamphleteering and preaching are ultimately "no use" (III,39); with Undershaft, that Parliament is a "foolish gabble shop" (III,151), a surrogate for Undershaft's real power; with Barbara, that to refuse Undershaft's offer would mean his reading reviews and her playing the piano, i.e., uselessness. Undershaft challenges him, "Turn your oughts into shalls, man. . . . Whoever can blow men up can blow society up" (III,175). His acceptance of the challenge is not capitulation. He takes Undershaft's accomplishments as foundations for greater and different work. What he accepts is power to act. To do otherwise would leave him an ineffectual intellectual. Seizing the opportunity to turn should into shall, he becomes a Platonic philosopher-king—"Plato says . . . that society cannot be saved until either the Professors of Greek take to making gunpowder, or else the makers of gunpowder become Professors of Greek" (III,178)—to save society in the sense of redeeming it, not preserving it.

Furthermore, he changes during the play, gradually becoming an agent of the Life Force. A prologue to the screenplay clarifies his interest in religion. He calls it "my life's work. . . . I am interested in the essence of all religions. . . ."[38] Shaw suggests his abilities in Act I, chiefly when he takes charge of the introductions to clarify identities for the long-absent father of the family. He becomes more prominent when he becomes Undershaft's confederate in Act II, but even here he does not understand the Life Force. At this stage, he believes, quoting Euripides' *The Bacchae*, "the spirit of God—whate'er it be—" is a "law that abides and changes not" (III,118). He later realizes that it does change, that a dead language and civilization cannot alter the world, but that power to blow up society and create anew can do so materially and spiritually. Regardless of possible personal consequences (the loss of Barbara), he surrenders to the Life Force. "I dare. I must. I will," he says (III,182), inaccurately. There is no "must" about it. Note the Devil's partly accurate words: "As to your Life Force, which you think irresistible, it is the most resistible thing in the world for a person of any character" (II,685–86). It is resistible, but not for a person of real character, like Cusins, who chooses to become its agent. His will accepts the dare and turns it to must. Like Juan's philosophic man, he contemplates, then acts upon his understanding of what to do.

What are the shalls to which he will try to change his oughts? To begin with, he repudiates the Armorer's faith, which is to sell arms to anyone who can pay for them, be that person aristocrat or republican, capitalist or socialist. "I shall sell cannons to whom I please and refuse them to whom I please." Undershaft replies, "From the moment when you become Andrew Undershaft, you will never do as you please again" (III,169). As Turco explains, this means "that the Professor will be in the grip of the Life Force, *not* that he will be under the thumbs of the very 'rascals' Undershaft proceeds to urge him to fight."[39] Also, Undershaft may back down, since he does not repeat the ultimatum that sparked Cusins's rejection: unless he keep the Armorer's faith he will not enter the business. Minutes earlier, Cusins demonstrated his abilities by persuading Undershaft that by a technicality he qualifies as a bastard and that the tradition the heir be uneducated is unimportant. To only one demand does he agree, a change of name, but "Would any man named Adolphus—any man called Dolly!—object to be called something else?" (III,166). Next, he defeats Undershaft in Undershaft's own province, business. Tenaciously, this University don who does not know whether three-fifths is more or less than half persuades the capitalist to raise his salary and add a percentage of the profits. Undershaft perceives his mettle: "You are a shark of the first order, Euripides. So much the better for the firm!" (III,167).

His renunciation of the Armorer's faith recalls his statement that like

Barbara he loves the common people. Although Undershaft scorns such
love, neither Cusins nor Barbara changes his mind. To the contrary,
Cusins reiterates it and goes further. For him, all do not have the right
to fight and he intends to judge who does have. By small but significant
changes, shown here in brackets, Shaw's screenplay clarifies Cusins's
principles:[40]

> As a teacher of Greek I gave the intellectual man weapons against the
> common man [I gave the rich man an intellectual weapon against the
> poor man]. I now want to give the common man weapons [give the poor
> man material weapons] against the intellectual man. I love the common
> people. I want to arm them against the lawyers, the doctors, the priests,
> the literary men, the professors, the artists, and the politicians, who, once
> in authority, are more disastrous and tyrannical than all the fools, rascals,
> and imposters. I want a power simple enough for common men to use,
> yet strong enough to force the intellectual oligarchy to use its genius for
> the general good.   (III,181)

The last sentence is particularly important. Work for the good of the
people differs from work for the profit of a few. Cusins, who will be
among the intellectual oligarchy, will try to use his genius for that good.
In a Fabian fashion, he aims to broaden the base of power, to build upon
Undershaft's social advance, to turn the capitalist Perivale St Andrews—
by extension and analogy, England—into a socialist democracy.

Will he succeed? Realistically, Shaw does not prophesy. He depicts a
dramatic present and a desire. At issue is whether social position shapes
the individual or the individual the position. Shaw does not simplisti-
cally choose: "What a man is depends on his character; but what he does
. . . depends on his circumstances" (III,46). Will Cusins report for work
at six the next morning, as Undershaft wants, or at eleven, as he wishes?
Each is determined, but Shaw is ambiguous. Although the play's final
line is Undershaft's command, "Six o'clock tomorrow morning, Euripides" (III,185), its final word, added in revision, is a reminder that the
Professor of Greek will take over the factory—mitigating the possible
impression of Undershaft Triumphant.[41]

"Every genuine religious person is a heretic and therefore a revolutionist," says Tanner's *Handbook* (II,737). Barbara learns that while, in
Undershaft's words, "All religious organizations exist by selling themselves to the rich" (III,121), they have no choice for, in Shaw's words,
"The notion that you can earmark certain coins as tainted is an unpractical individualist superstition" (III,35). No matter that Undershaft's factory manufactures instruments of death. "There is no wicked side," she
says: "life is all one" (III,183). Also, "There are no scoundrels" (III,90).
Names are irrelevant. What counts—as Bluntschli indicates in *Arms and*

the Man when Nicola denies his engagement to Louka—are the consequences of one's actions, not moralistic labels. It is irrelevant to call Undershaft wicked or a scoundrel. His elimination of poverty counts. For Shaw, the Salvation Army's military form of organization is apt: "Does it not suggest that the Salvationists must actually fight the devil instead of merely praying at him? At present, it is true, they have not quite ascertained his correct address" (III,37). Barbara finds it. In changing her locus of operations, she becomes, like Cusins, an agent of the Life Force.

According to Shaw, "there is no salvation . . . through personal righteousness, but only through the redemption of the whole nation from its vicious, lazy competitive anarchy" (III,36). Barbara and Cusins unite to accomplish both simultaneously. Like Cusins, she accepts the power Undershaft offers, like him she aims to use it for her own ends, and as with him the alternative is ineffectuality. He intends to create social redemption from without, she individual redemption from within. The absence of poverty enables her to eliminate the bribe of bread, concentrating her energies on hungry souls, not hungry bodies. Her job will not be easy. These workers are quarrelsome and uppish, like Bilton; some are atheists, like Shirley.

Barbara more than loves the common people, she is one of them. Early in the play her mother complains that she discharged her maid and lives on a pound a week. Late in the play Barbara asserts, "I have no class, Dolly: I come straight out of the heart of the whole people." She adds that Undershaft's workers think he "ought to be greatly obliged to them for making so much money for him—and so he ought." What the workers are to her biological father, she—a worker for God—is to her heavenly father: "When I die, let him be in my debt, not I in his" (III,183–84), i.e., let him be obliged to her as Undershaft is to his workers. Although Undershaft and Cusins are foundlings, Shaw links them with capitalism and intellectualism. He links Barbara with the proletariat. Perhaps her union with Cusins to create simultaneous social and spiritual redemption suggests a union of proletarian and Fabian.

Cusins's accession to power provides a new perspective on efficiency, which in *John Bull* characterizes scoundrels, of which Barbara says there are none. The month after Shaw completed *Superman*, he told Beatrice Webb, "efficiency is obviously not a final term and cannot be held up as an end."[42] In *Superman*, he suggests it may be a socially useful means. Straker wants "to do away with labor. Youll get more out of me and a machine than you will out of twenty laborers" (II,589). Juan regards the Life Force's creation of a brain as an efficient way to determine "the line of greatest advantage" (II,685). *John Bull* condemns efficiency as a means to serve "the cupidity of base money hunters" (II,1018). At issue is not efficiency but the end it serves. With Broadbent, the end is social harm;

with Undershaft, social beneficence. Although he operates efficiently—
even manufacturing explosives in separate small sheds so that if one
blows up little money and few lives are lost—he eliminates poverty and
lays the groundwork for greater and more efficient improvement by
Life Forcers who succeed him. As Charles Frankel perceives, *Barbara*
does not offer a choice "between Efficient Power and Inefficient Virtue. . . . The problem of Power, in a word, becomes the problem of dis-
tributing it, not of eliminating it." He effectively argues that Shaw demands recognition of the purpose for which power is used. Efficiency
and inefficiency differ, but power and virtue need not, and in *Barbara*
efficiency, like power, joins virtue. "Virtue without Power is empty," says
Frankel; "but Power without Virtue, without ideas, is blind." Among this
play's themes are that "Power is not something inherently immoral, and
that . . . the false dilemma of Power *versus* Virtue merely keeps us from
getting ahead with this job."[43]

But what of power used to kill? Like efficiency, killing is a means toward an end. Such a view may seem mad, and the question of madness,
with the readiness to kill, recalls another great English play that Shaw's
trilogy resonates—*Hamlet*, whose original rather than readymade morality, says Shaw, sets it above Shakespeare's other plays.[44] Shakespeare's
sympathetic, serious treatment of a madman is "an advance towards the
eastern consciousness of the fact that lunacy may be inspiration in disguise, since a man who has more brains than his fellows necessarily appears as mad to them as one who has less" (III,17). This explanation
characterizes the "madness" of the Life Force figures or visionaries in
this trilogy. A twentieth-century Don Juan, says Shaw, "is now more Hamlet
than Don Juan" in that he is "a true Promethean foe of the gods"; naturally, "the man whose consciousness does not correspond to that of the
majority is [considered by them] a madman" (II,502,510). Shaw says Jack
is *"possibly a little mad"* (II,541) and when he calls Ramsden "Polonius,"
Ramsden accuses him of considering himself Hamlet. Although Mendoza quotes Hamlet on Ophelia and Laertes, both he and Jack have the
dream of Hell. The Life Force visionary is Keegan, called mad by others
and himself. William Irvine's interpretation of Jack and *Superman* applies more to Keegan and *John Bull*: "a modern Hamlet who goes on
talking and philosophizing in the face of modern imperatives. . . . As a
Hamlet play, it condemns its most interesting character to relative inac-
tion."[45] In *Barbara*, Undershaft says that he, Cusins, and Barbara—all
Life Force figures—are mad.

Note the variations. Jack, who may be slightly mad and whose consciousness exceeds that of the others, writes about revolution. Although
Keegan's words may carry weight among the villagers, he seems deliberately to avoid using his influence. Reprimanding Patsy Farrell for gen-

uflecting to him, he calls himself "unfit and unworthy to take charge of the souls of people" (II,926). Nor, apparently, does he consider himself fit to take charge of their bodies. The visions of the ironically self-described madman transcend those of everyone else in the play, but he is unable or unwilling to act on his perceptions of the destructiveness of capitalism. Not only does he give no indication he will work against Broadbent and the syndicate the Englishman represents, he confesses—with more weariness than irony—that it might be "better" for him to vote for an Englishman who knows what he is doing than an Irishman who does not (II,1015). With a young face but white hair, he may look—as photographs of Granville Barker in the role look—older than his fifty years. His reference to himself as "an oldish man" (II,988) suggest a person who has given up. Not so Undershaft, Cusins, and Barbara. This trio, whose madness is explicitly characterized as superiority to the common mob, recognizes that the readiness to kill, a major theme in *Hamlet*, is "the final test of conviction, the only lever strong enough to overturn a social system, the only way of saying Must" (III,174). To Shaw, "Hamlet, who does not dream of apologizing for the first three murders he commits, is always apologizing because he has not yet committed a fourth" (IV,285). The reason is that though he was raised according to "the vindictive morality of Moses he has evolved into the Christian perception of the futility and wickedness of revenge and punishment," but he cannot comprehend this reason (V,688). In *Barbara*, one character's circumstances of birth resemble Hamlet's: Cusins, who like Hamlet is his own cousin, though unlike the Dane his father, not his mother, married the spouse's sibling and he is the product of the second not first marriage. Cusins grapples with "the moral question" (III,168). When Undershaft argues that poverty has withstood sermons and articles and urges him to kill it, not preach at or reason with it, Cusins initially repudiates this sentiment but finally admits Undershaft is right. Unlike Hamlet's murder of Claudius, such killing is not retributive. Circumstances alter cases. With weapons forged by fire and resulting in blood—recalling the Salvation Army's motto, "Blood and Fire," which Undershaft says might be his own and which Cusins accepts when he joins the Army and then the firm—such killing, of a pestilence more rotten than anything in Shakespeare's Denmark, is justified. With Shaw's Hamlet and Shakespeare's, readiness is all by the play's end, when both are willing and able to kill the rank offender of the commonweal.

In his preface to *Puritans*, written the year before *Superman*, Shaw anticipates Jack and Juan, Cusins and Barbara: "From Prometheus to the Wagnerian Siegfried, some enemy of the gods, unterrified champion of those oppressed by them, has always towered among the heroes of the loftiest poetry." He identifies "the Superman" as the newest such hero and adds, "Two and a half centuries ago our greatest English dramatizer of life, John Bunyan, ended one of his stories with the remark that there is a way to hell even from the gates of heaven, and so led us to the equally true proposition that there is a way to heaven even from the gates of hell" (II,33–34). This statement obviously relates to Shaw's trilogy, which discusses paths from hell to heaven. In *Superman*, the "great gulf" between them is a parable, "the difference between the angelic and the diabolic temperament" (II,647). The frontier "is only the difference between two ways of looking at things. Any road will take you across it if you really want to get there" (II,687). Recognizing that "the brain will not fail when the will is in earnest" (II,672), Juan leaves for the frontier. In *John Bull*, Keegan does not feel at home in a world he calls hell. Heaven may be close: "Could you have told me this morning where hell is?" he asks Larry. "Yet you now know that it is here." Heaven "may be no farther off" (II,1019). Yet without Juan's will, a being like him "can only look at Heaven from here: you cant reach it" (II,923). Barbara wishes she "could have the wings of a dove and fly away to heaven!" When she says, "I cant," she means that the journey is not that simple, for it requires both Juan's steadfast will and also work. She agrees with Cusins that "the way of life lies through the factory of death"— *through*, not *in*—and adds, "through the raising of hell to heaven and of man to God" (III,182–84). In the final scene, she becomes "*transfigured*," "has gone right up into the skies," and, dragging at her mother's skirt, becomes as a child again (III,184–85), a condition Matthew says is necessary for entry into heaven.

But Shaw changes metaphors, or rather gives different meanings to "heaven" and "hell," and "earth" as well. In Juan's words, "hell is the home of the unreal and of the seekers for happiness." Containing "nothing but love and beauty," it is—and one may infer the heartfelt anguish of Shaw, a recently retired theatre critic—"like sitting for all eternity at the first act of a fashionable play, before the complications begin." In hell, "Nothing is real"; it is merely "a perpetual romance, a universal melodrama." Earth "is the home of the slaves of reality," where people "play at being heroes and heroines, saints and sinners," but are made aware of their false dreams and true slavery by hunger, thirst, cold, age, disease, and death. Heaven is "the home of the masters of reality," where "you live and work instead of playing and pretending. You face things as they are; you escape nothing but glamor; and your steadfastness and your peril are your glory" (II,637,650–51,682). In Juan's view, like that of most people, what Keegan calls hell is earth, and the horrors he vividly describes are earthly. He sees neither heaven, though he hopes it may be near, nor what Juan calls hell, whose romantic indolence is leagues away from Rosscullen's poverty.[46]

Using Juan's definitions, *Barbara* contains all three places. Wilton Crescent is the hell he describes; West Ham the earth, where people play at being saints and sinners. The masters of reality work at Perivale St Andrews, where they abandon pretence and face facts amidst occasionally perilous explosions. In a passage discarded from the published text, Cusins explicitly says of its workers, "Compared to the West Ham proletariat theyre in heaven already."[47] While Undershaft's factory and town might seem a comparative heaven, with Peter Shirley at the gates, it is really a potential heaven, where Cusins and Barbara may forge it. In the heaven of his dreams, says Keegan, "the State is the Church and the Church the people: three in one and one in three. It is a commonwealth in which work is play and play is life: three in one and one in three. It is a temple in which the priest is the worshipper and the worshipper the worshipped: three in one and one in three. It is a godhead in which all life is human and all humanity divine: three in one and one in three" (II,1021). *Barbara* makes his vision concrete. Where Undershaft has used his power to eliminate poverty, his daughter works toward salvation and her intellectual fiancé, his adoptive son, aims to give power to the people. In the world they hope to create, men and women will do God's work for its own sake and human life will become divine. The three are so interconnected as symbolically to become one. Undershaft sires Barbara, is succeeded by Cusins; he hands on his torch of reality and power to his daughter and to his adoptive son, who assumes his name. Through blood and spirit, he fathers Barbara, who marries Cusins, who Dionysos-like is reborn via the man he calls "Dionysos Undershaft" (III,135). Undershaft looks after people's bodies, Cusins their minds and social needs, Barbara their souls. Only together can they become effective; they form a trinity of body, mind, and soul necessary for economic and spiritual salvation.[48]

Shaw's vision is not simple. Thus, to say as Turco does that "Barbara's 'life is all one' resorts to cliché to muddle the meaning" and that "Cusins's 'all power is spiritual' is only a paraphrase of Carlyle's disastrous aphorism 'All force is moral'" may seriously muddle Shaw's meaning, which insists on the interconnectedness of the different elements of his united trinity. Nor is it accurate to state, "It was Shaw's misfortune to have sensed that his view of life was tragic at precisely the moment when he was temperamentally least capable of facing tragedy."[49] Since all major characters get what they want, the play is comic, not tragic. Undershaft gets the type of heir he seeks, Cusins the chance to try to forge the type of world he envisions, Barbara the devil's correct address. Lady Britomart keeps the foundry in the family and Stephen, relinquishing what he does not want, reconciles with his father, whom he comes to admire. Snobby Price gets the small amount of money he wants, Mrs.

Baines the large amount the Army needs, the Bill Walker, who pays his debt as he wants to pay it, may find his soul saved, for as Undershaft asks, "Can you strike a man to the heart and leave no mark on him?" (III,156). The play is comic in another conventional sense. As Charles Frohman is reported to have said, "Shaw's very clever; he always lets the fellow get the girl in the end."[50] Perhaps one of the most cogent statements on Shaw and the culminating play of this trilogy is by Kingsley Martin, who edited *The New Statesman and Nation*: "He preferred debate in which no one won, though everyone scored." Challenging anyone to find an alternative ending to *Barbara*, he observed that while "Almost any other dramatist would have been content" with a conventionally dramatic solution of the personal situation, "Shaw had become so absorbed in the intensely difficult problem of power and its relation to ideas that he leaves his play and his players wrangling and his audience carrying on the discussion after the curtain falls."[51]

This trilogy connects in another basic sense. As Shaw says in the Epistle Dedicatory to *Superman*, "Money means nourishment and marriage means children; and that men should put nourishment first and women children first is, broadly speaking, the law of Nature and not the dictate of personal ambition." However, it is more than stupid to place "nourishment and children first, heaven and hell a somewhat remote second, and the health of society as an organic whole nowhere," since man's desire to be rich and woman's to be married inevitably produces, "without a highly scientific social organization," poverty, prostitution, infant mortality, and adult degeneracy. "In short, there is no future for men, however brimming with crude vitality, who are neither intelligent nor politically educated enough to be Socialists" (II,504–5). *Superman* deals not with nutrition but with sexual attraction, now left by men to women. *John Bull* dramatizes nutrition as handled by the stupid men to whom women now leave it, the result being the horrors just cited. *Barbara* dramatizes nourishment as practiced by sagacious people, at least one with socialist ideals, who provide true nutrients for the health, not stultification, of society.

Setting a theoretical groundwork, *Superman* shows possibilities of success and failure for the Life Force in the frame play and an abstract success in the inner play. *John Bull* dramatizes a probable failure, *Major Barbara* a possible success. Act I of *Barbara* corresponds to the frame play of *Superman*, Act II to *John Bull*, and the final scene to the Hell scene of *Superman*. Beginning with possibilities of the Life Force's success and failure, it moves toward a depiction of failure and concludes with a hope of success—a fitting finale to and culmination of Shaw's "big three."

Notes

1. Letter to Siegfried Trebitsch, 22 August 1919, quoted in Louis Crompton, *Shaw the Dramatist* (Lincoln: Univ. of Nebraska Press, 1969), p. 237.

2. Where I quote or specifically refer to these writers, I footnote them in the usual way. Rather than clutter this essay with footnotes, however, let me here cite the chief sources in chronological order: Bernard F. Dukore, "The Undershaft Maxims," *Modern Drama*, 9 (May 1966), 90–100; Dukore, *Bernard Shaw, Playwright* (Columbia: Univ. of Missouri Press, 1973); J. L. Wisenthal, *The Marriage of Contraries* (Cambridge: Harvard Univ. Press, 1974); Alfred Turco, Jr. *Shaw's Moral Vision* (Ithaca: Cornell Univ. Press, 1976); Robert F. Whitman, *Shaw and the Play of Ideas* (Ithaca: Cornell Univ. Press, 1977); Dukore, *Money and Politics in Ibsen, Shaw, and Brecht* (Columbia: Univ. of Missouri Press, 1980).

3. Letter to James Huneker, 9 May 1905, *Collected Letters 1898–1910*, ed. Dan H. Laurence (London: Max Reinhardt, 1972), p. 526. Hereafter, this volume will be cited as *CL*, II. *Collected Letters 1874–1897*, ed. Laurence (London: Max Reinhardt, 1965), will be cited as *CL*, I.

4. In "The Natural History of *Major Barbara*," *Modern Drama*, 17 (June 1974), 149, Kurt Tetzeli v. Rosador asserts, "Shaw was, when he started work on *Major Barbara*, in the midst of preparing *Man and Superman*" for production. While the chronology makes this questionable, my different conclusion also derives from inference. For dates of the composition of *Barbara*, see Shaw, *Major Barbara: A Facsimile of the Holograph Manuscript* (New York: Garland Publishing, 1981), pp. xiii–xiv, 2, 63, 64, 98, 155, 185, 239, 328.

5. *The Bodley Head Bernard Shaw: Collected Plays with their Prefaces*, Vol. III (London: Bodley Head, 1971), p. 186. Further citations from these seven volumes (1970–74) will appear parenthetically in the text.

6. Letter to Gilbert Murray, 14 March 1911, paraphrased in Wisenthal, pp. 232–33.

7. Crompton, p. 75.

8. Wisenthal, pp. 91–92.

9. Letters to Beatrice Webb, 30 July 1901, and Max Beerbohm, 17 December 1901, *CL*, II, pp. 232, 247–49.

10. *Everybody's Political What's What?* (London: Constable, 1944), p. 156.

11. E. Strauss, *Bernard Shaw: Art and Socialism* (London: Gollancz, 1942), pp. 38–40.

12. Letter to James Huneker, 4 January 1903, *CL*, II, p. 394.

13. Strauss, p. 43.

14. Sean O'Casey, *Drums Under the Window* (New York: Macmillan, 1950), p. 256.

15. Maurice Valency, *The Cart and the Trumpet* (New York: Oxford Univ. Press, 1973), p. 239.

16. Humanities Research Center, University of Texas, Austin, fols. 30–32.

17. Dukore, "Introduction," Shaw, *Barbara Facsimile*, p. xv. Is it coincidental that like *Barbara*, *Heartbreak House* resonates Shylock in *The Merchant of Venice*? His "there be land-rats and water-rats, land-thieves and water-thieves" is echoed by Shotover: "Land-thieves and water-thieves are the same flesh and blood. . . . Off with you both" (V,138). Subscribing to Proudhon's view, Shaw agrees. As Undershaft marches out of the Army shelter, he cries, "My ducats and my daughter!" (III,136), spoken by Shylock upon learning that his daughter has left home and taken his money. By contrast, Undershaft's daughter leaves her home for his. Whereas Shylock loses money and daughter, Undershaft invests money to gain his daughter. Wittily, Cyrus Hoy—"Shaw's Tragicomic Irony," *The Virginia Quarterly Review*, 47 (Winter 1971), 69—notes: "Captain Shotover, like Andrew Undershaft in *Major Barbara*, is a munitions maker, and Heartbreak House literally operates on the profits earned from

his death-dealing devices. If here it is not quite true that in the arts of life man invents nothing, the point is nonetheless made that in the arts of life man invents nothing that sells." I thank the anonymous reader of this essay for *Shaw* for calling my attention to Hoy's fine article, of which I was unaware when I completed the essay.

18. *The Collected Screenplays of Bernard Shaw*, ed. Dukore (London: Prior, 1980), pp. 334–35.

19. These stage directions are not in the original holograph or published text but were added when Shaw revised the play in 1930. See Dukore, "Toward an Interpretation of *Major Barbara*," *Shaw Review*, 6 (May 1963), 67–68.

20. Shaw, *Essays in Fabian Socialism* (London: Constable, 1949), pp. 139, 141.

21. Letter to Beatrice Webb, 30 July 1901, *CL*, II, p. 233.

22. Eric Bentley, *Bernard Shaw* (New York: New Directions, 1957), p. 56.

23. Turco, p. 205.

24. Shaw, *The Road to Equality*, ed. Louis Crompton (Boston: Beacon, 1971), pp. 101–2.

25. Bentley, p. 56.

26. *Shaw and Society*, ed. C. E. M. Joad (London: Odhams, 1953), pp. 31–32.

27. *Practical Politics*, ed. Lloyd J. Hubenka (Lincoln: Univ. of Nebraska Press, 1976), pp. 3–6.

28. *Sixteen Self Sketches* (London: Constable, 1949), p. 129.

29. Letters, 27 October 1896 and 26 April 1898, *CL*, I, p. 686 and *CL*, II, p. 37.

30. Charles A. Berst, *Bernard Shaw and the Art of Drama* (Urbana: Univ. of Illinois Press, 1973), pp. 150–51. In striking contrast to Berst's treatment of autobiographical elements in *Man and Superman* is that by Arnold Silver—*Bernard Shaw: The Darker Side* (Stanford: Stanford Univ. Pr., 1982)—who manages to be both farfetched and reductive (to conventional Freudian views). I restrict my comments to his chapter on this play. Arguing from what he admits are "Unascertainable causes" that shaped Shaw's marriage, he allows himself "to speculate on" some "less conscious" aspects of the marriage's early months (but provides no proof that Shaw was less or at all conscious of them) and to "wonder" whether Shaw "unconsciously" (how does Silver know?) rejected sex "in order to avoid the crime of incest and its attendant punishment of castration" (p. 136). From unascertainability, speculation, less consciousness, and unconsciousness, Silver's wonder leaps to such confident assertions as "Fearing in the depths of his being that he might be less than a man, he fantasizes himself as a Superman" (p. 172) but fails to cite a source wherein Shaw calls himself one. To Silver, Shaw's introductory description of Ann "clearly" indicates his "damaging ambivalence" toward her. What he regards as clarity is the statement that her mother does not agree with Octavius that she is enchantingly beautiful. What he calls ambivalence (different from complexity of character) is neither self-evidently true nor proved. In the same paragraph, however, he turns ambivalence to condemnation. "Unable to say unequivocally whether she is physically attractive or not, Shaw then seeks to make the issue irrelevant by declaring that however she looked, 'Ann would still make men dream.'" Partly for this reason and partly since Shaw says that weaker women might call this vital genius a cat, he concludes, with convoluted reasoning, that her role is "designed to discredit her" (pp. 127–28). Because I have greatly abbreviated his example, I invite readers to examine the stage direction *in toto* to decide for themselves whether Silver's interpretations are justified.

31. Bentley, pp. 55, 154; "Foreword," *Plays by George Bernard Shaw* (New York: Signet, 1960), p. xvii.

32. Letter to Josephine Preston Peabody, 29 December 1904, *CL*, II, p. 474.

33. Ibid., p. 475. In a book published the year before *CL*, II, Barbara Bellow Watson reaches the same concluson: *A Shavian Guide to the Intelligent Woman* (London: Chatto and Windus, 1964), p. 76.

34. Arthur H. Nethercot, *Men and Supermen* (New York: Blom, 1966), p. 279.

35. Turco, p. 190, claims that Larry grows "more isolated from the rest" in the final scene. This view is sustained by neither dialogue nor stage directions, which have Keegan leave Larry and Broadbent together. Noting that Broadbent's statement that Larry has "no capacity for enjoyment" repeats the Devil's about Juan (II,96,1005), Wisenthal concludes, p. 96, that Larry "is in some ways not unlike Juan." It seems to me that the repetition ironically emphasizes an *unrealized* potential.

36. Beatrice Webb, *Our Partnership*, ed. Barbara Drake and Margaret I. Cole (New York: Longmans, Green, 1948), p. 314.

37. *Collected Screenplays*, p. 284.

38. Ibid., p. 283.

39. Turco, p. 210.

40. *Collected Screenplays*, p. 349.

41. Dukore, "Toward an Interpretation," p. 70.

42. Letter, 30 July 1901, *CL*, II, p. 235.

43. Charles Frankel, "Efficient Power and Inefficient Virtue," *Great Moral Dilemmas in Literature, Past and Present*, ed. R. M. MacIver (New York: Institute for Religious and Social Studies, 1956), pp. 22–23.

44. Preface to *The Irrational Knot* (London: Constable, 1950), p. xvii. See also Dukore, "Shaw on *Hamlet*," *Educational Theatre Journal*, 23 (May 1971), 152–59.

45. William Irvine, *The Universe of G.B.S.* (New York: Whittlesey House, 1949), p. 239.

46. Hoy, p. 70, points out that Ireland is the materialization of Juan's conception of earth. See n. 17, last sentence.

47. *Barbara Facsimile*, p. 246.

48. What I call a trinity of Undershaft, Cusins, and Barbara, Hoy with a different emphasis, p. 72, suggests is a synthesis of Undershaft's and Barbara's goals "that satisfies the body's material needs and thereby frees the spirit to save itself. The play accomplishes this miracle of synthesis through that union of culture and power which is prefigured at the end when Cusins, who throughout the play has been affianced to the munitions maker's daughter, is designated heir to the Undershaft cannon works as well." In viewing the play this way, Hoy may follow the lead of Eric Bentley, *Bernard Shaw*, p. 167: "Probably the idea of making Cusins the synthesis of Barbara's idealism and her father's realism came to Shaw later, perhaps *too* late." Unlike Bentley, Hoy does not believe the idea came too late. Nor do I.

49. Turco, pp. 227–28.

50. Hesketh Pearson, *George Bernard Shaw: His Life and Personality* (New York: Atheneum, 1963), p. 236. Although "always" is untrue (e.g., *Captain Brassbound's Conversion*), Frohman's remark is generally correct.

51. *Shaw and Society*, p. 31.

Lisë Pedersen

DUCATS AND DAUGHTERS IN *THE MERCHANT OF VENICE* AND *MAJOR BARBARA*

Shaw's life-long interest in Shakespeare and his life-long battle against what he considered to be Shakespeare's "second-hand" philosophy influenced many Shavian plays. Often that influence appears only in the form of brief allusions or quotations, but sometimes it takes the form of rather thoroughly developed parallels between characters, situations, or themes of a Shakespearean and a Shavian play. An influence of the latter kind is suggested by certain similarities in the roles of Portia and Lady Cicely in the trial scenes of *The Merchant of Venice* and *Captain Brassbound's Conversion*. A comparison of the two plays reveals that *Brassbound* resembles *Merchant* not only in the heroine's clever manipulation of the trial to the outcome she desires, but also in Sir Howard's referring to himself as an "upright judge," in Brassbound's insistence on achieving justice though what he really wants is revenge, and in the play's repudiation of the concept of justice under law.[1] Struck by these similarities, Louis Crompton wondered whether Shaw had envisioned the two plays' being performed together, with the parallels in the plays highlighted by Ellen Terry's playing the roles of Portia and of Lady Cicely.[2] Portia was a role in which Ellen Terry had enormous success, and the role of Lady Cicely was written specifically for Miss Terry. Given the similarities in the plays, a pairing of the two in performance would seem logical.

Here, then, the parallel between the Shakespearean and the Shavian scenes is so close as to suggest that one may have been patterned quite consciously after the other. Elsewhere, however, the similarities between Shakespearean and Shavian treatments of characters, situations, or themes are more subtle and complex and may have been the product of Shakespearean influences on Shaw's subconscious. Such may be the case with the impact of *The Merchant of Venice* on *Major Barbara*.

At first glance the only relationship between the two plays seems to be Undershaft's cry "My ducats and my daughter," an echo of Shylock's lament for the loss of his daughter and of the ducats she has stolen from him. At the same time, since Undershaft's is a cry of triumph evoked by his success in winning his daughter away from the Salvation Army by using his "ducats" to corrupt it in her eyes, it inverts the meaning of Shylock's cry.[3] This echo is, of course, quite deliberate.

Another indication there was a connection between the two plays in Shaw's mind, whether consciously or not, is a similarity between a thought expressed in *Major Barbara* and a thought Shaw expressed a year earlier when he had *The Merchant of Venice* in mind. In *Major Barbara* Undershaft tells Cusins that although his partner Lazarus is "a gentle romantic Jew who cares for nothing but string quartets and stalls at fashionable theatres," Cusins will be able to blame his "rapacity in money matters" on Lazarus, as Undershaft has done (III, 167). In a letter to Ada Rehan dated 5 July 1904, Shaw asserted that in the author-actress business association between Rehan and Shaw she would have an advantage because, although he was "not nearly so disagreeable personally" as his writings might suggest, nevertheless people who had not met him would be likely to believe "anything unpleasant" about him and therefore if she were "forced to be disagreeable to the management" she could put the blame on Shaw.[4] The thought here is similar to that in Undershaft's words to Cusins. In both cases a person who is innocent of disagreeableness is to be used as a scapegoat for the disagreeableness of another and will be readily accepted in that role because of an established reputation, in the one case a racial reputation and in the other a personal reputation. Also, in *Major Barbara* the scapegoat is Jewish—indeed, in the screen version Undershaft states flatly that "the role of the Jew in modern Capitalism" is that of scapegoat[5]—and in the letter to Rehan the thought occurs in the same paragraph in which a reference is made to two Jewish characters in *Merchant*; thus a definite link in Shaw's mind between the two plays is established.

These two links invite a comparison between the two plays which is more fruitful than might initially be expected. Since Undershaft's triumphant cry about his ducats and his daughter is an inversion of Shylock's and since the Shakespearean influence on Shaw is often expressed through a Shavian inversion of Shakespeare's ideas and characters,[6] the question of whether or not Undershaft is in any sense an inversion of Shylock is pertinent.

The similarities between Undershaft and Shylock are surprisingly numerous. Both are referred to repeatedly as the devil or in terms suggesting the devil; both are rejected by one of their children—Shylock by his only daughter and Undershaft by his only son—because of their reputations in society; both attempt to trick someone through an offer which is disguised as an innocent and even good act; for both there comes a point where a literal interpretation of the law is important in a victory or defeat; both on occasion flaunt their ruthless brutality unashamedly; and both emphatically reject the concept of forgiveness. The most outstanding differences between the two are in their attitudes toward music and in their success at the end of the play: although Shylock has moments of victory, his role is primarily a descending one that leads to his complete defeat, whereas Undershaft's role seems to be an entirely ascending one leading to what may be a complete triumph at play's end.

The references to Shylock and to Undershaft as the devil have been noted so frequently that they hardly need further documentation here. To recapitulate, Shylock is called a devil by Antonio, Launcelot Gobbo, Salanio, Salarino, and Bassanio; even his own daughter, though she does not directly call him a devil, calls their house a hell before she leaves it. Though Adolphus Cusins is almost the only person who refers to Undershaft as the devil, because he is the only one who entirely sees through Undershaft and the only one to whom Undershaft confides his real purposes and methods, Cusins's references to Undershaft as the devil are numerous and varied. He calls Undershaft Mephistopheles, an "infernal old rascal," the "Prince of Darkness," a "clever clever devil," "you old demon," and "tempter, cunning tempter." Undershaft's daughter Barbara links him to the devil on three occasions—once in describing her idea of what his munitions works must be like and twice in echoing Cusins's epithets for Undershaft. There is an important difference, however, in these devil references: the references to Shylock as the devil are entirely condemnatory, and he is defeated because of his devilish qualities, whereas although Cusins is appalled by Undershaft's devilish qualities and seems unable to repress an unwilling admiration of them, these qualities do enable Undershaft to achieve his goals in the play.

Also, both Undershaft and Shylock are rejected by one of their own children—Shylock by his only child—and the reasons for this rejection are almost identical. Although Jessica leaves Shylock in order to marry Lorenzo, her words make it clear that her rejection of her father is entirely independent of her desire to marry Lorenzo. She acknowledges in a soliloquy that she is guilty of the "heinous sin" of being "ashamed to be [her] father's child," and adds "But though I am a daughter to his blood, / I am not to his manners" (II.iii.16–19). Undershaft's son Stephen also rejects his father because of the shame the relationship to his father has brought him through the constant appearance in the newspapers of the name Undershaft coupled with various newly developed murderous weapons. In his school and university days the other students called him names which reflected their disapproval of the source of his father's income, such as the description of him inscribed in his Bible by a student at Cambridge, a Christian "who was always trying to get up revivals": "Son and heir to Undershaft and Lazarus, Death and Destruction Dealers: address, Christendom and Judea" (III, 72).

As with the devil references, however, the effects which these rejections have on Shylock and Undershaft respectively and on their plays are quite different. Shylock loves his daughter and is deeply hurt by her rejection of him; Undershaft cares nothing for Stephen or Stephen's opinion. All the other characters in *Merchant* approve of Jessica's rejection of Shylock, whereas the other characters in *Major Barbara* have no more interest in Stephen's reaction to his father than Undershaft himself does. Jessica's rejection of Shylock is permanent and is an important part of his defeat in the play, whereas Stephen, after seeing the munitions works, undergoes a complete reversal of his opinion of his father. It is part of Undershaft's triumph that without even trying or caring to do so he has changed Stephen's attitude toward him.

A third similarity in Shylock and Undershaft is that each tries to trick someone through an offer which is presented in the guise of a good, and even self-sacrificing, act. When Shylock offers to lend Antonio money without usury, substituting instead a pound of flesh as forfeit, he asserts that this offer is intended to demonstrate his forgiveness of the "shames" that Antonio has "stained" him with, and he insists that "This is kind I offer" (I.iii.140–43). Similarly, when Undershaft offers the Salvation Army five thousand pounds, he presents it in the guise of a self-sacrificing gesture, arguing that the Army, in preaching against war, will reduce the need for munitions and thus ruin his business. Again, however, there is a difference in the ultimate effects of these two attempts at trickery. Although Shylock's stratagem is successful for a time, it is eventually defeated, and he is hoist by it. Undershaft's trick, on the other hand, causes Barbara's permanent disillusionment with the Salvation Army, a victory which is a necessary step in his eventually persuading her and Cusins to join forces with him in the munitions works.

Another similarity between Shylock and Undershaft is that both are faced with a legal question which is finally resolved by the resort to an extremely literal interpretation of the law. When Shylock wants to foreclose on the bond with Antonio, his insistence on a literal interpretation of the law and the bond is turned against him by Portia, and her strict application of the letter of the law and the bond in a way he had not foreseen causes him to lose everything and sink into utter defeat. When Undershaft finds himself barred from choosing Cusins as his heir by the requirement that his heir must be a foundling, Cusins finds a way around the difficulty by pointing out that a difference between the marriage laws of Australia and those of England could allow him to be considered a foundling under the laws of England, although in fact he is far from being one. The use of a legal technicality in *Major Barbara* inverts the one in *Merchant*, because Shylock is defeated by the literal interpretation of the law in *Merchant*, whereas for Undershaft such an interpretation is a necessary element in his success. Further, in *Merchant* the legal technicality provides the principal turning point of the play, whereas *Major Barbara* makes it clear that the legal qualification of Cusins is only a small difficulty to be gotten out of the way and that the more important test of Cusins's fitness to be Undershaft's heir is a test of his personal qualities. In this light *Major Barbara* seems to reflect Shaw's repudiation of a mere legal technicality as a proper way of providing a climax to a play and, more importantly, as a proper test for any significant human decision to turn on. That Shaw once gave *The Merchant of Venice* the substitute title "the Tricking of Shylock"[7] supports the view that he did not believe the problems posed by Shylock were properly resolved by the legal technicality.

A fifth similarity between Shylock and Undershaft is their occasional unashamed flaunting of a ruthless brutality. Lawrence Danson has demonstrated that the famous "Hath not a Jew eyes?" speech, which often brings great audience sympathy to Shylock, actually begins with his very brutal assertion that he will use Antonio's pound of flesh, if necessary, "to bait fish withal" rather than not foreclose on the bond, because "if it will feed nothing else, it will feed my revenge." It is an indication of Shylock's skill with words that he is able to move from the raw brutality of this assertion to the list of questions which brings him sympathy by linking him with all humanity, and then to make another illogical but effective bridge from this litany to the conclusion of the speech, in which he justifies his desire for revenge by blaming it on "Christian example"—"The villainy you teach me I will execute, and it shall go hard but I will better the instruction" (III.i.55–76).[8] Undershaft, whose motto is "Unashamed," similarly describes in brutal and graphic detail the source of the money which he is offering the Salvation Army—"Think of my business! think of the widows and orphans! the men and lads torn to pieces with shrapnel and poisoned with lyddite . . . ! the oceans of blood, not one drop of which is shed in a really just cause!"—and yet concludes with a justification which gains the acceptance of the Salvation Army and of most of the other characters in the play (III, 133–34).

In addition, both Shylock and Undershaft indulge in brutal gestures as well as brutal speech. When, at the same moment that he is exulting in the death of three hundred soldiers, Undershaft *brutally* kicks aside a dummy soldier that looks *like a grotesque corpse* (III, 158–59), it is as though he were kicking one of the real soldiers whose death means only that his new weapon is a success. The effect is thus brutal callousness like that which Shylock displays as he ostentatiously whets his knife during the trial in anticipation of using it on Antonio.

One of the most important characteristics shared by Shylock and Undershaft is their repudiation of the concept of Christian forgiveness. In demanding the pound of flesh from Antonio, Shylock is demanding justice through fulfillment of the letter of the law and the bond, and to the repeated appeals to him for mercy he responds that there is nothing in the law or the bond which requires him to be merciful. Both the Duke and Portia link their pleas for mercy to the Christian doctrine of forgiveness of sins, the Duke by implication in his question "How shalt thou hope for mercy, rendering none?" and Portia more explicitly in her statement "That in the course of justice none of us / Should see salvation. We do pray for mercy, / And that same prayer doth teach us all to render / The deeds of mercy" (IV.i.88,199–202). Shylock's rejection of the need for mercy constitutes an assumption of responsibility for his own actions and their consequences and a denial of the Christian doctrine that all human beings require forgiveness because they all sin and fall short of perfection.

Undershaft rejects forgiveness with equal vigor and with the same assumption of personal responsibility for his actions. Having verbally destroyed Cusins's arguments in favor of pity and love, qualities Cusins finds missing in Undershaft's philosophy, Undershaft taunts him to resort to a plea for the quality of forgiveness. To Cusins's response "No: forgiveness is a beggar's refuge. I am with you there: we must pay our debts" (III, 178), Undershaft gives wholehearted approval. Undershaft's motto, "Unashamed," carries the same implication that he takes responsibility for his own deeds and seeks no forgiveness for them.

This repudiation of forgiveness is perhaps the most significant quality shared by Shylock and Undershaft because it reflects a major theme of each play. A central concern of *Merchant* is the opposition between justice and mercy, with mercy linked to the Christian doctrine of forgiveness of sins.[9] The Christian doctrine of the forgiveness of sins is also a fundamental concern of *Major Barbara*, but here it is completely rejected. Sidney P. Albert has pointed out that "the language of debt and repayment . . . permeates *Major Barbara*."[10] This is hardly surprising, since the central conflict in the play is between the Salvation Army's philosophy of religion and Undershaft's. In contrast to Undershaft's rejection of forgiveness and insistence on the paying of debts, the fundamental tenet of Christianity, and thus of the Salvation Army, is that all humans are sinners and therefore subject to eternal punishment were it not for the infinite mercy of God, who allowed his Son to pay for the sins of all those who seek salvation by asking for forgiveness and acknowledging that Christ has paid their sin-debts for them.

The battle lines in this conflict between two views of forgiveness are drawn early in the play. Shortly after Undershaft meets his family for the first time in Act I, he rejects Cholly Lomax's offer of an excuse for his means of earning a living, indicating that he is not ashamed of this means and rejecting both the paying of conscience money (a way of asking for forgiveness for one's actions) and the turning of the other cheek (a way of expressing forgiveness for the actions of others). The opposing view is introduced a few lines later, when Barbara says that all men are sinners and "theres the same salvation ready for them all" (III, 90). The "salvation ready for them all" is of course brought about by the forgiveness of their sins.

Act II, set in the Salvation Army shelter, demonstrates the ways in which the Army tries to convert sinners by leading them to acknowledge their sinfulness and seek the forgiveness of God; the act concludes with the destruction of the audience's—and then Barbara's—faith in this approach to salvation. First, Rummy Mitchens and Snobby Price reveal that as a repayment for the bread and treacle they have received from the Army they are confessing to sins they have never committed, thus undermining the validity of the Army's concept of forgiveness. It is, however, through Bill Walker's reactions to forgiveness that the main burden of this theme is carried in Act II. Walker is a man of independent spirit who prides himself on what he conceives to be his manliness, and he is consequently tormented by Jenny Hill's insistence on forgiving him for striking her. Unable to bear this torment, he attempts unsuccessfully to escape it by paying for his sin, first by exposing himself to an almost certain beating by a professional boxer and later by offering money to square his debt.

Barbara objects to the Army's acceptance of Walker's or Undershaft's money because if they are allowed to feel that they have paid for their sins with money, they will not feel the need to accept God's offer of salvation by seeking forgiveness for these sins. That Barbara has seen this seeking and accepting of forgiveness as the essential means to salvation is confirmed by her telling Undershaft, in Act III, that she will never forgive him for turning Bill Walker's soul "back to drunkenness and derision" after she had "set him in the way of life with his face to salvation" (III, 155–56). As Albert has demonstrated, however, by the end of the play Barbara is completely won over to Undershaft's rejection of forgiveness as a way to salvation.[11] After Undershaft has pointed out to her the unfairness of trying to convert starving people with the bribe of bread, she accepts the much greater challenge of trying to convert the well-fed people who live in the middle-class comfort of Undershaft's factory town. In addition, she declares that she wants to do "God's work" in such a way that when she dies God will be in her debt and she will be the one to forgive Him (III, 184). Here she is clearly rejecting not only the Salvation Army's means of converting souls, but also the entire concept of forgiveness.

Thus, although Shylock and Undershaft are alike in their rejection of mercy and forgiveness, their respective plays take directly contradictory positions on this important theme, *The Merchant of Venice* insisting on the need for mercy and forgiveness and *Major Barbara* rejecting that need.

A marked contrast between Shylock and Undershaft exists in their attitudes toward music. Shylock on several occasions expresses his dislike of music, as when he warns his daughter to lock his doors and windows against the sound of "the drum / And the vile squealing of the wry-necked fife" (II.v.29–30). Undershaft, on the other hand, is by his own account "particularly fond of music" (III, 87). In the Elizabethan view, of course, music represented harmony, and the dislike of music would mark Shylock as a villain. Precisely what Undershaft's love of music signifies is not so easy to say, but Shaw's own well-known love of music suggests it should be considered an admirable trait.

In connection with the musical processions in the two plays, an important contrast should be noted. The procession which Shylock rejects, citing particularly his dislike of the drum and fife, is used as a cover for Lorenzo's stealing Shylock's daughter away from him, a theft which constitutes a rejection of his way of life; the procession which Cusins and Undershaft join, playing the drum and trombone respectively, is for Undershaft a celebration of his victory in stealing his daughter away from the Salvation Army, the first step in persuading her to accept his way of life.

The most important contrast between Shylock and Undershaft is one that has been evident throughout the above discussion of their similarities: despite all these similarities, Shylock's role is primarily a descending one, whereas Undershaft's is entirely ascending. Shylock is looked upon with opprobrium from beginning to end of his play, and although he experiences some moments of apparent triumph, they are rendered bitter for him by the defection of his daughter, and they are soon turned into defeat by his enemies. For Undershaft, on the other hand, even the initial disapproval of his way of life by all the other characters in the play is mixed with a grudging respect, and by play's end he has routed all opposition to himself and has won all the major characters to an acceptance of his way of life, at least as a proper means to their own ends. The very qualities which have brought defeat to Shylock have brought victory to Undershaft.

A consideration of the similarities between Shylock and Undershaft leads to the discovery of other similarities between *The Merchant of Venice* and *Major Barbara*. Sham or hypocritical Christians abound in both plays;

the proper uses of money is an important theme in both plays; and both playwrights use contrasting settings for the symbolic values with which they invest these settings.

Shylock is not the only character whose values are questioned in *The Merchant of Venice*. Most of the play's supposed Christians display at times some very unchristian attitudes and behavior.[12] Antonio, who later learns better, in the first part of the play continually heaps abuse upon Shylock, calling him names and spitting on him. Even as Antonio is asking for the loan of money from Shylock, he asserts that he will continue to abuse Shylock in this manner. Salanio and Salarino taunt Shylock mercilessly about the loss of his daughter. And in the trial scene Gratiano taunts him with an equal lack of mercy after he has been defeated. In fact, Gratiano expresses the same desire for revenge that has motivated Shylock throughout the play. Furthermore, there is never the slightest indication that Jessica's desire to convert to Christianity has any spiritual component. It seems to stem entirely from her desire to marry Lorenzo and from her desire to dissociate herself from her father's reputation. In leaving Shylock she steals large sums of money from him. She even trades (for a monkey) a ring which is the symbol of her mother's love for her father, and through the rest of the play she never once expresses any concern for him or even any curiosity about his fate. She benefits materially from her conversion to Christianity, but the spiritual gain is hard to detect.

Major Barbara also has an abundance of sham or hypocritical Christians. Rummy Mitchens and Snobby Price pretend to have been converted by the Salvation Army. The words and actions of Lady Britomart, Stephen, and Charles Lomax betray a lack of any real understanding of basic Christian doctrines and suggest that they perceive their adherence to the Church of England largely as a matter of fulfilling the obligations of their class. Lady Britomart finds religion both an unpleasant and an improper subject for discussion, and when Undershaft calls it the only subject "that capable people really care for" she insists "on having it in a proper and respectable way" and orders Lomax to "ring for prayers," thus indicating that she conceives of religion solely as the performance of certain ceremonies. That she sees such ceremonies as class obligations is suggested by her protesting that it would be "most improper" for Undershaft to leave just as the prayers are to begin because it would make a bad impression on the servants (III, 91–93). Further, although Lady Britomart often speaks of wickedness and wicked people, she does not relate wickedness to the Christian concept of sin and forgiveness. Quite the contrary: the idea of wickedness reminds her of the duties of class and country. To Stephen she says, "In our class, we have to decide what is to be done with wicked people" (III, 73), and to Cusins she says that if he inherits the munitions works he "must simply sell cannons and weapons to people whose cause is right and just, and refuse them to foreigners and criminals" (III, 168), implying in the first case that the aristocracy are themselves immune to wickedness and in the second that those "whose cause is right and just" are the English and that foreigners and a class called "criminals" are the wicked. No Christian beliefs color such attitudes.

Lomax sees religion as something consonant with respectability, and he is willing to respect anything that goes by the name "religion," regardless of its philosophical or spiritual content. He belongs to "the Established Church"—the most formal and respectable one for an Englishman—and feels that there is "a certain amount of tosh about the Salvation Army," but he respects the Army because "you cant deny that it's religion; and you cant go against religion, can you?" (III, 89). His ideas about wickedness, like Lady Britomart's, reflect little understanding of Christian beliefs and, furthermore, are easily swayed by material considerations. On two occasions he implies that although "we cant get on without cannons" nevertheless "it isnt right" to manufacture them and therefore Undershaft cannot expect to get into heaven (III, 89, 153), but later, impressed by the cannon works, Lomax asserts that "there is a certain amount of tosh about this notion of wickedness" and implies that Undershaft should not be condemned simply because he manufactures munitions. Lady Britomart interprets the latter statement to mean that "because Andrew is successful and has plenty of money to give to Sarah," Lomax "will flatter him and encourage him in his wickedness," and Lomax acknowledges the validity of her interpretation (III, 175–76).

Stephen has little to say about religion except to assert that there is only "one true morality and one true religion" (III, 90). Questions of morality he sees in absolute terms—he does not, in fact, acknowledge that there can be questions of morality, because "right is right; and wrong is wrong; and if a man cannot distinguish them properly, he is either a fool or a rascal" (III, 76). However, he is subsequently so favorably impressed by the material prosperity of the munitions works and the factory town dependent on it that he entirely reverses his earlier condemnation of his father.

Related to this lack of true Christian values and beliefs on the part of many characters in both plays is the overriding concern with money which they exhibit. Both plays are in fact very much about money and its impact. Both open with discussions of money. *Merchant* opens with Salarino and Salanio attempting to account for Antonio's sadness. The first and the most persistent explanation they offer is that Antonio is worried about the safety of his fortune, which is all tied up in ventures at sea. Almost immediately they are joined by Bassanio, with his request for money from Antonio to enable him to undergo the casket test for the hand of Portia, who will bring to her husband an enormous fortune. Although Bassanio indicates that he loves Portia, he does so only secondarily. His first explanation of his "plots and purposes" in connection with the money he is requesting from Antonio is that it will enable him to pursue a way "to get clear of all the debts" he owes (I.i.133–34). It is Portia's money that has caused her father to set up the casket test so that she will not fall prey to the first fortune-hunter who seeks her hand, and certainly her fortune is at least part of the motivation of her suitors. It is less Shylock's religion than the usury he exacts as a moneylender which has made him hated. Though Jessica may leave her father for love of Lorenzo, she does not depart empty-handed; she takes large amounts of her father's money and jewelry with her. The princes of Morocco and Aragon lose their bid for Portia because they value gold and silver too highly. The Duke cannot break the law to save Antonio from Shylock's revenge because the "trade and profit of the city" would suffer if merchants from other cities could not depend upon the Venetian law to uphold all contracts of debt (III.iii.26–30). Only in the last act does all this concern about money diminish, probably because the characters who appear in that act have by now become the possessors of assured wealth. Even in this act, however, the ultimate importance of money is underscored when the play itself closes with the news that three of Antonio's argosies have "richly come to harbor" (V.i.277) and with the giving of Shylock's deed of inheritance to Lorenzo and Jessica.

The obsession of *Major Barbara* with money never abates.[13] The play opens with Lady Britomart's explanation to Stephen of the need to ask Undershaft for an additional annual income for Sarah and Barbara now that they are to be married. Stephen learns to his horror that he has been dependent all his life on Undershaft's money and that his father wants to disinherit him in favor of a foundling. The rest of Act I expresses the repudiation by Undershaft's family and prospective sons-in-law of his means of earning money but their simultaneous dependence on this money. Act II opens by demonstrating through Rummy Mitchens, Snobby Price, and Peter Shirley the desperate plight of those who do not have access to enough money, and moves from there to a discussion between Cusins and Undershaft of Undershaft's religion of money and gunpowder. It concludes with Undershaft's successful attempt to buy the Salvation Army. Act III is given over mainly to the demonstration of what Undershaft's millions can do for a city and its inhabitants and to the arguments between Cusins and Undershaft and between Barbara and Undershaft that end in their accepting his millions as the means

of reforming the world and saving souls. It is clear, then, that the need
for money and the question of the proper uses of money are dominant
motifs in both plays.

A comparison of the conclusions which the two plays reach about the
need for and use of money is complicated because both playwrights have
used the technique of moving their characters back and forth between
and among several settings, each of which represents certain concepts
and values. In *Merchant* the two settings are the realistic, commercial
world of Venice, where people must struggle to earn a living, and the
fairy-tale world of Belmont, where money flows freely from an undeter-
mined source (we never learn how Portia's father amassed his apparently limitless fortune) and all needs are met as if by magic.[14] Though
the movement is back and forth between the two settings, the play begins in the real world of Venice and ends in the unrealistic world of
Belmont. Thus, the money problems of the real world are not actually
resolved; the characters are merely moved to a fairy-tale world in which
these problems do not exist. The question of the taking of usury, the
initial reason why the Venetians hate Shylock, is never resolved but instead the ground for the hatred of Shylock is shifted to his ruthless
desire for revenge, and its moral and spiritual bankruptcy demonstrated easily by Portia. The other characters then join Portia and Bassanio in Belmont, where all have wealth showered upon them and no
one has to consider the moral questions involved in earning a living.
Except for the lesson that money should not be used as an instrument
for gaining revenge, the questions posed by the play about the proper
uses of money are simply evaded when the playwright magically provides the characters with so much money that the problems disappear.
Since Shylock has been so thoroughly condemned in other respects, the
play leaves the impression that his means of making money, by usury,
has also been condemned.

In *Major Barbara*, on the other hand, the movement is among three
settings, the first two of which are, in one way or another, escapist worlds,
and the third of which represents the real world.[15] In some respects
Wilton Crescent, the world of Lady Britomart, is like Belmont, the world
of Portia. For its inhabitants an easy, gracious, and fashionable life has
been made possible by an apparently unlimited supply of money furnished by an absent father. For the younger members of the family the
source of the money is even unknown, as is the source of the money in
Belmont, but Lady Britomart does know that the money comes from
her husband's detested armaments works. When Barbara does learn of
the source of her income, she is "revolted" by Undershaft's claim that
his money saved her from the "seven deadly sins," which he identifies as

"food, clothing, firing, rent, taxes, respectability and children," the "millstones" that keep the human spirit from soaring (III, 171–72).

Nevertheless, Barbara had already come to see the world of Wilton Crescent as an escapist world even before she learned that it was founded on money earned by killing and destruction. Barbara had rejected the useless life of this world for what seemed to her at the time to be the more significant and more spiritual world typified by the West Ham Salvation Army shelter. Though this setting is far from perfect materially— it is marred by desperate poverty and hunger—it gives Barbara useful work to do in feeding the hungry, and it satisfies the needs of her spirit by allowing her to feel that she is saving souls. In the first scene in the West Ham shelter, however, the audience is made aware of the deceit upon which this world is founded. The audience hears the real opinions of Rummy Mitchens and Snobby Price with respect to the work of the Salvation Army and thus is not taken in by the behavior they adopt in the presence of the Army workers. Through her father's success in buying the Army, Barbara also comes to realize that the world of the West Ham shelter has a foundation as questionable as that of Wilton Crescent: "I was happy in the Salvation Army for a moment," she later tells Cusins. "I escaped from the world into a paradise of enthusiasm and prayer and soul saving; but the moment our money ran short, it all came back to Bodger: it was he who saved our people: he, and the Prince of Darkness, my papa" (III, 182).

The third setting, Perivale St Andrews, the world of Undershaft's munitions works and factory town, represents the real world, the only world in which people can effectively work toward a better world. Though it seems ideal to those who see only its material side—Lady Britomart, Stephen, Sarah, and Lomax—both Barbara and Cusins are aware of what it lacks as well as what it has. Nevertheless, Barbara has come to agree with her father that the precondition for saving souls is saving bodies. As Undershaft puts it, the souls of his factory workers and their families "are hungry *because* their bodies are full" (emphasis added; III, 173). In this world there is no secret about the source of the money which keeps these people well-fed, well-clothed and well-housed. It is the "factory of death," Undershaft's munitions works. The source of this money is not evil, however, because "there is no wicked side" of life; "life is all one." The money from the munitions works is necessary to lay the groundwork for the saving of souls, and thus "the way of life lies through the factory of death" (III, 183–84).

In this respect also, then, *Major Barbara* inverts the theme and direction of *Merchant* which, while actually evading the issue, gives the impression that Shylock's occupation, usury, is evil. *Major Barbara*, contrarily, demonstrates that the way Undershaft has acquired wealth (through death and destruction) is of no moral consequence—earning money by any means is simply a necessity. This inversion of the money theme goes hand in hand with the difference in direction the two plays take between the real world and the escapist worlds. In *Merchant* the characters move from the struggle of the real world to a conclusion in the fairy-tale world, while in *Major Barbara* the characters move from two escapist worlds to a conclusion in the real world where the struggles of life go on.

The similarities between *Merchant* and *Major Barbara* are so numerous that the influence of Shakespeare's play on Shaw's can hardly be ignored. The inversions, however, raise the question of how the influence of Shakespeare operates in Shaw's work and what significance it has for the understanding of Shaw and his work. One answer to these questions is that Shakespeare's influence manifests itself in Shaw's plays in such a way as to reinforce Shaw's criticisms of Shakespeare and to illuminate the ways in which Shaw's philosophy contrasts with what he considers to be Shakespeare's philosophy.

When Barbara expresses despair over her loss of faith in the Salvation Army, Undershaft advises her that since she has discovered that her morality or religion "doesn't fit the facts" she should "scrap it. Scrap it and get one that does fit" (III, 170–71). Shaw's fundamental criticism of Shakespeare was that Shakespeare failed to follow the practice advocated by Undershaft. "Shakespear's morality is a mere reach-me-down," Shaw asserted in the Preface to *The Irrational Knot*, where he distinguished writers of the first order, who write "fictions in which the morality is original and not ready-made" from writers of the second order, who accept a "ready-made morality . . . as the basis of all moral judgment and criticism of the characters they portray."[16] Therefore, in spite of his belief that "In manner and art nobody can write better than Shakespear,"[17] Shaw placed Shakespeare in the second order of writers because he felt that Shakespeare simply adopted and reflected the moral, political, and religious thought of his time instead of examining this thought, challenging what was unrealistic in it, and offering in its stead a morality or philosophy that was more realistic. The inversions in *Major Barbara* of the characters, motifs, and themes of *Merchant* are therefore a Shavian criticism of Shakespeare's moral philosophy.

Danson has discussed in detail the evidence from Shakespeare's time which demonstrates that although there were hardly any Jews in Elizabethan England and although the great majority of the moneylenders in England at that time were not Jews but Christians, the image of the moneylender as a rapacious Jew nevertheless persisted. Instead of acknowledging that the change from the feudal land-based economy to the mercantile economy of the Renaissance required a change in the

attitudes toward usury since the lending of money at interest is essential
to a merchantile economy, the Christians of Shakespeare's time continued to condemn usury as unchristian and used the Jew as a scapegoat
for their own practice of usury.[18] In his depiction of Shylock, Shakespeare was obviously following the conventional thought of his time rather
than devising a new morality that would take these facts into account.

   In his comments on Shylock Shaw repudiated Shakespeare's depiction
of Shylock in this stereotype of the rapacious, heartless moneylender.
For example, although Shaw again and again condemned actor-manager
Henry Irving's altering Shakespeare's plays in production to suit his own
taste, on one occasion Shaw praised Irving's transformation of the role
of Shylock from villain to sympathetic victim. In Irving's hands, Shaw
said, "The Merchant of Venice became the Martyrdom of Irving, which
was, it must be confessed, far finer than the Tricking of Shylock."[19] On
another occasion Shaw remarked that Irving had taught Shakespeare a
lesson in his interpretation because he "gave us, not 'the Jew that Shakespear drew,' but the one he ought to have drawn. . . ."[20] Thus Undershaft's unseen partner, Lazarus, the "gentle romantic Jew" upon whom
Undershaft's alleged rapacity in money matters is blamed—a character
to whom no reference was needed for the play's action but who seems
inserted—several times—into the dialogue to recall us to the Shylock
tradition.

   In Undershaft Shaw has drawn a character who earns his living not
by usury, but by a means looked upon with as much condemnation in
Victorian England as usury was in Elizabethan England—Shaw himself
referred to it as "the most sensationally anti-moral department of
commerce"[21]—yet a means which was considered essential to England's
existence, the making of munitions. In depicting Undershaft neither as
villain nor as martyr but as a victor who wins not only the acceptance
but the admiration of his society for his activities as munitions maker,
Shaw was doing for Undershaft and his society what he felt Shakespeare
should have done for Shylock and Shylock's society. He was setting before his audience the real facts and the real situation in England and
showing them the inappropriateness of their condemnation of "money
and gunpowder" in a world entirely dependent upon money and gunpowder. To satisfy Shaw Shakespeare should have taken a similar line in
Merchant, showing his audience the inappropriateness of their hatred
and condemnation of Shylock for his taking of usury when they were
living in a world entirely dependent on the system of usury for its continued economic survival.

   Shaw's insistence on the importance of facing the facts of life realistically is also reflected in the almost wholesale repudiation of the theme
of mercy and forgiveness in Major Barbara. Behind this repudiation is

Shaw's feeling that the concept that a wrong act can be wiped away simply by repenting of it and asking for forgiveness is totally unrealistic. In the Preface to *Major Barbara* he flatly states:

> Forgiveness, absolution, atonement, are figments: . . . You will never get a high morality from people who conceive that their misdeeds are revocable and pardonable, or in a society where absolution and expiation are officially provided for us all.   (III, 43)

The Preface to *Androcles and the Lion* expresses a similar view: ". . . to encourage a man to believe that though his sins be as scarlet he can be made whiter than snow by an easy exercise of self-conceit, is to encourage him to be a rascal" with consequent ill effects for society (IV, 567). The man who is not offered this forgiveness for his sins must endure the torments of his conscience until these torments prod him into reforming himself. This man, then, by reforming himself improves society, whereas the sinner whose sins are forgiven does not. Thus, the inversion of *Merchant*'s theme of mercy, an inversion implicit in the repudiation of forgiveness in *Major Barbara*, again reflects Shaw's belief that Shakespeare's plays often fail to face facts realistically and shape their morality to fit these facts. *Major Barbara* seems to be a repudiation of the moral thought of *The Merchant of Venice* and thus to be an embodiment of Shaw's principal objection to Shakespeare's plays.[22]

Notes

1. *The Bodley Head Bernard Shaw: Collected Plays with Their Prefaces*, ed. Dan H. Laurence (London: Max Reinhardt, 1970–74), II, 365. Subsequent references to Shaw's plays will be to this edition, and volume and page number will be given parenthetically in my text.

Another Shakespearean influence is suggested by the many references in *Brassbound* to Sir Howard, the judge, as a thief and a rascal and to the human qualities of judges under their ermine robes. *King Lear*'s concern with the hypocrisy of human systems of justice comes immediately to mind, especially Lear's "Change places and, handy-dandy, which is the Justice, which is the thief?" *Shakespeare: The Complete Works*, ed. G. B. Harrison (New York: Harcourt, Brace & World, 1968), IV.vi.156–57. Subsequent references to Shakespeare's plays will be to this edition, and act, scene, and line citation will be given parenthetically in my text.

2. In his helpful comments as one of the editorial readers of this article, comments for which I am very grateful.

3. Bernard F. Dukore has pointed out this ironic inversion in "The Undershaft Maxims," *Modern Drama* 9 (May 1966), 94.

4. *Bernard Shaw: Collected Letters 1898–1910*, ed. Dan H. Laurence (New York: Dodd, Mead, 1972), pp. 431–32.

5. *Major Barbara: A Screen Version* (Baltimore: Penguin Books, 1951), p. 127.

6. See, for example, Gordon W. Couchman, "Comic Catharsis in *Caesar and Cleopatra*," *Shaw Review* 3 (Jan. 1960), 11–13; Stanley Weintraub, "Shaw's 'Lear,'" *Ariel: A Review of International English Literature*, 1 (July 1970), 59–68, revised and augmented in *The Unexpected Shaw* (New York: Unger, 1982). I have investigated this Shavian inversion of Shakespeare in two articles: "Shakespeare's *The Taming of the Shrew* vs. Shaw's *Pygmalion*: Male Chauvinism vs. Women's Lib?" *Shaw Review*, 17 (January 1974), 32–39, reprinted in *Fabian Feminist: Bernard Shaw and Woman*, ed. Rodelle Weintraub (University Park: Pennsylvania State University Press, 1977), pp. 14–22; and "From Shakespearean Villain to Shavian Original Moralist: Shaw's Transformation of Shakespeare's Richard III and Edmund the Bastard," *McNeese Review*, 22 (1975–76), 36–50.

7. In an obituary of Henry Irving written for the *Neue Freie Presse* of Vienna, reprinted in *Pen Portraits and Reviews* and in *Shaw on Shakespeare: An Anthology of Bernard Shaw's Writings on the Plays and Production of Shakespeare*, ed. Edwin Wilson (New York: E. P. Dutton, 1961), p. 262.

8. *The Harmonies of "The Merchant of Venice"* (New Haven: Yale University Press, 1978), pp. 105–8.

9. See, for example, Frank Kermode, "The Mature Comedies," *Early Shakespeare*, Stratford-upon-Avon Studies, 3 (London: Arnold, 1961), pp. 221–24, reprinted in *Twentieth Century Interpretations of* The Merchant of Venice: *A Collection of Critical Essays*, ed. Sylvan Barnet (Englewood Cliffs, N.J.: Prentice-Hall, 1970), pp. 97–100; Nevill Coghill, "The Basis of Shakespearean Comedy," *Essays and Studies*, 3 (1950), 1–28; and Barbara K. Lewalski, "Biblical Allusion and Allegory in *The Merchant of Venice*," *Shakespeare Quarterly*, 13 (1962), 327–43.

10. "The Lord's Prayer and *Major Barbara*," *Shaw and Religion* (*Shaw*, vol. 1), ed. Charles A. Berst (University Park: Pennsylvania State University Press, 1981), p. 120. In addition, Albert's article "The Price of Salvation: Moral Economics in *Major Barbara*," *Modern Drama* 14 (Dec. 1971), 307–23, demonstrates that throughout the play moral and religious views and actions are expressed in terms appropriate to financial balance sheets.

11. "The Price of Salvation," p. 321.

12. See, for example, C. L. Barber, *Shakespeare's Festive Comedy: A Study of Dramatic Form and Its Relation to Social Custom* (Princeton: Princeton University Press, 1959), pp. 168–69; H. B. Charlton, *Shakespearian Comedy* (London: Methuen, 1938; rptd. 1966), pp. 123–60; A. D. Moody, "An Ironic Comedy," in *Shakespeare: The Merchant of Venice* (London: Arnold, 1964), reprinted in *Twentieth Century Interpretations of* The Merchant of Venice, pp. 100–8; and John Palmer, *Political and Comic Characters of Shakespeare* (London: Macmillan, 1964), pp. 433–35.

13. In "The Price of Salvation" Albert provides a thorough summary of *Major Barbara*, demonstrating that in every scene money is an important consideration.

14. Many critics have examined the two worlds of *Merchant* and the significance of these worlds. Prominent among them are John Russell Brown, in his "Introduction" to the Arden edition of the play (New York: Random House, 1964), pp. liii–lviii; Sigurd Burckhardt, *Shakespearean Meanings* (Princeton: Princeton University Press, 1968), pp. 211–36; Danson, *Harmonies*, passim; Peter G. Phialas, *Shakespeare's Romantic Comedies: The Development of Their Form and Meaning* (Chapel Hill: University of North Carolina Press, 1966), pp. 143–44, 167; and Theodore Weiss, *The Breath of Clowns and Kings: Shakespeare's Early Comedies and Histories* (New York: Atheneum, 1974), pp. 111–57.

15. Bernard F. Dukore, in *Bernard Shaw, Playwright: Aspects of Shavian Drama* (Columbia: University of Missouri Press, 1973), p. 90, has discussed the significance of the three set-

tings in *Major Barbara*, noting particularly Albert's identification of them with the three settings of *Man and Superman*: hell, "the home of the unreal and of the seekers for happiness"; earth, where "men and women play at being heroes and heroines, saints and sinners" but their bodily needs drag them "down from their fool's paradise," making them "slaves of reality"; and heaven, "the home of the masters of reality," where "you face things as they are" and work towards improving life.

16. Postscript to the Preface to *The Irrational Knot*, reprinted in *Shaw on Shakespeare*, pp. 229, 230.

17. Letter published in *The Daily News* of London in April 1905, reprinted in *Shaw on Shakespeare*, p. 4.

18. Danson, pp. 141–48.

19. *Shaw on Shakespeare*, p. 262.

20. Ibid., p. 38.

21. In a letter of 7 October 1905 to Gilbert Murray, *Collected Letters*, p. 566.

22. I would like to acknowledge with gratitude the assistance of Bernard F. Dukore, who made many valuable suggestions for the improvement of this article.

Martin Quinn

WILLIAM ARCHER AND *THE DOCTOR'S DILEMMA*

The late spring of 1906 saw the death of Henrik Ibsen. In early July, a month later, Ibsen's translator and champion in England, William Archer, would challenge Bernard Shaw, his friend and former collaborator (on *Widowers' Houses*), to face the "King of Terrors" in his own drama, implying that a play could not be serious unless someone died in it. The result was the Shavian "tragedy" *The Doctor's Dilemma*, written in August and September and first produced in November 1906 by J. E. Vedrenne and Harley Granville Barker at the Court Theatre. Although Shaw's friendship with the famed bacteriologist Almroth Wright as well as an ingrained antipathy to medical superstitions provided the major substance and thrust of the play, it was Archer's pointed criticism that brought such experience into dramatic focus—against the background of Ibsen's much written about departure from the world stage.

Ibsenist Shaw and Ibsenite Archer observed the passing of the Norwegian playwright with long articles, both written within days of their subject's demise. Shaw's piece, entitled simply "Ibsen," published as an obituary in *The Clarion* on Friday, 1 June 1906, argued for Ibsen's recognition as "the greatest dramatist of the nineteenth century."[1] Archer's retrospective, "Ibsen As I Knew Him," appeared in the June number of *The Monthly Review* and reconstructed the leading impressions of his many meetings with the "old min" from the first timid introduction at Rome in 1881 to the parting salute at Christiania (Oslo) in 1899.[2] Archer endeavored to reveal both the character and personality of the deceased, setting to rest much rumor and distortion, while Shaw assessed the motive power behind Ibsen's art and the nature of his influence upon the modern age.

In a letter to Archer on 7 June 1906, Shaw complained of problems with his own translators and expressed the fear that Archer was about "to let loose on the Continent a selection from the staggering hallucinations which you firmly believe to be a sound critical biography of my unfortunate self." Having registered surprise at the detail that his friend divulged of the long association with Ibsen, Shaw concluded with a mild taunt, "I had no idea that you had seen so much of him. It throws a light on the gross secretiveness of your disposition. Apparently the only person you ever tell anything to is Charles [Archer, William's brother, fellow translator and eventual biographer]."[3] (Owing to his "total ignorance of Norwegian," Shaw himself had foregone an opportunity to meet Ibsen in Munich and "to explain his plays to him" during an 1890 journey with Sidney Webb to the Passion Play at Oberammergau.)[4] Archer replied with advice on the "enormities" of Siegfried Trebitsch's translations of Shaw's work, pointing up the defects in G. B. S.'s own rudimentary German, but reassuring his old colleague that he intended only to give "some purely external data as to the performances of your plays" during the course of an interview on the German stage.[5] On July 7, a few days after a balloon ascension, eventually to be transmuted into the airplane crash in *Misalliance*, Shaw again wrote Archer, taking issue on historical grounds with a recent *Tribune* article on Gilbert and Sullivan. And on 10 July Shaw urged the formalist-minded Archer to accept a new, somewhat fanciful definition of a dramatic masterpiece: "a play whose faults you learn to endure . . . a perfect breath-bereaver."[6]

Under this steady barrage of Shavian barbs and perhaps with half an eye to good copy, Archer went public. In *The Tribune* on Bastille Day 1906 Archer examined Shaw's "notable utterance" on the death of Ibsen, in particular the passage which observed that "Ibsen seems to have succumbed without a struggle to the old notion that a play is not really a play unless it contains a murder, suicide, or something else out of the Police Gazette." Shaw had gone on to paint Dickens and Ibsen as typical nineteenth-century morgue-haunters and claimed that the extinctions of "Little Nell and Paul Dombey, the Brand infant and Little Eyolf are each as tremendously effective as a blow below the belt; but they are dishonorable as artistic devices because they depend on a morbid horror of death and a morbid enjoyment of horror."[7] While such a pronouncement may be second nature to an ironist capable of recording his mother's cremation and sister's death from tuberculosis with philosophic sangfroid, Archer—whom Shaw often accused of being a sentimentalist—had other ideas. Although Archer ignored Shaw's indictment of Dickens, he exonerated Ibsen from complicity in any gratuitous or deliberate slaughter of innocents—observing that in twenty-five plays Ibsen kills just three children. However, the real problem, according to Archer, was that Shaw not only failed to appreciate Ibsen's poetry (partly because of the language barrier) but that his own plays shrank from confronting the "affirmation and confirmation of destiny which only death can bring."

Until death itself were banished or until the mass of mankind found themselves living to the age of Methuselah (in due course Shaw would address this contingency), Archer argued, a dramatic poet who omitted mortality as a subject would be proclaiming his own limitations.

In a press release drafted for *The Tribune* in September 1906 (a copy of which G. B. S. duly sent to Archer with the inscription "What price tragedy now? Yah!") Shaw confessed to having been "stung by this reproach from his old friend" and described the forthcoming production of *The Doctor's Dilemma* as "the outcome of the article in which Mr. William Archer penned a remarkable dithyramb to Death."[8] Archer's article of 14 July 1906, the proximate cause of Shaw's play—it was begun 11 August 1906—is reprinted here in its entirety for the first time since it appeared more than three-quarters of a century ago. The dithyramb in question is the long periodic sentence which begins "But in the meantime . . ." under the sub-heading "Death the Illuminant."

ABOUT THE THEATRE.

BY WILLIAM ARCHER.

Death and Mr. Bernard Shaw—Tragedy as a Relic of Barbarism—"The Illumination of Life"—"Killing a Baby."

One of the most notable utterances called forth by the death of Henrik Ibsen was an article by Mr. Bernard Shaw, which appeared in the "Clarion" for June 1st. Of course, Mr. Shaw has his own peculiar Ibsen, as he has his own peculiar universe. He would not be Mr. Shaw if he saw anything at quite the normal angle. No doubt we have all our personal equation to allow for; but his is so personal as to be unique, and, far from allowing for it, he insists on it as the essential fact. Nor is there any reason to complain of this; for the image he presents to us of any given object is always a suggestive distortion, and, placing it alongside of our own less distorted, but less vivid image, we may sometimes obtain from their fusion a stereoscopic effect of reality. However, I am not now concerned to contrast or combine my Ibsen with Mr. Shaw's. What I wish to consider is the lesson he draws for the dramatists of the present and future from the work of the great dramatist, now, alas! of the past. That lesson, it seems to me, is too much coloured by Mr. Shaw's idiosyncrasy to be entirely sound, at any rate as a general rule of conduct. I cannot but find in it a certain savour of the aestheticism of the fox without a tail.

Ibsen the Morgue-Haunter.

Practically, though not explicitly, Mr. Shaw adopts M. Maeterlinck's famous contention that tragedy is a relic of barbarism—that what art should now aim at is the reproduction of "life itself," as distinct from "a violent, exceptional moment of life." This is how Mr. Shaw puts his point:—

"Ibsen seems to have succumbed without a struggle to the old notion that a play is not really a play unless it contains a murder, a suicide, or something else out of the "Police Gazette." The great men born in the early nineteenth century were all like that: they visited the Morgue whenever they went to Paris; and they clung to Ruskin's receipt for a popular novel—kill a baby. Little Nell and Paul Dombey, the Brand infant, and Little Eyolf are each as tremendously effective as a blow below the belt; but they are dishonourable as artistic devices because they depend on a morbid horror of death and a morbid enjoyment of horror."

We have here two distinct, or partially distinct, theses: first, that any dealing with crime, or violence, or death under what the newspapers call "tragic circumstances" is beneath the dignity of drama; second, that the pathetic effects obtained by the death of children are particularly vulgar and reprehensible. Let us, now, examine a little into these theses. Are they "eternal verities"? Or are they the instinctive self-justification of a dramatist so fatally at the mercy of his impish sense of humour that he cannot keep a straight face long enough to write a scene of pathos or of tragedy?

Mr. Shaw's Ideal.

Perhaps it may help us to answer this question if we can place beside Mr. Shaw's statement of what drama should not do his exposition of what it should do. And here the same article helps us. Towards the end we come upon this passage:—

"What we might have learned from Ibsen was that our fashionable dramatic material was worn out as far as cultivated modern people are concerned; that what really interests such people on the stage is not what we call action . . . but stories of lives, discussion of conduct, unveiling of motives, conflict of characters in talk, laying bare of souls, discovery of pitfalls—in short, illumination of life for us."

In the clause I have omitted Mr. Shaw gives as instances of the "action" which we do not want, the duel in "The Dead Heart" between Sir Henry Irving and Sir Squire Bancroft and the scene of attempted "rapine" in "Peril." Very well; for my part, I accept his statement of what we want on the stage, with one obvious but essential proviso—namely, that the stories of lives shall be told, and the discussions of conduct conducted, in such form as to give us that peculiar order of emotion which the theatre alone can give, and which is the solo justification of its complex and unwieldy mechanism. Now it is manifest that we do not go to the theatre to listen to exhaustive biographies—to Boswell's "Johnson," or Morley's "Gladstone," or even to the shorter compilations of Plutarch or Suetonius. What is meant by the "story of a life," for theatrical purposes, is the story of some episode in a life, which may be chosen, no doubt—indeed, ought to be chosen—so as to throw as much light as possible upon the life as a whole. This is only a rather cumbrous way of saying that we go to the theatre primarily for the revelation of character, and secondarily, I may add, to deduce those general conclusions as to the social and metaphysical order of things which are implicit in any vital presentment of individual character and destiny. Observe that in this "secondarily" I am traveling beyond Mr. Shaw's record; for this, or something very like it, must be what he means by "illumination of life."

Comedy v. Tragedy.

Here it may be noted that our premises rule out the futile discussion as to whether character or action is the essential element in drama. We have admitted that, so far as we are concerned, character is the great essential; it only remains to determine in what way character is best exhibited on the stage. Now, without begging the question, we may say that the whole experience of mankind tends to show that, for theatrical purposes, character is best exhibited in an ordered series of events, or more briefly, an action. In the dialogues of Plato the characters of Socrates and others are admirably presented: but because they have little or no action they have never been placed on the stage. An intrepid Society proposes to recite on a stage the Dialogue in Hell from Mr. Shaw's "Man and Superman," and I am far from saying that it may not prove an amusing entertainment: but if all drama were to take this form, the theatre would soon cease to exist; for why should its costly machinery be applied to producing an effect which could equally well be produced by intelligent recitation in any hall or private room? Mr. Shaw, indeed, has shown, what Molière had shown before him, that, by a particular sort of intellectual dexterity, a dramatist may make a very little action the vehicle, so to speak, for a great deal of discussion. But even in "Le Misanthrope" and "Les Femmes Savantes," even in "John Bull" and "Major Barbara," there is an ordered series of events through which, and in relation to which, the characters are displayed and developed. And these plays are, after all, only brilliant comedies—a form of art, which, however engaging, is placed by universal consent a little lower than the other form of art which deals seriously, and even sombrely, with the more serious and even sombre aspects of human destiny. When we speak of the great dramas of the world, it is not of these or of such plays that we think, but of the "Agamemnon," the "Oedipus," the "Medea," of "Othello" and "Lear," of "Polyeucte" and "Phedre." It is much if "Le Misanthrope" as a sort of tragi-comedy, and in courtesy to the great name of Molière, may find a place on sufferance in the tail-end of the list.

Death the Illuminant.

"But do you not see," Mr. Shaw may say, "that it is precisely against this 'universal consent' of yours that I am protesting? Do you not see that I am urging what Nietzsche would call a re-valuation of dramatic values?" Oh, yes, I see that well enough; and I am now going to state the reasons why I do not think that the re-valuation will commend itself to the mass of mankind, for many a generation to come. The reader may or may not have noticed a little word which, in paraphrasing Mr. Shaw's ideal of drama, I somewhat disingenuously slipped in. I described drama as "a vital presentment of individual character *and destiny*," and then pretended that I had not travelled beyond Mr. Shaw's record. But, in fact, I had. That totalization of human experience which is implied in the expression "destiny" is not contemplated in Mr. Shaw's philosophy of drama. He gives us glimpses of life, dissertations on psychology, sometimes penetrating, always amusing. He gives us "discussions of conduct, conflict of characters in talk," enough and to spare. But he eschews those profounder revelations of character which come only in crises of tragic circumstance. He shrinks from that affirmation and consummation of destiny which only death can bring. Death is, after all, one of the most important incidents of life, not only to him or her who dies, but to those who survive. Not the least momentous problems of human conduct are those concerned with the facing of death for ourselves and the enduring of it in others. If, in Mr. Shaw's own phrase, "the illumination of life," is the main purpose of drama, what illuminant, we may ask, can be more powerful than death? To compare a tragic dramatist's preoccupation with death to a morbid tourist's haunting of the Morgue is, with reverence be it spoken, to talk very idly.

There may come a time, perhaps, when, in the vast majority of men, death will be scarcely more tragic than falling asleep: a time when almost everyone shall live to extreme old age, and flicker out like a spent flame: a time when any other ending will rank as a sort of monstrosity to be hushed up, and at all events remote from the domain of art. When that time comes, I venture to prophesy that drama, too—except, perhaps, in the form of farce, idyll, or spectacular ballet—will flicker out like a spent flame. A world which has no use for either pity or terror will have no use for tragedy. But in the meantime, while death is still the touchstone of character, the supreme test of fortitude, the refuge of despair, the consecrator of greatness, the decorator of loveliness, the crass intruder and the deliverer yearned for in vain, the matchless stimulant, the infallible anodyne, the signature to the slave of life, the mystery and the solution, the problem and the key—so long will the dramatic poet have recourse without shame to what is, in fact, the most penetrating searchlight in the armoury of his craft. It is not the glory, but the limitation, of Mr. Shaw's theatre that it is peopled by immortals.

The Massacre of the Innocents.

And now as to "killing a baby." Only the other day, I suggested, in these columns, a Society for the Prevention of Cruelty to Imaginary Children. It seemed to me (rightly or wrongly) that, in a play I happened to see, the death of a child was dragged in without sufficient reason, as a cheap device for piling up the agony. Than this, nothing can be more inartistic—so far I quite agree with Mr. Shaw. On the other hand, it is one of the almost intolerable and unforgivable facts of life that children do die—that innocent, and beautiful, and happy creatures are, by a greater Dramatist than Henrik Ibsen, or even Bernard Shaw, condemned to suffering and extinction. And is it not one of the unquestionable functions of drama to help us, so to speak, to make up our accounts with that supreme Dramatist? And how are we to do so if this crucial item be omitted? To dwell on it morbidly is of course inartistic, like any other disproportion or excess. To comment on it smugly, as a providential "chastening" for the survivors, is, to my mind, disgusting; and I won't say that the end of "Little Eyolf" may not be in some measure open to this reproach. But Ibsen was certainly not, on the whole, Herod among the playwrights. In twenty-five plays he kills three children (including Hedvig)—no extravagant percentage. In no single instance does he harrow us by representing, or otherwise dwelling upon, the physical suffering of a child. Mr. Shaw's comments on "the 'Brand' scene," which he calls "infamously morbid," show a curious absorption in its surface aspect, and heedlessness of its inner meaning, which I cannot but attribute in part to the fact that he reads the play only in translation. But the ultimate fact is—and this explains much more in his article than the passage on the child question—that Mr. Shaw has a partly instinctive, partly cultivated, horror of poetry. He is so diabolically clever that he can, on occasion, and for dramatic purposes, almost transform himself into a poet. But he always does so with his tongue in his cheek: and he holds it a weakness in Ibsen—and Shakespeare—that they can refrain from "guying" their own imagination.

The Doctor's Dilemma's opening run of nine matinées at the Court Theatre, beginning 20 November 1906, attracted a range of hostile and mixed reviews. Playwright St. John Hankin, writing half a year later, was moved to compare Shaw's fate at the hands of dramatic critics to Ibsen's in the nineties: "In each case, I suppose, it is the novelty, the breaking away from old methods and conventions, which they find so galling. The Athenians, according to St. Paul, always desired some new thing. The English dramatic critic, on the contrary, is always craving for an old one."[9]

The anonymous critic for the Morning Post found the actors at the Court perfect and the scene in which it is discovered that the dying artist Louis Dubedat borrows money from the dinner party of doctors—sparing neither the poorest nor the richest—"a delightful bit of exposition." Nevertheless, the same writer saw the play as "decidedly unpleasant," faulting in particular the "dramatically ineffective" and offensive death scene as well as the epilogue which "made the impression of a harlequinade."[10]

Desmond MacCarthy, critic for the Speaker, using a tactic reminiscent of Archer's 1893 piece "The Mausoleum of Ibsen,"[11] compiled a catalog of contemporary reaction. The Daily Mail suggested that if Shaw wrote the work "to prove that his sensibilities are so dulled that he can see nothing beautiful, nothing sacred, in the dying moments of a man, whose head is pillowed in the breast of the woman who loves him, he has succeeded." The Mail went on to describe the death scene as "offensive and theatrical." Similarly, The Times complained of the play's "discursiveness" and condemned the presentation of Dubedat's demise as an example of bad taste which appealed only to the morbid. The *Daily Graphic* noted the work's vulgarity and lack of feeling.

Not all critics yielded to the conventions of Victorian sentimentality, according to MacCarthy. The *Daily Telegraph* called the death scene "very harrowing . . . pathetic and almost tragic," adding that the playwright "has paid a greater attention than it is his wont to pay to the process of construction"—an observation with which Archer concurred. The *Standard* even noted that Shaw seemed to recline "almost timidly . . . on the more conventional props and stays of stagecraft," while the *Westminster*, on the other hand, brought accusations of "lack of form and precision of idea." The *Globe* found the satire on the medical profession "worthy of Molière" although the *Pall Mall* uttered the familiar cry that Shaw's characters were merely "amusing puppets" about whom the audience cannot "in the least care."

MacCarthy himself, though he declared *The Doctor's Dilemma* "the most interesting play now running," resisted any comparison with Molière. "Mr. Shaw's satire," he wrote, "is amusing and often witty, but it is essentially satire upon contemporary and temporary types. . . . It is not airy, permanent satire upon human ignorance and pretence; but hilarious, thumping, obvious fun, made at the expense of prevailing prejudices, very good of its kind, but overdone." MacCarthy responded to the necessarily "chilly, quiet, matter-of-factness" of Dubedat's expiration and to the artist's devastatingly successful "pose upon his wife." Yet, like Archer, he confessed exasperation that Shaw's irrepressible wit and instinct for caricature rendered him unable to deliver "a perfect and splendid play." In fine, MacCarthy conceded that "glimpses of dramatic excellence" in Shaw's works afforded the very "light [by] which we manage to find fault with him."[12]

Avowing that he had read none of the reviews when he compared Louis Dubedat to Henry James' Roderick Hudson, Max Beerbohm prophesied that the artist's death scene would cause Shaw to be "more or less violently attacked for lack of taste." Although the death-bed pathos is real, according to Beerbohm, in a way that the Dickens who led Little Nell to the slaughter could never achieve, Shaw's error was neither of art nor of taste. Instead, Shaw merely forgot that Bloomfield Bonington's post-mortem effusions were inappropriately addressed to his unemotional colleagues. Furthermore, Shaw's "deep-rooted disgust for the unmoral artist" made it impossible for an audience to mourn Dubedat in the way that James led the reader to mourn a near cousin in fiction, Roderick Hudson. To Beerbohm the only other fault in the play lay in the characterization of Dubedat as a painter of masterpieces. The problem is that he talks too much and too well. "Indeed," Beerbohm maintained, "it is generally the quite bad painters who are most fluent. Good painters think rather with their eyes and hands than with their brain, and thus have a difficulty in conversation. . . . we disbelieve in him as a genius. Only as a scamp is he real to us."[13]

Archer's own appraisal of the work that he challenged Shaw to write professed admiration for the play's intellectual quality mixed with severe reservations about its structure—especially the uncomfortable resolution of the fourth act and, to Archer, the superfluous epilogue. But again let William Archer have the floor, in a review published in *The Tribune*, 21 November 1906.

Court Theatre.

"THE DOCTOR'S DILEMMA."

A Tragedy in Four Acts, and an Epilogue.

BY BERNARD SHAW.

Sir Patrick Cullen	Mr. William Farren, jun.
Sir Ralph Bloomfield Bonnington [*sic*]	Mr. Eric Lewis
Sir Colenso Ridgeon	Mr. Ben Webster
Cutler Walpole	Mr. James Hearn
Leo Schutzmacher	Mr. Michael Sherbrooke
Dr. Blenkinsop	Mr. Edmund Gurney
Louis Dubedat	Mr. Granville Barker
Redpenny	Mr. Norman Page
The Newspaper Man	Mr. Trevor Lewis
Mr. Danby	Mr. Lewis Casson
Jennifer Dubedat	Miss Lillah McCarthy
Emmy	Miss Clare Greet
Minnie Tinwell	Miss Mary Hamilton

Up to the end of the second act "The Doctor's Dilemma" is the most brilliant thing Mr. Shaw has done. Up to the end of the fourth act it is daring, original, and, to my mind, admirable. Unfortunately, Mr. Shaw failed to observe when the fourth act was over, and kept the curtain up and the characters repeating themselves for about ten minutes (which seemed like twenty) after the interest was exhausted. Then came an epilogue, which was absolutely dull, explaining all over again things that we knew by heart, and existing, it would seem, for the sake of a momentary surprise at the close. With the dribbling out of the theme, the pleasure of the audience also dribbled away. And the mischief of it is that Mr. Shaw will doubtless make this "nuciform sac" of the play (as one of his characters would call it) the very apple of his eye, and decline to apply the necessary knife to it. This is a pity; but it would be a still greater pity if the public were to let his obstinacy stand between it and the keen intellectual enjoyment which three-fourths of the play are capable of giving. Mr. Shaw has never been more witty, more penetrating, or (in a sense) more human.

Havoc in Harley-Street.

Some people will no doubt understand the play as an attack on the medical profession. I should be sorry to trust myself in the hands of any doctor who could take serious offence at it. A satire, certainly, it is. Many of the undeniable foibles of the profession are caricatured, many hits are made which, if they were taken too seriously, would doubtless be unfair. But the satire is always good-humoured, and almost all of it is placed in the mouths of the doctors themselves, especially of one wise, sceptical, kindly veteran whom I take leave to think a quite delightful character. One of the doctors, no doubt, is a pompous nincompoop, but even he is genially drawn. Another is the monomaniac of his speciality; but will any reasonable doctor maintain that neither nincompoops nor monomaniacs exist in his profession? The others are capable, sensible men of whom no profession need be ashamed. And, far from following previous satirists, from Molière onwards, in making the whole healing art a delusion, Mr. Shaw actually bases his plot on the assumption that the opsonin theory (in what I presume to be its latest phase) is infallibly right. What is this opsonin theory? Well, we shall see.

Phagocytes and Opsonin.

The play opens in the consulting room of Dr. Colenso Ridgeon. The birthday honours have just been published, and the Doctor is now Sir Colenso. Several of his colleagues call to congratulate him, among the first being Sir Patrick Cullen, the Nestor of the profession. To him Sir

Colenso expounds what I have called the latest phase of his theory, which is, briefly, this: In cases of tuberculosis the hypodermic injection of a vaccine known as opsonin acts as an appetizer to those phagocytes, or white corpuscles of the blood, whose business it is to eat up the disease-germs. But—there is a very important "but"—in certain states of the blood, which are known as negative states, the action of the opsonin is the reverse of beneficent. It destroys instead of whetting the appetite of the phagocytes, and so leaves the disease-germs to germinate at their own sweet will. Before opsonin can safely be injected, then, the patient's blood must be examined. If it is in a positive state, you inject and he recovers; if it is in a negative state, you wait until the rhythm of nature brings about a positive state. This is, roughly, the theory which Sir Colenso expounds to Sir Patrick Cullen. Then enters Sir Ralph Bloomfield Bonnington (commonly known as B.B.), who flatters himself that he is a perfect master of Ridgeon's theory, but who has no notion of the essential distinction between positive and negative states, and cannot be got to pay the slightest heed to it. Other congratulators are Mr. Cutler Walpole, M.R.C.S., whose one cure for everything is the removal of the "nuciform sac"; and Dr. Blenkinsop, a poor local practitioner in the East End, who has been a fellow-student of Ridgeon's. The conversation between these worthies is one of the most brilliant pieces of writing on the modern stage, as full of humour as of thought and character.

Enter the Plot.

But all this time a lady is waiting to see Sir Colenso Ridgeon. He has declined to see her, for his "klinik" is full, and he can take no more patients; but at last he is won over to admit her and hear her case. She is Jennifer Dubedat, and she is pleading for the life of her husband, Louis Dubedat, a consumptive artist. Sir Colenso tells her that if he takes her husband into his "klinik" he must turn some one else out, and that the lives he is trying to save are picked lives which he believes to be worth saving. She pleads that Louis's genius is supremely worth saving, and produces some of his sketches in proof of the point. The doctor is struck by the sketches, and still more struck by the lady. He consents to see this wonderful artist, and judge whether someone ought to be thrown off his life-saving "raft" in order to make room for him. He invites Mrs. Dubedat to bring her husband to a dinner of his professional friends, which he is giving at Richmond in a few days.

When the curtain rises on the second act, the dinner is over, and Mr. and Mrs. Dubedat are just taking their leave. Both of them have won golden opinions, and the young man's charm is thought to be not inferior to his genius. But when they have gone it quickly appears that golden opinions are not the only golden harvest Mr. Dubedat has reaped. He has borrowed money from almost every one of the party, even from poor shabby Blenkinsop; and he has pocketed Cutler Walpole's gold cigarette-case. Moreover one of the maids at the hotel has seen him driving off and rushes in to declare that she is his deserted wife. The man is, in short, an engaging blackguard; and the question now comes to be: Ought Ridgeon to sacrifice another life in order to save his? If we admit the conjuncture imagined by Mr. Shaw—admit the impossibility of saving one life except at the expense of another—the problem is an extremely dramatic one. Moreover, the last scene of this act, in which Ridgeon and Sir Patrick Cullen discuss the situation, is an admirable and really profound piece of writing, worthy of a great dramatist.

Superman or Subterman.

In the third act, the character of Dubedat is fully developed. He is a man born with a very real artistic sense and faculty, but without a glimmer of moral sense. The capacity for shame is omitted from his composition. He proclaims himself "a disciple of Bernard Shaw," and supposes himself a Superman because he is, in all moral regards, a Subterman. But his wife (she is really his wife, for his other marriage was bigamous) believes him to be a hero without fear and without reproach; and in order to "save her hero for her," Ridgeon hands over his case to "B.B.," well knowing that there is every chance that that eminent authority's haphazard method of dealing with vaccines will kill him off. Here, again (admitting Mr. Shaw's premises), we have a most dramatic complication—all the more so because Ridgeon is now clearly aware that he loves the romantic, high-souled Jennifer—the Cornish form of Guinevere, we are informed.

In Articulo Mortis.

What Ridgeon foresaw speedily comes to pass; and in the fourth act we assist at that death-scene which Mr. Shaw has told us that he was determined to produce, in order to rebut the present writer's assertion that he could not keep a straight face long enough to deal with death on the stage. The rebutment, I own, escapes me; for assuredly it is not with a straight face that he acts about suppressing his "vibrion" as Dumas fils would have called Dubedat. At the same time, the death-scene is enormously clever in an uncanny fashion. Dubedat dies in the odour of aestheticism, professing his faith in "Michael Angelo, Velasquez, and Rembrandt, in the might of design, in the mystery of colour." Some people, I fancy, were shocked; but there are people who will be shocked at anything. Others began to be bored; and here I cannot hold Mr. Granville Barker quite blameless. His Dubedat is exceedingly clever, but a long course of Shaw heroes, from Eugene [Marchbanks] onward, has got him into an unreal, preachy method of delivery which he must unlearn if (as an actor) he is to save his soul alive. Miss Lillah McCarthy, who played Jennifer, was charming in the earlier acts, and very good in the death-scene up to a certain point. From that point onwards I cannot help suspecting that truth and feeling had been stage-managed out of her. Certain it is that the last five minutes or so before Dubedat's end struck me as quite unreal. If at this point Mr. Shaw had had the courage to be human, had briefly led up to the parting between Jennifer and the doctors (an admirable piece of irony), and had ended the play there, all might have been well. Instead of this, he sent Jennifer off the stage for an absurd change of dress, and allowed the doctors to fill up the time by sinking into sheer farce. As for the "Epilogue," I shall not reveal the surprise with which it ends, thus leaving intact its one spark of interest.

The acting was, in the main, as admirable as it always is at this theatre. Mr. Eric Lewis's "B.B." is a quite monumental and delightful performance—so that one doubly resented the buffoonery into which he is made to sink at the close. Mr. Ben Webster's Ridgeon is firm, polished, tactful; and nothing could be better than Mr. William Farren, jun.'s Sir Patrick—it had really memorable moments. Mr. James Hearn, Mr. Edmund Gurney, Mr. Michael Sherbrooke were all as good as could be; and Miss Clare Greet deserves special praise for a most original performance of a small part.

W.A.

While Archer's admiration for *The Doctor's Dilemma* may have been sharply qualified, the play was one of the few in which the critic saw Shaw fulfilling "his real duty." Another such triumph, asserted Archer in a 1907 essay entitled "G. B. S. on the Warpath," had been *John Bull's Other Island*.[14] Earlier he observed that the same drama "may be said to have revealed [its author], once for all, to the intelligent public. The political world especially it took by storm."[15]

Widowers' Houses, upon which the Scot and the Dubliner originally collaborated, had been completely disowned by Archer. It "fails," he wrote, "to produce any illusion of real life."[16] A similar note had been struck in his review of *Arms and the Man*: "By attempting to fix his action down to the solid earth he simply emphasizes its unreality."[17] Although Archer noted that *Man and Superman* "swarms with quips and cranks in his best manner," the play was seen finally as "primitive in invention and second-rate in execution."[18] Moreover, *Major Barbara* was too "patently allegorical" for Archer's taste, "fascinating entertainment" but "There are no human beings . . . only animated points of view."[19]

Of *Plays: Pleasant and Unpleasant* in general Archer offered the caustic opinion that "If Mr. Shaw had wanted a really descriptive title for his dramatic works, he should have called them 'Plays, Wise and Silly,' or 'Intelligent and Unintelligent,' or 'Admirable and Despicable.'" Indeed, he continued, "Two out of the seven plays are works of genius [*Candida* and *Mrs. Warren's Profession*] . . . while one of the remaining five [*The Philanderer*] is an outrage upon art and decency." Archer admitted that his reaction to Shaw's work tended to run to exaggeration—even hysteria. Thus he recorded the intensity of his response: "An hour ago I was reading *Candida* for the third time, with bursts of uncontrollable laughter, not unmingled with tears. The thing is as true a poem as ever was written in prose, and my whole soul went out in admiration and gratitude to the man who had created it. Then I re-read an act of *The Philanderer*, and I wanted to cut him in the street."[20]

In the years that followed *The Doctor's Dilemma*, a degree of estrangement developed between the two friends and proponents of Ibsen. Although both were strong public advocates of a national theater, Archer lost patience with Shaw's unwillingness to become enmired in the detailed planning of the enterprise to which the critic sacrificed so much energy over the years. Archer conveyed to Granville Barker his disappointment that G.B.S. had proved a "broken reed," noting of one meeting of the Shakespeare Memorial National Theatre Committee that "Shaw was in his most unhelpful and impossible mood—very funny at times."[21] On the issue of the cutting of Shakespeare's plays for performance the old friends also fell out. Archer pleaded that "To pretend that every line Shakespeare ever wrote possesses meaning and vitality for modern audiences is to say that which is not; and to insist that modern audiences be forced to listen to every line printed under his name . . . is to carry Shakespearean idolatry to the verge of the grotesque."[22] Shaw, with an eye no doubt to the sanctity of his own texts, argued from a different perspective: "The simple thing to do with a Shakespear play is to perform it. The alternative is to let it alone. If Shakespear made a mess of it, it is not likely that Smith or Robinson will succeed where he failed."[23] In the campaign for spelling reform to which he bequeathed his estate, Shaw predicted that "before Mr. Archer is an old man he will be ridiculed as a fogey unless he yields to the overwhelming currency of modern mispronunciations founded on the phonetic suggestions of our half phonetic spelling. . . . If Archer were spelt Ariqricher, the familiar name 'William Ought-jer' would be unknown in London."[24]

World War I saw yet another parting of their paths. Surging with patriotic fervor, Archer—born in the same year as Shaw and fifty-eight in 1914—attempted to enlist in the army. When that effort failed, he devoted much of his time to the service of the Propaganda Ministry, producing a series of lengthy tracts in defense of civilization against the presumed barbarities of the "Huns." Through the bitter years of the war such titles appeared under Archer's name as "The Thirteen Days, July 23–August 4, 1914: A Chronicle and Interpretation"; "501 Gems of German Thought"; "An Die Neutralen" ("To Neutral Peacelovers: A Plea for Patience"); "The Villain of the World-Tragedy: A letter to Professor Ulrich von Mollendorf"; "The Pirate's Progress: A Short History of the U-Boat."[25] Shaw, meanwhile, wrote his inflammatory "Common Sense About the War," stewed over *Heartbreak House*, and lamented the circumstances which had led Englishmen to exult "in the death of Beethoven because Bill Sykes had dealt him his death blow."[26] The years 1917–1918 show a marked gap in their correspondence.

Perhaps triggered by the loss of his son Tom at the front in 1917, Archer's own creative instincts were revived late in the war, and in 1919 his *War is War; or The Germans in Belgium: A Drama of 1914* was published. The play was never performed. Of his friend's attempt to memorialize wartime atrocities Shaw observed: "If neither the Germans nor the British had ever done worse than the worst Mr. Archer showed, they would be armies of angels—comparatively."[27] Indeed, Archer's heroic Lieutenant Kessler, who blows out his own brains rather than order a firing squad to execute civilians, might be thought almost the direct antithesis to Shaw's practical chocolate soldier of the Balkans, Captain Bluntschli, conceived when war was remote.

The breach was felt by the critic (now also playwright) even in his subconscious. In a posthumously published volume, *On Dreams*, Archer recorded that after reading the proofs of an essay on Shaw he had a dream of which he made the following note:

> The beginning is quite vague. I think I had been at some meeting where G.B.S. was speaking—at all events at some place where I had come more or less in contact with him. I left the place, wherever it was, went to the house where I supposed him to be living and sat down outside it, with a book or MS. on my knee. Presently G.B.S. came along, and without seeing me, went up the steps that led to his door. I called out to him, "Halt! are you going to sleep?" He replied, "Yes, I am very tired," or something to

that effect; and then, without any words that I can recollect, I seemed to arrange to have a talk with him when he had rested.

Archer's analysis of the event is even more revealing of the state of their relationship: "My lying in wait for G.B.S., and arrangement for a subsequent meeting, was certainly the result of the regret I had been feeling for finding my treatment of his work, on the whole, unsympathetic, and of my vague desire to talk things over with him, as I would have done years ago."[28]

This urge for reconciliation manifested itself in September 1919 as Archer wrote excitedly to Shaw that "a tolerably complete scheme for a romantic melodrama" had come to him in a dream and lacked only the Shavian touch to become "infallibly THE PLAY OF THE CENTURY." Archer attempted to lure his old colleague into a renewed partnership and outlined the plot of what would become his only box-office success, *The Green Goddess*.[29] Shaw declined the offer but encouraged Archer to go it alone. Happily for his fortunes, he did.

Archer's last appraisal of Shaw was published as the lead article in the Christmas 1924 number of *The Bookman*, which appeared almost simultaneously with the author's death. Entitled "The Psychology of G.B.S.," the essay recapitulates judgments made during the forty years of their friendship. Owning himself "deeply indebted" to Shaw "for many lessons taught me in the years of our early intimacy," Archer avowed that G.B.S. "never succeeded in imbuing me with his inflexible devotion to ideals." His chief regret was that Shaw had made "so great noise and so little mark." Archer professed to reveal "the inmost secret of Mr. Shaw's whole psychology[:] His perception of fact is absolutely at the mercy of his will. The world without has no existence for him, except in so far as it can be, and is, fitted into the pre-existent scheme of his world within. . . . The most honorable of men, the most incapable of telling a falsehood for his own advantage, or even in furtherance of a cause or an argument, he is equally incapable of seeing, reflecting, expressing things as they objectively or historically are. . . . The plain common sense of his world-wide audience tells them that there is something indefinably but fundamentally wrong with his statement of things. He presents a vivacious distortion of life at which they laugh consumedly; but, having done so, they go on their way, unconvinced and uninspired."[30]

Although Archer believed that Shaw the idealist had lost touch with reality, the critic who challenged his friend to create what was to become *The Doctor's Dilemma* remembered their old alliance as he was about to face a medical dilemma of his own—surgery for the removal of a cyst or tumor in December 1924. With more than an intimation of approach-

ing mortality, Archer wrote feelingly to Shaw that "though I may sometimes have played the part of all-too candid mentor, I have never wa-
vered in my admiration and affection for you, or ceased to feel that the
Fates had treated me kindly in making me your contemporary and friend.
I thank you from my heart for forty years of good comradeship."[31]

A few days later he entered a nursing home and after a week he was
dead. Denied any opportunity for a deathbed oration in the manner of
Dubedat, Archer the rationalist and closet-poet, facing his own doctor's
dilemma, scribbled in pencil on the evening before the operation the
following fragment of verse:

> Dread not, my soul, the ether's drowsy breath;
> Quail not, my flesh, before the surgeon's knife;
> Rather exult—"Where is thy sting, oh Death?
> How blunted are thy ruthless fangs, oh Life!"
>
> My brother-men I praise, those men divine
> Who fought with Pain and hurled it back to Hell;
> From Nature wrung her balsams anodyne,
> And told the secrets God forgot to tell.
>
> The Fates I thank, too, who delayed my birth
> Till Pain was bridled for all time to come—
> But oh! what anguish has the groaning earth
> Endured for aeons because God was dumb.
>
> And oh! what spiritual bugbears—worse
> Than torments of the flesh—haunted of yore
> The men who, cowering 'neath a fancied curse,
> Approached, as I do now, Death's mystic door.
>
> If I with brow serene can face to-night
> The Great Perhaps, whose praise shall be my theme?
> The men's, God wot, who said: "Let there be light!"
> Where God left Ignorance and Fear supreme. . . .[32]

Shaw had once warned Archer in his most energetic days that unless he
began to age naturally he would "collapse some day like a one-horse-
shay."[33] The casual remark proved prophetic.

True to his suspicions of doctors and the healing profession, Shaw
concluded in a 1927 preface to *Three Plays by William Archer*, a volume
which contained a legacy of the critic's unperformed works, that "the
operation had killed him. . . . I have never been able to regard a death
caused by an operation as a natural death." Thrown into a towering rage
against the surgeons, Shaw admitted that his fury "carried me over the
first sense of bereavement" as he returned to "an Archerless London
[that] had entered a new age in which I was lagging superfluous."[34] He
had completed *Saint Joan* in August 1923, but would not begin his next

play, *The Apple Cart*, until November 1928. The impact of William Archer's loss may not have been exaggerated; however the positive effect is the more important yardstick. To him Shaw owed the beginning of his career as playwright, in the abortive collaboration on *Widowers' Houses*. And to Archer's taunts, in the spirit of friendly rivalry which always characterized their long and close association, is owed *The Doctor's Dilemma*.

Notes

1. Bernard Shaw, "Ibsen," *The Clarion*, Friday, 1 June 1906, p. 5. Reprinted in *Shaw and Ibsen: Bernard Shaw's 'The Quintessence of Ibsenism' and Related Writing*, ed. J. L. Wisenthal (Toronto: University of Toronto Press, 1979), pp. 239–45.

2. William Archer, "Ibsen As I Knew Him," *The Monthly Review*, no. 69, XXIII, 3 (June 1906), pp. 1–19.

3. Bernard Shaw, *Collected Letters: 1898–1910*, ed. Dan H. Laurence (New York: Dodd, Mead, 1972), pp. 626–28 (7 June 1906).

4. Bernard Shaw, *Collected Letters: 1874–1897*, ed. Dan H. Laurence (New York: Dodd, Mead, 1965), p. 258 (17 August 1890).

5. William Archer to Bernard Shaw, 8 June 1906 (British Library Add. MS. 50528, f. 173). Quoted in *Collected Letters: 1898–1910*, p. 628.

6. *Collected Letters: 1898–1910*, pp. 633–35 (7 July 1906); Bernard Shaw to William Archer, 10 July 1906 (British Library AD. MS. 45296, f. 175).

7. Shaw, "Ibsen," *The Clarion*, Friday, 1 June 1906, p. 5.

8. "Mr G. B. Shaw's Next Play," *Bernard Shaw: Collected Plays with their Prefaces*, ed. Dan H. Laurence (New York: Dodd, Mead, 1971), vol. 3, p. 437.

9. "St John Hankin on the position of Shaw," *Shaw: The Critical Heritage*, ed. T. F. Evans (London, Henley and Boston: Routledge & Kegan Paul, 1976), p. 173. Reprinted from "Mr. Bernard Shaw as Critic," *Fortnightly Review*, vol. LXXXI, ns 1057, June 1907.

10. "Unsigned notice, *Morning Post*," 22 November 1906, 41963, 4, *Shaw: The Critical Heritage*, p. 167.

11. Archer, "The Mausoleum of Ibsen," *Fortnightly Review*, July 1893.

12. "Desmond MacCarthy, notice, *Speaker*," 24 November 1906, XV, 373, 226, *Shaw: The Critical Heritage*, pp. 168–72.

13. Max Beerbohm, "Mr. Shaw's Roderick Hudson," 24 November 1906, *Around Theatres* (New York: Simon and Schuster, 1954), pp. 442–46.

14. Archer, "G. B. S. on the Warpath," *The Tribune*, Saturday, 23 March 1907, p. 2.

15. Archer, *The Vedrenne-Barker Season: 1904–1905* (London: D. Allen & Sons, 1905), p. 4.

16. Archer, "The Theatre: *Widowers' Houses*," *The World*, 14 December 1892, pp. 14–15.

17. Archer, "Arms and the Man," 25 April 1894, *The Theatrical World of 1894* (London: Walter Scott, 1895), pp. 109–18.

18. Archer, "Mr. Shaw's Pom-Pom," *The Critic* (New York), October 1903, pp. 311–12.

19. Archer, "The Theatre: 'Major Barbara'—'Dodo'—'Jimmy's Mother'—Irish Plays,"

The World, 5 December 1905, pp. 971–72. To Archer's piece Shaw replied: "Your article on 'Major Barbara,' the worst you ever wrote, delighted me. The complete success with which I wrecked your mind and left you footling—simply footling—was really the greatest proof of your fundamental sensibility to my magic." *Collected Letters: 1898–1910*, p. 599 (1 January 1906).

20. Archer, "Mr. Bernard Shaw's Plays," *Study and Stage: A Yearbook of Criticism* (London: Grant Richards, 1899), pp. 1–2.

21. William Archer to Harley Granville Barker, 21 August 1922 (British Theatre Association).

22. Archer, "On 'Cutting' Shakespeare," *Fortnightly*, June 1919, pp. 965–73.

23. Shaw, "On Cutting Shakespear," *Fortnightly*, August 1919, pp. 215–18.

24. Shaw, "A Plea for Speech Nationalisation" (To The Editor of the *Morning Leader*, 16 August 1901), *Shaw on Language*, ed. Abraham Tauber (London: Peter Owen, 1965), p. 15.

25. "Bibliographic Appendix," *William Archer: Life, Work and Friendships*, by Lieut.-Colonel C. Archer (New Haven: Yale University Press, 1931), pp. 428–29. See also British Library General Catalog.

26. Preface to *Heartbreak House, Bernard Shaw: Collected Plays with their Prefaces*, vol. V, p. 32 ("Evil in the Throne of Good").

27. Shaw, "The Imperialism of Bernard Shaw," *The New Witness*, 6 June 1919, p. 117. Archer had written to Shaw on 22 April 1919: "I'm delighted to hear that Lynd has sent you *War is War*. I have no doubt you will 'deal faithfully' with it; but it's far better to be murdered than to be still born" (British Library Add. MS. 50528, f. 254).

28. Archer, *On Dreams*, ed. Theodore Besterman (London: Methuen, 1935), pp. 65–66.

29. William Archer to Bernard Shaw, 17 September 1919 (British Library Add. MS. 50528, f. 61). *The Green Goddess* ran for more than 850 performances in 1920, 1921 and 1923.

30. Archer, "The Psychology of G. B. S.," *The Bookman*, No. 399, vol. LXVII (December 1924), pp. 139–41.

31. "How William Archer Impressed Bernard Shaw," *Three Plays by William Archer*, with a personal note by Bernard Shaw (London: Constable, 1927), p. xxxix.

32. C[harles] Archer, *William Archer: Life, Work and Friendships*, pp. 403–4.

33. Bernard Shaw to William Archer, 28 July 1908 (British Library Add. MS. 45296, f. 207).

34. *Three Plays by William Archer*, pp. xxxix–xl.

W. R. Martin

GBS, DHL, AND TEL: MAINLY *LADY CHATTERLEY* AND *TOO TRUE*

Has anyone noticed the similarities between Shaw's *Too True to be Good* and D. H. Lawrence's *Lady Chatterley's Lover*?[1] T. E. Lawrence is in both. Shaw himself declared that T. E. Lawrence was the original of Private Meek, and Stanley Weintraub has argued that he was a model for Shaw's Aubrey too.[2] But TEL crops up significantly in the novel as well: Connie herself says that Mellors "is like Colonel C. E. Florence, who preferred to become a private soldier again," though her father "had no sympathy with the unsatisfactory mysticism of the famous C. E. Florence" (p. 294). Shaw makes Meek the perfect pragmatist, and leaves something like mysticism to Aubrey, "a preacher" who has "no creed" (p. 287). So one might say that TEL is in some sense a hero of both the novel and the play.

It may be a coincidence that, as Blanche Patch tells us, Shaw began to write *Too True* "between the islands of Corsica and Sardinia on March 5, 1931" on the Shaws' way back to Venice,[3] but one notices the date (one year and a few days after D. H. Lawrence's death), the place (not very far from Vence, where DHL died, and near Sardinia, about which he wrote a book), and the destination (which features quite prominently in the novel). It wouldn't be very surprising if Lawrence was in Shaw's thoughts as he wrote the second half of the play.

Not long after this, Shaw was in South Africa, and it was in early 1932 that, as Sarah Gertrude Millin records, "I . . . brought Shaw and [Field-Marshal] Smuts together one day in Cape Town and Shaw, thinking to startle Smuts, said every schoolgirl of sixteen should read *Lady Chatterley's Lover*; to which Smuts, knowing about neither Lawrence nor Lady Chatterley, said politely, 'Of course. Of course.'"[4]

There are many things in the play that might recall Lawrence. When

Col. Tallboys "brings down his umbrella whack on poor Mrs. Mopply's helmet" (p. 279), striking her "with unmixed enjoyment" (p. 283), and with the stroke radically altering the old lady's life and outlook, one might think of Hermione striking Birkin "crash on his head" with the ball of lapis lazuli, feeling as she does so "unutterable consummation, unutterable satisfaction" (in Chapter VIII of *Women in Love*) and causing a fundamental change in Birkin's life. Shaw has transposed the incident into a comic key, but they are remarkably similar, and both central to the plots of *Too True* and *Women in Love*.

But the loudest chords are made by the host of similarities between the play and *Lady Chatterley's Lover*. Both *Too True* and the novel present us with pretty desperate waste lands in which there is little confidence, faith, or sure sense of purpose: the phrase "bottomless pit" (or "abyss") appears in the novel (p. 77) and echoes throughout the latter half of the play (pp. 278, 279, 284). Both works confront and discuss urgently, at length, and with detailed analysis, the crisis in civilization and the sense of breakdown that pervades twentieth-century writing.

Oddly enough, the heroines of both works achieve early on a sort of freedom: for Connie there is the somewhat ironically presented "beautiful pure freedom of a woman" (p. 7); the Patient receives "the priceless boon of . . . emancipation" (p. 242), but says later, "I am free . . . and I am utterly miserable" for want of "something sensible to do" (p. 260); Connie's mother "wanted her girls to be 'free,' and to 'fulfil themselves'" (p. 8), but the novel shows how great a distance there can be between the first achievement and the second.

Shaw's Aubrey has been deeply unsettled by the war, having been "hardly more than a boy when I first dropped a bomb on a sleeping village" (p. 274), and Lawrence's Sir Clifford has been "shipped home smashed" from the war, though his impotence is seated more deeply than his physical incapacity—"the sex part did not mean much to him" (p. 13).

It is on the question of the relation between mind and body, including especially the matter of sex, that the thematic parallels between the novel and the play are most striking. In *Lady Chatterley* this relation is the emphatically high-lighted focus of the whole novel, and the conflict has been made explicit as early as Chapter II when we are told that Clifford lives by talk and not at all by "touch" (pp. 16–17): "He was so very much at one with her, in his mind and hers, but bodily they were non-existent to one another" (p. 19). In *Too True* the conflict is clear by at least the middle of Act II, where we hear Aubrey dilating on the "higher" and "lower centres" (pp. 256, 258, 261), and the different demands that they make. Sweetie, always out for "a bit of fun" (p. 268), is the embodiment of the lower center, and we have the comedy of the Sergeant, devoted to the Bible, Bunyan, and the traditionally sanctified higher center, having to rationalize himself out of his "mess" (p. 269) and Sweetie into his program, which he does by saying: "This young woman has no conscience; but I have enough for two" (p. 282). Sweetie seems to echo Clifford's "marry-and-have-done-with-it" (p. 36) when she says, "Oh, well, kiss me and have done with it" (p. 271), though she is of course using the phrase for an opposite effect—for the purpose of seduction.

The Patient, Shaw's heroine, "did fall in love" with Aubrey, but is soon "tired of him" (p. 278), and, rising above sex, if not love (because she is said by the perhaps unreliable Sweetie to be "interested in Private Meek"— p. 257), she wants to found a "sisterhood" (p. 286), to find "something sensible to do" (p. 260). Shaw has much fun at the expense of the lopsidedly higher-centered characters—the Sergeant, the Elder, and even Aubrey—but his "own favorite" (p. 288) is the Patient, presumably because she is active at both centers but directed ultimately by the higher one, which is not only the seat of the intellect but also of moral passion and, in Shaw's view, the Life Force.

But Shaw doesn't seem to be trying to dissociate his view from Lawrence's entirely. That the Patient "lifts her foot vigorously waist high, and shoots it hard into [Aubrey's] solar plexus" (p. 238) and is capable of at least a brief physical infatuation with Aubrey are not the only signs in the play that the lower center is important in his heroine and must be accommodated. Shaw has the Patient saying, "Sweetie is bad enough, heaven knows, with her vulgarity and her low cunning: always trying to get the better of somebody or to get hold of a man; but at least she's a woman; and she's real. Men are not real: they're all talk, talk, talk" (p. 261). She is here almost paraphrasing what Lawrence makes Tommy Dukes say about "the mental life" and "talk" (p. 58). We might recall what Lawrence himself wrote in "A Propos of *Lady Chatterley's Lover*": "I stick to my book and my position: Life is only bearable when the mind and the body are in harmony."[5]

There are several other points in the play at which the ear picks up echoes of Lawrence's work. "Mothers cling" (p. 277) might bring to mind *Sons and Lovers*; the parent/child relation (in Mrs. Mopply/the Patient and the Elder/Aubrey) could remind one of Will/Ursula in *The Rainbow* and *Women in Love* and Thomas/Gerald Crich in *Women in Love*; the Sergeant's "When men and women pick one another up just for a bit of fun, they find they've picked up more than they bargained for because men and women have a top storey as well as a ground floor" (pp. 268–69), is parallel to, or the reverse of, the truth Lawrence utters in "A Propos of *Lady Chatterley's Lover*": "You can fool yourself for a long time about your own feelings. But not forever. The body itself hits back at you, and hits back remorselessly in the end";[6] the Sergeant's argument that like should not marry like (p. 282) sounds like an echo from *The Rainbow*, where there is an emphasis on the foreignness, strangeness and mystery that Lydia, for example, holds for Tom; Mrs. Mopply's invitation to her daughter to "come with me as my companion" and to enter into a new relationship "on trial" (p. 285) might be a more prosaic, Shavian version of "two very separate beings, vitally connected" in Chapter I of *The Rainbow* and of "freedom together" in Chapter XI and elsewhere in *Women in Love*; Aubrey's eloquent rhetoric, "We have outgrown our religion, outgrown our political system, outgrown our own strength of mind and character" (pp. 287–88), hits a note struck by Lawrence as early as 1915 when, in his "Note to 'The Crown'," he wrote: "The whole great form of our era will have to go."[7] Certainly the main thrust of the play coincides with Birkin's assertion in Chapter III of *Women in Love* that mankind must free itself from the prison of "a limited, false set of concepts"; divers concepts in the play, variously held by the doctor, Mrs. Mopply, Tallboys, the Sergeant, and the Elder, are outmoded.

Some or all of these last similarities are perhaps accidental. The views expressed might in a sense be native to both Shaw and Lawrence and independently cultivated by each for his own purposes. But how can one explain the striking fact—it can hardly be a mere coincidence—that the play and *Lady Chatterley* each give such prominence to pentecostal flame in the last page or two? In his letter Mellors mentions his little flame of "Pentecost" four times (p. 316), and in the last sentence of his peroration, which concludes the play, Aubrey proclaims: "I must preach . . . no matter whether I have nothing to say—or whether in some pentecostal of revelation the Spirit will descend on me." Shaw's last stage direction immediately follows this and in it "Pentecostal flame" is referred to twice, though here again, as in Aubrey's peroration, the flame is something that will declare itself to choicer "spirits" (p. 288)—to higher centers— rather than in the physical manifestations that Mellors pins his hopes on.

Critics and biographers, impressed by the many wide differences between the two writers, have tended to assume a simple and straightforward antipathy, or at least lack of sympathy, for Lawrence in Shaw. S. Winsten reports that Shaw "admitted once he had ploughed through . . . *Sons and Lovers* but found this dreary,"[8] and Frank Harris that Shaw said the same novel was "hard reading," but also that it was "the work of a man of genius." Of *Lady Chatterley* Harris has Shaw saying that it "should be on the shelves of every college for budding girls. They should be forced to read it on pain of being refused a marriage licence. *But it is not as readable as 'Ivanhoe' or 'A Tale of Two Cities.'*"[9] Shaw was revising and touching up Harris's biography of himself while he was working on *Too True*, and it is tempting to believe that he wrote this passage into the biography at this time (March–June 1931); if he did, it is another sign that the novel was very much in his mind.[10] In any event, the passage corroborates the substance of the Millin story, but not Mrs. Millin's interpretation: she, accepting the opinion of her husband, who became a Judge, that the novel was obscene, and honoring his wish that she shouldn't read it, merely assumed that Shaw was trying to "startle" Smuts. The passage in Harris's biography, however it got there, suggests that Shaw, beneath his characteristic buoyancy of spirit, actually meant what he said.

Though the differences are striking, there are, as David J. Gordon has shown,[11] important similarities and identities within the differences between the two great writers. Elsie B. Adams has even gone as far as suggesting it is "possible" that in writing *Lady Chatterley* Lawrence "borrowed from or rewrote" Shaw's early novel, *Cashel Byron's Profession.*[12] Be that as it may, Lawrence certainly does lambaste Shaw and his views on sex for two whole pages of "A Propos of *Lady Chatterley's Lover,*"[13] which Shaw might have read before writing *Too True*, because the essay was published in 1930. But Shaw does not, I think, show any resentment; the veteran of debate and controversy was always remarkably devoid of rancor. *Too True* can indeed, I think, be seen as a moderate reply to Lawrence's attack. The play shows a regard for Lawrence and *Lady Chatterley*, not as enthusiastic as Yeats's,[14] but nevertheless a sort of respect; some of the features of the Pan-like Lawrence are discernible in Shaw's shrubbery.

Shaw's respect for the novel is all the more remarkable in view of his well-documented fastidiousness about the body. Hesketh Pearson reports that Shaw "once told Cecil Chesterton . . . that the sexual act was to him monstrous and indecent,"[15] and S. Winsten has Shaw saying that the life of Sidney and Beatrice Webb "convinced me that life would one day culminate in brain work reaching the same kind of ecstasy now obtained through sexual orgasm."[16] One might here in contrast remember the passage between Clifford and Connie in *Lady Chatterley*: Clifford says, "I think there is something in the idea that the universe is physically wasting and spiritually ascending," to which Connie replies: "Then let it ascend, so long as it leaves me safely and solidly physically here below" (pp. 244–45).

Shaw's *Too True* is of course far from being a mere reflection of *Lady Chatterley*, but it is I think a rewriting of the novel, not primarily in a spirit of hostility or contradiction, because the play endorses much of the novel, but with the intention of changing the emphasis. What the play and the novel agree on are the fact of the crisis in civilization, the need for a new vision and a radical renewal of faith in order to restore a sense of serious purpose, the importance of both the higher and the lower centers and the necessity for harmony between them. It is a large

measure of accord. Shaw felt the rewriting was necessary though, because he wanted to make a fundamental change of emphasis: Lawrence's Clifford becomes Shaw's Patient, and the pentecost is to work in
the spirits of Aubrey and the Patient, not—as in the novel—through
the bodies of Mellors and Connie. Colin Wilson has put it well: "Shaw
would agree [with Whitman or Lawrence] that man must evolve as a
whole, emotionally, intuitively, as well as intellectually. But what is necessary at this point in evolution is a sense of conscious purpose."[17]

Notes

1. The page numbers that will be given in parentheses in the text refer to the Penguin,
1960, edition of *Lady Chatterley's Lover*, and to the edition of *Too True to be Good* that appears
in *Bernard Shaw's Plays*, ed. Warren S. Smith (New York: Norton, 1970).

2. "The Two Sides of 'Lawrence of Arabia': Aubrey and Meek," *The Shaw Review*, 7
(May 1964), 54–57; reprinted in *Bernard Shaw's Plays* (see footnote 1).

3. *Thirty Years with G.B.S.* (London: Gollancz, 1951), p. 67.

4. *The Measure of My Days* (London: Faber and Faber, 1955), p. 90.

5. *Phoenix* II (New York: Viking, 1968), p. 492.

6. *Phoenix* II, p. 494.

7. *Phoenix* II, p. 364.

8. *Days with Bernard Shaw* (London: Hutchinson [194?]), p. 72.

9. *Bernard Shaw* (New York: Simon and Schuster, 1931), pp. 238–39.

10. See items 710 and 711 in Dan H. Laurence's Catalogue, *SHAW: An Exhibit* (Austin:
Humanities Research Center, University of Texas at Austin, 1977). The galley proofs of
Harris's book on which Shaw made his corrections have been destroyed, and as Stanley
Weintraub makes clear in his recent book—*The Playwright and the Pirate; Bernard Shaw and
Frank Harris: A Correspondence* (Pennsylvania State Univ. Press, 1982), p. 257—no such
letter from Shaw to Harris has come to light. Could Harris have been relying on his mem-
ory of a conversation?

11. "Two Anti-Puritan Puritans: Bernard Shaw and D. H. Lawrence," *The Yale Review*,
LVI (Oct. 1966), 76–90.

12. "A 'Lawrentian' Novel by Bernard Shaw," *The D. H. Lawrence Review*, 2 (Fall 1969),
251.

13. *Phoenix* II, pp. 498–500.

14. Letter to Olivia Shakespear, 22 May 1933; *The Letters of W. B. Yeats*, ed. Allan Wade
(London: Rupert Hart-Davis, 1954), p. 810.

15. *G.B.S.: A Full Length Portrait* (New York: Garden City, 1946), p. 90.

16. *Days with Bernard Shaw*, p. 178.

17. *Bernard Shaw: A Reassessment* (London: Hutchinson, 1969), p. 163.

Marianne Bosch

MOTHER, SISTER, AND WIFE IN
THE MILLIONAIRESS

Literature does not exist in a vacuum—impressions and experiences from the life and environment of every writer deeply influence his literary productions. Moreover, in the act of writing, the author is guided by motives unknown to himself. Thus, the text is not simply the author's conscious organization of material but reveals unconscious motives and impulses which have entered into his conscious considerations, the underlying power of which cannot be overestimated. These motives create dynamic relationships within the basic structure of the text which can lead to a deeper understanding of the writer's work; indeed they not only show his conscious organization of the material but also uncover the unconscious organization as well.

The interweaving of the unconscious with the conscious can be demonstrated well in *Millionairess*. Shaw himself has asserted (*Sixteen Self Sketches*) that the "best autobiographies are confessions; but if a man is a deep writer all his works are confessions." There is no question that, despite his attempts to conceal himself, Shaw was such a "deep writer."

One of the prevailing unconscious motifs working in Shaw's plays is his penchant for juxtaposing weak and helpless male characters with exceptionally independent female characters who dominate the men and are given leading roles. This combination is so consistent it can almost be regarded as a trademark of Shaw's dramas. Even by today's standards, Shaw's heroines seem emancipated and for his own time they were prototypes of the "new women" as opposed to the "womanly women."

Since Shaw was one of the first and most persistent defenders of equal rights for women (equal rights not only at the ballot box and in public

This article was translated from German by Kirby Richards and edited by Suzanne Wills.

life, but also in private life), that his opinions have found expression in his art and in his female characters is not surprising. But, if the author is working out his own problems consciously and unconsciously in his dramas, his particular characterization of women and his efforts on their behalf may be ascribed to more than his goals of a just society and of the rejuvenation of the theater through incorporation of new values.

In order to find further motives unknown to himself for these things, a look at the women in his environment who necessarily impressed and influenced him from his childhood on is useful, because they served as models for his characters. Also, their most important qualities *taken together* suggest the "new woman." However, although Shaw himself has claimed that "all the characters are really composites," he does allow that in one or another of the characters, some traits of one person who served as his model are apparent.[1]

The women who come to mind for such an inquiry (since they were closest to Shaw) are not only his mother and his sister, Lucy, but his wife Charlotte. Shaw's mother, Lucinda Elizabeth Gurly, with whom (with a short interruption) Shaw lived until he was forty-two years old and who certainly influenced his view of women in no small way, is remembered as an independent, strong-willed, often obstinate and selfish person. Even Shaw himself (*Sixteen Self Sketches*) agreed indirectly with this view of his mother: "Misfortunes that would have crushed ten untrained women broke on her like waves on granite."

Although not intentionally a stern and unemotional woman, the early "misfortunes" which formed her left her stoical. When Elizabeth Gurly was nine years old, her mother died and she was given to the care of an iron-willed great-aunt who raised her with unmerciful austerity. Thus, growing to hate her great-aunt and spartan upbringing, Elizabeth turned her own unbending will against her great-aunt's influence. In this attitude of defiance and from disappointment about her father's remarriage, she decided to marry George Carr Shaw, who stood below her in social position. Although she had been warned of his alcoholism, she believed his assurances that he had reformed and was a teetotaler.[2] Yet even on their honeymoon, she discovered to her bitter regret that her husband was a drunkard and that her marriage was a disastrous mistake. Her husband could offer her neither the financial security nor the social status to which she had been used. She was sure of only one improvement: she had married a man who could not stand up to her strong will and, after his lies about drinking, his lack of professional ambition, and his business failures gave rise to her unbridled contempt, he did not even dare to do so. Even after George Carr Shaw later overcame his alcoholism, this did not change: "Mr Shaw, always ready to retire to the corner, was an unexceptionally undemanding man, who seldom asserted himself or fussed about anything."[3] Indeed, George Carr Shaw, always presented as ineffective, was also—according to his son—good-natured, peaceful, and a kind person with a profound sense of humor. Shaw's mother, in contrast, had ambition through which she compensated for the frustrations of her marriage by taking singing and music lessons from a well-known Dublin teacher, George Vandeleur Lee. The extent of their relationship (beyond the field of music) can no longer be determined exactly, but when Lee moved to London in 1873, she followed him.

Her motive for inviting Lee into the Shaw household may have been to ease their straitened finances or it may have been a conscious or unconscious act of revenge against her husband and against the moral conventions imposed upon her by her great-aunt. Whatever the cause, she got her way even here, regardless of whether or not the arrangement benefitted other members of the family. G.B.S., asked whether his father liked Lee, admitted that "he certainly did not, and would not have tolerated the arrangement if he could have afforded a decent house without it, or if he could have asserted himself against my mother. . . ."[4] This "ménage à trois" also led to a "schizophrenic" situation (in the truest sense of the word) for the children, especially for George Bernard Shaw.

While Shaw's mother was never selfless and to her children often indifferent, inspired by Lee, she found more and more fulfillment in music and spared even less time, attention, and love for her children, who were left to fend for themselves or cared for by a servant. When Shaw speaks of his childhood, it is usually with bitterness. That his mother paid him even less attention than his two sisters may be traced back to his outward similarity to his father, which may have caused an unconscious antipathy in the mother to her son.[5] Shaw himself wrote: "What was done to me in my childhood was nothing at all of an intentional kind. . . . No direct ill treatment was added by anybody to the horror of the world. . . . I was taken—and took myself—for what I was: a disagreeable little beast. Nobody concerned himself or herself as to what I was capable of becoming . . . far from being conceited, I hadn't even common self-respect. . . . My shyness and cowardice were beyond all belief."[6] The feelings of inferiority were not the only effects of parental behavior on the young Shaw. Identifying with his mother's opinions, he began to despise his incompetent father. This was easy since, besides his mother's open contempt, George Carr Shaw himself advised Shaw "very earnestly never to follow his example in any way; and his sincerity so impressed me that to this day I have never smoked . . . and never used alcoholic stimulants. He taught me to regard him as an unsuccessful man with many undesirable habits, as a warning and not a model. . . ." G.B.S., who freely admitted in his preface to *Misalliance* that in his youth he had three fathers,[7] really did not have even one whose clear-cut example would have made possible the kind of identification necessary for a young person's development. The mother example, on the other hand, was clearly outlined and unchallenged. The Shaw family lived, by necessity, such a socially isolated life that Shaw's mother could be in the beginning his only point of orientation and since she practically never concerned herself about him, she became an unreachable, untouchable, yet admirable (as opposed to his father) object of identification to which his imagination clung tightly. As Shaw later complained, "Oh a devil of a childhood . . . , *rich only in dreams*, frightful and loveless in realities."[8]

That the dreams of the young Shaw made the unreachable female person superior to the male and more heroic than she really was, is, under the circumstances, hardly surprising. Shaw claimed in his preface to *London Music* (1937) that "almost complete neglect of me had the advantage that I could idolize her [his mother] to the utmost pitch of my imagination and had no sordid or disillusioning contacts with her." On the other hand, that his male figures—even in his plays—seldom reach the dimensions of the women, is, obviously, because he lacked an exemplary male with whom to identify.

Occasional physical punishment by his parents could have had no worse effect than the total indifference of Shaw's mother. For a child, blows are at least a sign of attention. Thus in Shaw's play *The Music Cure* (1914), to which he added (perhaps deceptively) the subtitle *A Piece of Utter Nonsense*, the exchange between a woman and a youth who has fallen in love with her is significant:

> STREGA: My child: I am a hard, strong, independent, muscular woman. How can you with your delicate soft nature, see anything to love in me? I should hurt you, shock you, perhaps—yes . . . even . . . beat you.
> REGINALD: Oh do, do. Dont laugh at this ridiculous confession; but ever since I was a child I have had only one secret longing, and that was to be mercilessly beaten by a splendid, strong, beautiful woman.

The masochistic desire expressed here to get attention from women in the form of beatings shows the degree of Shaw's need for love, which only found fulfillment in his daydreams. According to Shaw, he could not remember when he did not use his imagination to invent stories about women. His dreams were both an expression of a mother fixation and a means to bear an unmerciful reality of which Shaw claimed: "I don't think a soul really cares for me. The word care is the most wonderful word. To have one who really cares! My mother never cared. . . ."[9] But in his desperate attempts to draw his mother's attention to himself was also the unconscious desire to punish her for her indifference toward him. Shaw recalled in an interview how, in his childhood, he purposely left his window open at night, in spite of the warning that he would catch a fatal cold, but "I was so wretched that I wanted to die. If I were ill my mother would take notice of me. An open window was a short cut to sympathy. You can't imagine the plight of an unloved child."

The combination of aloof mother figure and ineffectual father figure led, in Shaw, to feelings of weakness, of resigned helplessness, and even of powerlessness, which led Frank Harris to remark: "He was excessively sensitive and found his eyes filling with tears at the slightest rebuff."[10]

A further consequence of his mother's indifference was the self-depreciation which covered a profound hostility towards her: "I rather despised her for having brought such a miserable specimen as myself into the world."[11] The concomitant need for a good mother and frustration and anger which he felt towards his own mother's failures produced, like his attempts at revenge, feelings of guilt, which then were compensated for by his idealizing women.

Hence the dynamics of Shaw's neurotic attachment to his mother appear in his plays in the relationships between a weak, insecure protagonist seeking identity who falls in love with an emancipated, mature woman (who obviously represents a mother substitute). The youth, trying desperately to attract her attention, is always more willing to put up with rejection than with indifference. But, while Shaw fantasized about an all-loving, all-powerful mother figure, he had to be in real life his own source of support and thus developed a strong narcissism which, in Daniel Dervin's opinion, "cannot be taken in the ordinary sense of passive, complacent self-love, or clinically as lingering autoeroticism . . . [but] must have stemmed from fears of abandonment and a desperate striving for independence."[12] Yet fear of his own unconscious wish for complete passivity led to a restless striving to be useful in his profound aversion to every kind of ineffectiveness.

In London, in the 1870s, Shaw found himself in a household dominated by two women whom he loved and idealized, but whose affection he could not win. Thus aggressive feelings arose against their indifference, feelings which could not be expressed, but rather had to be compensated for in his imagination. Lucy, who in Dublin felt as little sympathy for Shaw as his mother did, in London openly professed she would prefer to be rid of her (in her eyes) useless brother; she "nattered and nagged about his sponging on his mother to all who would listen."[13]

Shaw's feeling of inferiority was only strengthened by her contempt, but the partial truth in her complaints left him with a permanently bad conscience:

> I was an ablebodied and ableminded young man in the full strength of my youth; and my family then heavily embarrassed, needed my help

urgently. That I should have chosen to be a burden to them instead was . . . monstrous. Well, without a blush I embraced the monstrosity. I did not throw myself into the struggle for my life: I threw my mother into it.[14]

The feeling of guilt, which was added to by Lucy, originated in Shaw's love/hate of his mother. Of his unknowingly driving his mother to distraction by playing his favorite selections from Wagner's *Ring* cycle, he said later: "She never complained at the time, but confessed it after we separated, and said that she had sometimes gone away to cry. *If I had commited a murder I do not think it would trouble my conscience very much; but this I cannot bear to think of.*"[15] Thus, Shaw's involvement in the women's movement and his idealized female characters may be understood as, at least in part, *unconscious* acts of reconciliation with his mother whom, he believed, he had wronged.

As soon as Shaw established himself in London, he met women in socialist and in theatrical circles who undoubtedly strengthened his view of women as powerful. The respect and admiration which he had felt for his mother and sister were now transferred to certain women in his group; they were often independent types who—like his mother and sister—had found a task or profession, worked hard at it, and were utterly devoted to it. Beatrice Webb, Ellen Terry, Annie Besant, Florence Farr, for example, had certain traits in common with the female characters of Shaw's plays: they were intelligent, strong-willed and self-assured, and endowed with some clearly masculine traits. Shaw himself described Florence Farr as "an 'emancipated woman' of her day, who had had quite enough with four years' experience of conventional marriage." She represented the "new woman" who Shaw imagined for his "New Drama," the plays which he intended to write.

But, in his relationships with women, Shaw really hoped to find his *own* identity: "All my love-affairs end tragically because the woman can't use me. It is only when I am being used that I can feel my own existence, enjoy my own life. They . . . let me imagine things about them but in the end a frightful unhappiness, and unspeakable weariness comes; and the Wandering Jew must go on in search of someone who can use him to the utmost of his capacity. . . ."[16] The parallels between Shaw as child and Shaw as young man show the same searching for security and identity through first his mother and later other women, but the reality failed always to live up to his fantasies.

When Shaw felt he was not useful, he tried to be indispensable, and when he was useful, he gave his all to show himself in the best light. Winning affection through writing and political activities was the unconscious driving force behind his life: art was a kind of courtship.

Daniel Dervin contends that Shaw continued to idealize his mother, "through a succession of actresses, or rather generations of actresses," but that "these attachments to actresses—fixations if you will—were actually defences against a much earlier fixation to his mother, who indeed serves as creative model."[17] Also, Shaw's marriage to Charlotte Payne-Townshend was a further defense against the power of his mother, but he recognized her as a replacement: "I could not have been married to any other type of woman." Charlotte, in taking the ailing Shaw away from his mother's apartment to nurse him back to health, was clearly a woman who was concerned about him.

Similar in many respects to Shaw's mother, Charlotte's dominating character, strong will, pride, and explosive temper were—as she herself recognized—traceable to her childhood:

> I had a perfectly hellish childhood and youth. . . . My mother was a terribly strong character—managing and domineering. She could not bear opposition: if it was offered she either became violent, or she cried. . . . My father was gentle & affectionate well-educated & well-read, very, VERY good, honourable & straight. He was a marvel of patience with my mother, which was terribly bad for her. I think, now, she ought to have been BEATEN; it would have been better for us all, especially for herself. As it was, my father led a most unhappy life & died . . . of sheer tiredness. It was a terrible home. . . . I am, in some ways, like my father, but I have a lot of my mother's managing, domineering strain in me. I used to stand between my father & her, & stand up against her on my own account. . . . Well, I needn't go on. . . . It warped my character & spoiled my life & my health & my mind. . . ."[18]

Mrs. Bernard Shaw, like Shaw's mother, obviously played the role of a "Maitresse femme who rules in the household by a sort of divine right" ("Preface on Bosses"). She had also, according to Shaw, developed a father fixation in her childhood comparable to Shaw's mother fixation.

Thus, Shaw failed to free himself from his complex by marrying Charlotte: in reality, he had simply shifted his allegiance to another difficult and dominating woman whose problems—in addition to his own—were dealt with in the later plays, as his mother's had been in the earlier ones. Therefore, in *The Millionairess*, Charlotte's father fixation is a dynamic element which replaces the mother fixation of some earlier plays.

In the light of Shaw's psychological background, the contrast in *The Millionairess* between Epifania and the weak men—Sagamore, Adrian, Alastair, the "sweat shop" owner, and the hotel manager is not surprising. Even the doctor succumbs to her strong pulse.

Alastair, of course, resembles Shaw's father as a failure in financial matters, and in his impotence in maintaining his wife's interest in him. The doctor, on the other hand, resembles George John Vandeleur Lee in his ability to awaken a woman's interest not only in living but also giving her "a Cause and a Creed to live for." [19]

However, a Shaw character is not simply based on *one* real person, but, in his creative process (consciously or unconsciously) is fashioned from several people. Since, in his youth, Shaw had no one exemplary male role model, his male characters tend more strongly to be composite than not. Thus, the male figures in his plays combine negative and positive traits of Shaw's father figures plus those of characters springing from his own imagination (which were based on Shaw's ideal self), and parts of himself which could not be accepted by his ideal self (which were negative traits).

Alastair, for example, while bearing negative traits possibly from Shaw's father, is also an amateur tennis champion and heavyweight boxer. These latter elements were from the boxer, Gene Tunney, with whom Shaw and his wife were on friendly terms at the time he wrote *The Millionairess*. In boxing, Shaw himself said that "one is up against physical facts as in economics. . . ." [20] Shaw's "addiction to knockabout scenes of crude physical violence," Margery M. Morgan has observed, "farcially underlines the equal aggressiveness in the verbal assaults and conflicts the plays contain." [21]

There are, however, deeper causes for the many scenes of crude violence in the plays. Shaw admired the masculinity, bodily strength, and courage which he himself lacked. Although he took up boxing himself in his twenties, his childhood feelings of inferiority and fits of cowardice left him a legacy of shame, openly admitting "that he was no paragon of manliness in his youth. . . ." But Shaw, in giving his characters a physical strength which he himself had lacked, sometimes succumbed to unconsciously revenging himself on his characters. For example, Alastair is, according to Epifania, an "irresistible athlete" whom she thought "would be an ardent lover. He was nothing of the kind. All his ardour was in his fists." And in stage directions introducing Alastair, Shaw wrote, "*He is a splendid athlete, with most of his brains in his muscles.*" Shaw's private revenge on the muscular hero also compensated for his own frustrated dreams as a child: "GBS described himself as a 'cowardly little brat'. . . . But at night there came a wonderful change; the realities of the unhappy day slipped away and the cowardly little brat was transformed into a triumphant hero. . . ." [22]

In bestowing Alastair with strength, another unconscious wish is fulfilled which developed from Shaw's inner revolt against his mother's, his sister's, and Charlotte's power: the wish to dominate them at least once with his fists, as Alastair had done. But this wish is immediately suppressed; Shaw protects the woman from the man and (thereby) from the fulfillment of his own wish:

ALASTAIR: . . . What are you learning now, may I ask?
EPIFANIA: All-in wrestling. When you next indulge in your favourite sport of wife beating, look out for a surprise. . . ."

Just as Shaw combines consciously and unconsciously the character traits of several people to make male stage characters, he develops his female characters in the same way. But, although they are composites of women who made an impression on him, and of fantastic idealizations, they reflect only that Shaw had more suitable female role models than male ones.

For example, referring to Act III of *Millionairess*, St. John Ervine has shown that the Fabian, Beatrice Webb, who grew up in a cultivated and well-to-do household, went at twenty-nine to the East End of London disguised as a factory girl—just like Epifania—to work in a "sweat shop," which no doubt impressed Shaw deeply.[23] But Beatrice Webb is not the only prototype for Epifania; in fact, his wife Charlotte is the principal model. First, Epifania's temperament corresponds exactly to Charlotte's, which according to Beatrice Webb was that of "an anarchist—feeling any regulation or rule intolerable—a tendency which has been exaggerated by her irresponsible wealth . . . she is by nature a rebel" and ". . . an 'original' with considerable personal charm and certain volcanic tendencies."[24] Shaw's description (from the play) shows similar traits in Epifania:

SAGAMORE: Do be reasonable, Mrs Fitzfassenden. Can one live with a tornado? with an earthquake? with an avalanche?
EPIFANIA: Yes. Thousands of people live on the slopes of volcanoes. . . .

Epifania's strong will is also characteristic of Shaw's wife who, although she "did not often display her fighting mood . . . when she did, submission was the result."[25] Also, like Epifania, Charlotte was ready to wait for the right man, declaring that she would marry a "genius," and though to her mother's vexation she had shown little inclination to marry, she was one of the "new women" of her day, with ideas of having a life of her own and developing herself. Unlike Epifania, however, Charlotte did not have the experience of an unfulfilling marriage behind her but after observing the unhappy marriage of her parents, her caution was understandable: Charlotte "is a clever woman," Shaw wrote. "She knows the value of her independence, having suffered a good deal from family bounds . . . the idea of tying herself up again by a marriage . . . before she has exploited her freedom and money power to the utmost—seems to her intellect to be unbearably foolish . . ." Like the doctor, who says to Epifania, "You talk to me as if you were a man," Shaw found in Charlotte a woman who "had none of the feminine traits that I had expected, and all the human qualities I had only hoped for."[26]

Not only do Epifania's character traits correspond to Charlotte's, but parallels in the external circumstances of both are also apparent. For instance, Shaw had indeed married an "Irish millionairess," as he used to call her. More important, however, events in the play—Epifania's anger in the first act and her intention to commit suicide after she is disappointed in Alastair and after he has chosen Polly over her—correspond to real events in Charlotte's life. When Shaw's love affair with Mrs. Patrick Campbell threatened her marriage, Charlotte "flared into ferocious and jealous fury" and, according to Shaw, did talk of murder and suicide.

Before joining the Fabians, Charlotte was a rich, unsatisfied person lacking motivation, just as Shaw portrays Epifania in the first and second acts of the play, before she meets the Egyptian doctor. (Charlotte's doctor, with whom she fell in love before she married Shaw, was the Swedish Axel Munthe. He failed to respond appropriately.) The Webbs particularly fascinated Charlotte because they had discovered something she lacked—"some employment or purpose which would occupy and interest her to be generally useful."[27] For Epifania, it is the doctor who, by asking her what she most wants, and receiving the answer, "Everything. Anything," focuses in his answer on the real problem: "Everything and anything is nothing." Epifania and Charlotte both need "something" to live for. Beatrice Webb appears to echo the doctor's thoughts in a journal entry: ". . . he [Shaw] is annoyed at her lack of purpose. . . . If she would set to do and even do the smallest . . . task . . . I believe she could retain his interest and perhaps develop his feelings for her. Otherwise he will drift away. . . ." But Charlotte, like Epifania at the end of Act IV, was "more than eager to use what talents and capacity she possessed in the service of some worthwhile cause."[28] What both lacked was motivation and a fixed goal. The Webbs, and especially Shaw, helped Charlotte to set that goal. Just as Vandeleur Lee had done for Shaw's mother and the Egyptian doctor for Epifania, Shaw gave Charlotte's life purpose by involving her in the work of the Fabians and in his goal of world improvement. Thus, her highest aim became helping people in *her* way and she forthwith applied herself energetically to that end, using her financial resources liberally. For instance, she supported the newly founded London School of Economics, saying: ". . . what I hope to do is this: with all my power, physical, financial and intellectual, to study sociology . . . and to help and encourage others cleverer than myself to study it. If I only make the way one little bit easier for the students who are with me and come after me . . . that will be reason enough for me devoting my life to it."[29] Charlotte, in wanting to contribute to economics, realized, like Epifania, that progress and change began with educating the young: "The average educated person knows nothing of the financial system under which he lives. He sees that certain persons are millionaires and others are paupers, but ask him 'why', he does not know. . . . We must know something of all these things before we can begin to think about answering the question why the poor are so poor and the rich so rich."[30]

Like Epifania, too, Charlotte, with the choice between an "untroubled" life of "beautifying and expanding [her] own life" and an active, selfless life with a humanitarian goal, picked the latter: ". . . a person situated as I am ought to give *her time and her money* to trying to make things more even between the 'Haves' and the 'Have nots'. . . ." By ending her "good-for-nothing existence," Charlotte proved that she could *earn* her own living as Epifania did through the doctor's test. She learned, through Shaw, how she could use her "talents" significantly, and, hence, she *needed* him for her development. Similarly, the "patient," Epifania, needed the Egyptian doctor to help her realize herself. Therefore, Charlotte could hold onto Shaw not only because she corresponded to his female ideal but because she fulfilled Shaw's deep desire to be useful and thereby to be really loved. Alternatively, thanks to Shaw, Charlotte was no longer a useless millionairess: her financial resources could provide the author and reformer, Shaw, with better working conditions and be used to help people in general. In a similar but simplified fashion, Epifania's money becomes useful when the doctor gives it to the widow of his former teacher.

Parallels between Epifania and Charlotte, however, go further. For example, the Egyptian doctor, because of his origins and religion, would have been interesting to Shaw's wife, who "was attracted to all things Eastern" and "intensely interested in religions."[31] Even the choice of profession is not coincidental since Charlotte found the occupation attractive: "I go, several times a week, to the London School of Medicine for Women. I have taken up Anatomy and Physiology. . . . I think medicine the finest of all professions and I would like to help women to get into it. . . ."[32]

Its charm for her, however, did not only stem from rational conviction but was also motivated by her having fallen in love with Dr. Axel Munthe, who was practicing in Italy when she met him: "der Arzt" "had been the only man in her life to make her feel helpless, no longer mistress of herself." Her feelings had not been reciprocated, and in her disappointment, she had turned to Shaw. As Epifania had, in the doctor, found someone with whom she could talk, so Charlotte found that "Bernard Shaw was the first man she had met since Munthe who talked to her as a human being and not merely as a woman to be flattered."[33] Naturally, she confessed, as Shaw wrote later: "Just before we married she had a serious love affair with Axel Munthe in Italy, and she told me her heart was broken. I answered, 'Rubbish! Your heart is certainly not broken.' And from then on she seemed to attach herself to me."[34]

Other elements from Charlotte's life appear in the play also. For instance, her trip in 1894, when she met Munthe, included an Egyptian tour. Years later, Charlotte travelled to Italy for a research project: "G.B.S. had teased her into declaring that she would show him that she could apply herself to work if she tried. . . ."[35] Similarly, Epifania is provoked by the doctor into undergoing her ordeal.

When Shaw heard nothing for a few days during Charlotte's trip abroad, he became unreasonably jealous: "All this time no letter from Rome. Some Italian doctor, no doubt, at the bottom of it."[36] When Charlotte returned from Italy, she proved to Shaw—just as Epifania proved to the doctor—that she could work very well if she had chosen a task and was motivated: "Charlotte came back . . . with a gigantic collection of documents concerning the Roman municipality . . . I insisted on her setting to work at once. . . . Her lady-like instincts strongly urge her to a dry official report for the use of students at the school. I, on the other hand, insist on a thrilling memoir, giving the whole history of a *lady of quality* suffering from a broken heart (with full particulars) *and being rescued from herself by the call of public work*. The extent to which the call was reinforced by the renewed activity of the mended heart is to be described . . . Charlotte sees dimly that the accomplishment of such a magnum opus would be indeed the conquest of a profession for herself, and consequent *salvation*. . . ."[37] Therefore, *Millionairess* is, in a sense, the "magnum opus" Shaw wanted Charlotte to write, and his choosing a doctor for Epifania's partner is not mere chance.

Indeed, Axel Munthe had other characteristics in common with the Egyptian doctor besides his profession. Shaw had learned from Charlotte that he was a brilliant and attentive conversation partner, and, like the Egyptian doctor, obviously had "the most fascinating ideas and theories."[38] Munthe also dedicated himself selflessly to the needy and sick and avoided taking most rich patients. In a letter to Charlotte he explained his motivation and plans: ". . . more than ever I am struck by the terrible misery . . . and by my impossibility to help as I wanted to do and ought to do according to my unfortunate theories of life and its duty. When I see sights like these I feel ashamed to keep a penny to myself. I do not KEEP it but . . . I might eat less myself. . . . What I would like to do would be to start a dispensary here. I could then have the feeling of being *useful* to somebody. . . . Up til now I have been able to give away a good deal of medicine and money—all I have earned in fact. . . . But alas! The realisation of my dispensary plan costs a good deal of money and I have not got it. . . . If ever you decide to do good in grand style let me know and I shall put you on the right track."[39] Like the doctor in *Millionairess*, Axel Munthe had a life goal to use all his physical and financial means to lessen suffering and ease sickness, a "useful" activity, which, corresponding to Shaw's own ideal, impressed him to such a degree that he saw in Munthe a possible rival. Munthe could have succeeded in winning Charlotte to his cause and in motivating her if he so chose, and the Egyptian doctor has a similar influence on Epifania. Indeed, Munthe had a personality so powerful that he seemed to bewitch even those who disliked him.

Although primarily attributable to Munthe, the stage character of the doctor has the qualities of several persons. Indeed, Shaw himself is represented in his inability to forego Epifania's pulse and, in consequence, a relationship with her. Shaw, writing about his strong desire to see Charlotte immediately after her return, exposes his ambivalence: "I MUST: and that 'MUST' . . . TERRIFIES me. If it were possible to run away—if it would be any good—I'd do it. . . ." But whereas the Egyptian doctor obeys the Life Force by not running away, Axel Munthe could leave a Charlotte who was thereby threatened in her very existence: "Nothing seemed to matter to her any more. She was rudderless: without direction. What could she turn to? Social work? She did not know where to begin. Here she was, a wealthy woman, with a terrible sense of guilt. She had been in the slums of Rome, but there were slums in London and other cities which were almost as bad."[40] In the vacuum, "doctor" Shaw could take hold of the rudder, lead her to a task and give her life purpose.

While Shaw consciously works out his political and philosophical thoughts in *Millionairess*, he unconsciously deals with private matters at the same time. Shaw's compulsion to write was, however, a mystery even to himself: ". . . but whence and how and why it comes to me, or why I persisted, through nine years of unrelieved market failure, in writing instead of in stockbroking . . . I do not know," he wrote in the preface to *Buoyant Billions*. Writing did bring, nonetheless, "moments of inexplicable happiness. . . . To me they have come only in dreams not oftener than once every fifteen years or so." In fact, Shaw, often unable to find happiness except in dreams, was in the *act of writing* searching unconsciously for sublimation of his unhappiness, and this unconscious element is the cause of his "unceasing" activity as a writer: "I cannot hold my tongue nor my pen. As long as I live I must write." Yet although his creative activity relieved tension through wish-fulfillment (idealizing his mother in some female characters and identifying with male heroes), his controlling rational consciousness was too strong to permit a lasting gratification or a complete feeling of happiness. In the plays, however, he also rationalized his choice of topic and his characters which distorted the true motives beneath them so "They are *not transparent* attempts to come to terms with . . . feelings. . . ."[41] Even so, Shaw's psychological needs found no genuine solution in literary creation, and remnants of them survive which never left his psyche in peace and which surfaced again and again in his work. Hence, as late as his eighties Shaw was still dealing with autobiographical material from his earlier years. Even his last play, *Why She Would Not* (1950), shows, except in the switch of the female character to a male one, a perfect parallel in content to *Millionairess*!

The relationship between unsolved psychological problems and art did not escape Shaw's attention: "If I were not a chaos of contradictions, I could not have written plays. . . . I *escaped* into the writing of plays because I could not resolve the inherent contradictions of existence. . . ."[42] And, in spite of proposing apparently sober, enlightened, clever, and theoretically practical solutions in his plays, Shaw compensates by introducing playful elements to overcome uncontrolled emotions.

The Egyptian doctor is lucky because the emancipated Epifania, in the process of getting a divorce, is willing to marry him. But, for Shaw himself, the women in whom he took a romantic interest were often already married, and he claimed that the "frightful sensation of being always on guard with another man's wife used to develop itself to such a devilish intensity that I could only release my feelings by writing plays. All my plays were heavily charged with feelings; one man's distress is another man's laughter." The audience's laughter, therefore, has a cathartic effect on the writer which gives him the motivation to continue writing: ". . . the more serious I am, the more they laugh. Nobody laughs when Beethoven's Ninth is played, why do they laugh when I play my ninetieth?" The poignancy of this plea throws light on Shaw's main character, G.B.S. himself. Through his rationalizations, his humor, his irony, and his playful paradoxes, Shaw used his psychological difficulties and learned to laugh doing it: "The impossible is the only practical solution to all our troubles. Don't take this nightmare of a world too seriously. I was like that once but I've learnt to laugh since. . . ."[43]

Notes

1. Stephen Winsten, *Jesting Apostle* (London, 1956), p. 34. Much of this introductory argument will be familiar to Shavians yet is necessary here as background.

2. Daniel Dervin, *Bernard Shaw, A Psychological Study* (London, 1975), p. 32.

3. St. John Ervine, *Bernard Shaw* (New York, 1956), p. 16.

4. Quoted from a letter to T. D. O'Bolger, in B. C. Rosset, *Shaw of Dublin* (University Park, Pa., 1964), p. 105.

5. Ervine, p. 17.

6. "In the dreams of the superfluous child," says Dervin, "begins the Superman." He adds that Shaw's narcissism was "after all an early response to what he missed from his parents" (pp. 93, 135).

7. George Carr Shaw, G. J. Vandeleur Lee, and Dr. Walter Gurly, Mrs. Shaw's brother.

8. Ervine, p. 18.

9. Quoted by Stephen Winsten in *Shaw's Corner* (London, 1952), p. 81.

10. *Bernard Shaw* (London, 1931), p. 67. It is important to remember here that Shaw saw the proofs through the press after Harris's death and approved this line.

11. Winsten, *Shaw's Corner*, p. 23.

12. Dervin, p. 73.

13. Ervine, p. 99.

14. Quoted by Ervine, p. 99.

15. Hesketh Pearson, *George Bernard Shaw* (London, 1963), pp. 50–51.

16. Quoted in G. C. L. DuCann, *The Loves of Bernard Shaw* (London, 1963), pp. 99–100.

17. Dervin, p. 317.

18. Janet Dunbar, *Mrs. G.B.S.* (London, 1963), pp. 281–82.

19. Quoted in *Sixteen Self Sketches* (London, 1949), p. 14. My argument here with respect to Charlotte Shaw parallels, but takes up different biographical details to, the article by Rodelle Weintraub, "The Irish Lady in Shaw's Plays," *Shaw Review*, 1980. Arnold Silver, in his essay in *The Shavian*, V (1975), has also made a connection between *The Millionairess* and the facts of Shaw's life.

20. Quoted by Winsten in *Days with Bernard Shaw* (London, 1949), p. 196.

21. Margery Morgan, *The Shavian Playground* (London, 1972), p. 3.

22. Rosset, p. 136.

23. Ervine, p. 559.

24. Dunbar, pp. 115–16, 121.

25. Ervine, p. 573.

26. Shaw to Ellen Terry, in their *Correspondence* (New York, 1931), p. 109.

27. Quoted in Ervine, pp. 304, 302.

28. Quoted in Dunbar, pp. 141, 142.

29. Quoted in ibid., p. 148.

30. Quoted in ibid., p. 150.

31. Winsten, *Jesting Apostle*, p. 149.

32. Dunbar, p. 122.

33. Ibid.

34. Pearson, p. 456.

35. Dunbar, p. 161.

36. Ibid., p. 160.

37. Winsten, *Jesting Apostle*, p. 40; italics are the author's.

38. Dunbar, p. 118.

39. Ibid., pp. 107–8.

40. Ibid., pp. 129, 108.

41. Dervin, p. 58.

42. Winsten, *Days with Bernard Shaw*, p. 118.

43. Ibid., pp. 47, 69, 71.

Jean-Claude Amalric

SHAW, HAMON, AND
RÉMY DE GOURMONT

In 1913, Augustin Hamon sent his first volume of translations of Shaw's plays[1] to Rémy de Gourmont, the eminent writer and critic, exponent of the Symbolist movement, and one of the contributors to and editors of *Le Mercure de France*. Hamon received in reply a very enthusiastic and friendly letter, which he then sent to Shaw. Shaw made a copy and returned the original. This copy reads as follows (the translation is mine):[2]

> My dear Hamon.
> I have received the first volume of your Bernard Shaw. It interested, amused, elated me more than I can say. What a mirror of English manners. You had a really fine idea when you translated these very curious plays *which do not sound translated anyway, so natural does the French style seem.* Please convey my congratulations to your collaborator. With kind remembrances—the Sarine period, how far away it all seems now.
> Very sincerely. RdG.

A week later, Rémy de Gourmont published a short article, "Bernard Shaw," in "Les Idées du jour" column of *La France*, in praise of Shaw's theatre, calling Shaw "the only dramatic genius at the present time in Europe."[3] Here is a translation of the article:

> I know very well what kind of successor Mr. Claretie should have. It should be a man who will include the theatre of Ibsen and that of Shaw in the repertory. As far as I am concerned, I would ask nothing else of him, and I would esteem that, having done so, he would serve well, not the French dramatic authors, doubtless, but Dramatic Art—which is not quite the same thing. Dramatic genius is the most rare of all. It has not been seen in France since the seventeenth century. Perhaps it will raise its head again tomorrow or the day after. That is possible. We know nothing at all about that. In any case, what is obvious is that it has emerged in Norway with Ibsen and that after being all the rage for a while, we are now treating it as though it had never existed and that it is a crime against

the gifts of the mind. The beginning of Bernard Shaw's career in France looks even less promising. Some bold theatre from time to time puts on one or another of Shaw's plays but Shaw does not even have the benefit of that sort of momentary enthusiasm which has not succeeded in letting Ibsen hold his own against the vanity of the French. Yet he is the only dramatic genius at the present time in Europe and his is the only theatre which gives expression to a somewhat elevated life and to a life which is profoundly original. His French translator has called him "the Molière of the XIXth century," which tends to crush him rather. Molière! Ibsen is not Shakespeare and Shaw is not Molière, but there are in his comedies strokes worthy of Molière, who did not invent a medical man more comically medical than Dr. Paramore, or any females more female than those in the same play *(The Philanderer)* who claim to have no femininity. They possess all the bovarism of the *Bourgeois Gentilhomme* himself. It is quite admirable. Life still keeps fine surprises for us if we look far enough.

Here some remarks are called for, to throw light on the friendship between A. Hamon and R. de Gourmont, the judgment on Hamon's translations, and the possible influence of Gourmont on Shaw.

In the letter, Gourmont alludes to "the Sarine period." To the best of my knowledge, "Sarine" has no significance, as far as literary history is concerned.[4] There may be a mistake in the reading of Gourmont's letter or in the copying of it, and perhaps "Savine" should be substituted for Sarine. Savine was the publisher both of Hamon and Gourmont in the early part of their careers, in the 1890s. Savine was a republican and a socialist who published many books on various subjects, polemical pamphlets and social studies such as *L'Algérie, Souvenirs Militaires* and *Au Palais: moeurs judiciaires.* Among those books were some of Hamon's works: *L'Agonie d'une société: histoire d'aujourd'hui* (1889, written in collaboration with G. Bachot), *Ministère et mélinite, étude sociologique* (1891), a new edition of *La Psychologie du Militaire profesionnel* (1895, "with a vindication"), *La France Sociale et politique en 1891* (1892). It was also Savine who published Rémy de Gourmont's first novel, *Sixtine, roman de la vie cérébrale,* in 1890.

Rémy de Gourmont was a free, independent, vigorous spirit, critic and scholar, refined and pessimistic, with a taste for lucid analysis and a hatred of prejudices. He had a straightforward, almost brutal way of renewing the questions he dealt with. In 1891 he wrote a violent essay for *Le Mercure de France,* "Le joujou patriotisme" (Patriotism, that plaything), in which he denounced, in a pacifist perspective, the idea of revenge against Germany. France and Germany had complementary qualities; the artistic, spontaneous friendship that should link both countries, he declared, was hindered by the question of the provinces of Alsace and Lorraine, and thwarted on both sides by patriotism. This article raised a general outcry in the press, and Gourmont was removed from his post as librarian at the Bibliothèque Nationale, in spite of vigorous protestations from such writers as Octave Mirbeau and Alfred Vallette. In his work, *La France sociale et politique en 1891*, published in 1892 by Savine, a kind of year-book summary and critical comment upon the main political and social events of the year, Hamon recalled the incident and said that he supported Gourmont in *l'Egalité*.[5] In his own survey of the situation, Hamon agrees that the idea of the mother-country is much inferior to the idea of mankind. Universal brotherhood, that Christian law and socialist ideal, does not admit of the idea of the mother-country, which inevitably implies hatred of all that is alien, that is, of the enemy. And, besides, as Vallette had remarked, Gourmont had condemned not the mother-country but patriotism. Therefore, the "Savine period" which Gourmont alludes to in his letter might refer to that period when the two men shared the same opinions, the same attitudes to life, and the same publisher.

In his 1913 article in *La France*, Gourmont states that the successor of Claretie should be a man who would stage or at least recommend Ibsen's and Shaw's plays. Jules Claretie, who had just died that year, had been a novelist, a dramatist, a journalist, and for years a witty chronicler and columnist of Parisian life. He had been administrator of the Comédie Française. He had also written two books on the drama of his time: *La Vie moderne au théâtre*, and *Profils de théâtre*. The most urgent task of such an arbiter of dramatic taste, Gourmont argues, would be to support the courageous plays of Ibsen and Shaw. Ibsen's plays had been introduced into France thanks essentially to the efforts of Antoine and Lugné-Poe. Between 1890 and 1900, fifteen plays were produced, some of them on several occasions (*Ghosts*, *The Master Builder*). But between 1900 and 1913, there were only seven or eight Ibsen plays produced and they were revivals of already known works. As for Shaw, though some serious critical studies of his drama had already appeared,[6] only four plays had actually been produced, by Georges and Ludmila Pitoeff and their troupe: *Candida*, *Mrs Warren's Profession*, *Arms and the Man*, and *You Never Can Tell*. The critical and popular response was varied, from praise to complete lack of understanding and disapproval. Gourmont's article did not seem to spark off a reaction in France about Ibsen and Shaw, since between 1914 and 1920, no Shaw play was produced, and, except for two Ibsen revivals in 1913, *The Wild Duck* and *A Doll's House*, no Ibsen play was produced until 1919. R. de Gourmont had died in 1915. The administrator who succeeded Jules Claretie at the Comédie Française, Albert Carré, only stayed two years because of the war. Then Emile Fabre, a dramatist, was appointed in late 1915. At last two plays by Ibsen were introduced into the repertory between 1918 and 1925, *An Enemy of the*

People and *Hedda Gabler*, but no Shaw play was chosen or considered for production. Only in 1925 did Shaw triumph with the Pitoeffs' *Saint Joan*, and that production was not at the Comédie Française.

Gourmont mentions Shaw's translator without naming him and admits that to say Shaw equalled Molière is an exaggeration but contends that some characters in Shaw's plays are worthy of Molière. Thanks to his connection with Augustin Hamon, Rémy de Gourmont was then well aware of the value and the importance of Shaw's works. The enthusiastic praise of Hamon's translations is all the more surprising as their literary and dramatic qualities, if not their literal accuracy, was often questioned by the critics. Gourmont insists on the French style, so natural that the plays do not seem to have been translated from another language. At the same period, several writers and critics, particularly Abel Hermant and Robert D'Humières, strongly disagreed on that point, regretting the poor quality of the translations. Georges Pitoeff himself is said to have struggled in vain to persuade Shaw to change his translator.

> Pitoeff fought all his life against the Hamons' texts which obviously prevented Shaw from becoming a success in France. Georges could not get the great Irishman to authorize his use of another translation. And it was not from blindness that the poet remained faithful to his tyrants but from friendship and similar ideological leanings.[7]

But the controversy was so hot about the time of, and after, *Saint Joan*, that it led to a rejoinder by Shaw. Louis Thomas, and after him R. de Smet, criticized Hamon's translations very violently:

> The only man who ruins Shaw's work in France is his translator, A. Hamon, who writes theatre dialogue without any wit, verve or naturalness, all of which is most prejudicial to the man that Mr. Hamon naively calls the Molière of the XXth century. . . .[8]

> Mr. Hamon's translations are a veritable treachery. . . . The dialogue produced by the collaboration of the two Hamons is not only harsh and incorrect, but abounds in misinterpretations. We wonder why Shaw, who knows French, tolerates such a scandalous state of affairs.[9]

Shaw replied in a long letter to questions asked by Mr. Borgex, the London correspondent of *Comoedia*. Borgex had asked Shaw his personal ideas on Joan of Arc, on the reception of his play in the States and in Europe, and, finally, whether he thought that the French translation was a faithful reflection of his thought and wit. After stating that he had educated London, New York, Berlin, and Vienna, and that he was too old to educate Paris if that city was too backward to understand his plays, Shaw answered the last question:

When, as most often happens, the gentleman who denounces Hamon shows the most disastrously complete ignorance of my work and sometimes undisguised hostility, I begin to ask myself if Hamon has not created trouble for himself by wishing to be too faithful to me. His translation seems all the more revolting because it is better.[10]

But Antoine, the great actor-manager, who had appreciated Shaw from the beginning, said he was not convinced:

We thought we should acknowledge the evident unsatisfactoriness of the translations presented to us; Bernard Shaw comes very diplomatically to the defence of his collaborators, but our conviction that he has been badly served remains. . . . It is a useless hurting of his admirers among whom I could be counted from the very first.[11]

Rémy de Gourmont, as the article in *La France* shows, was delighted and fascinated by certain characters in Shaw, and the example he gives is Dr. Paramore in *The Philanderer*. He had always been interested in English literature, and he had written, in his *Promenades littéraires* (1904–1913), a perceptive study on English literature in France from the beginning to Kipling and Wells, including a chapter entitled "Marginalia sur Edgar Poe et Baudelaire." He was a friend of Richard Aldington and also followed the development of the Imagist movement and the review, *Poetry*. He is acknowledged to have been a formative influence on Ezra Pound. But he was probably more attentive to ideas or psychological types than to the problems of dramatic translation. Augustin Hamon knew more scientific and technical English than literary idiom, but his wife, Henriette, who became his collaborator, had a much better knowledge of English. Quite naturally, Hamon protested to Shaw in the beginning that he was unable to do justice to his work, but the dramatist, for whom ideas were of paramount importance, insisted on being translated by a kindred spirit rather than by someone who had only dramatic know-how. As Shaw could not choose the actors and directors in foreign countries, at least he could choose a translator who could safeguard the quintessence of Shavianism, or so he thought. And it is true that the Hamons spared no pains to spread Shaw's ideas, to explain and promote his plays, to translate prefaces and plays conscientiously, and to make audiences and critics appreciate him, all activities for which Shaw was rightly grateful.

This leads us to the possibility of some influence of Rémy de Gourmont on Shaw. In his book,[12] Martin Ellehauge suggested the possible influence of Gourmont and Léon Blum, and of the two reviews, *Le Mercure de France* and *La Revue Blanche*. Some of Gourmont's ideas and theories are in keeping with Shaw's. Here are a few examples. In *Le Chemin de velours* (1911), Gourmont points to the utilitarian origin of modern morality, which demolishes its abstract value. The monogamous marriage is found to be a practical compromise between chastity and promiscuity. Modern morality has become antagonistic to the development of life. The cause of evolution requires evolutionary and relative ethics, but Gourmont—and this is not Shavian—insists on the irresponsibility of man for deterministic reasons. In *La Dissociation des Idées* (1899), Gourmont contends that ideas and concepts that are traditionally associated should be separated in modern analysis, the best example being the three notions of sexual pleasure, generation, and love in a general sense. This involves new views of marriage, free love, sexual instinct, and their place in society. In the same way, the ideas of justice, hatred, and envy should be dissociated; so also should militarism, sacrifice, and heroism be kept distinct. All these attitudes, Shaw could have supported and shared.

In *La Physique de l'Amour* (1903), Gourmont lays emphasis on the animal side in man:

> There is not a single instinctive way of behaving in man which is not found in such and such an animal species: and this is not difficult to understand since man is an animal subjected to the same essential instincts that govern all animality, since everywhere the same matter is animated by the same desire: to live, to perpetuate life.[13]

The natural functions of man and woman produce contrasting interests; the maternal function of woman and the economic and intellectual function of man often lead to a struggle between man and woman. Men and women must obey the commands of natural instincts and not the rules of an outmoded morality. Finally, the Shavian idea that man can be superseded and replaced by the Life Force if he does not fulfil his purpose is also to be found in *La Physique de l'Amour*:

> Finally, if man was to abdicate, which seems improbable, animality is rich enough to produce an heir to him. Candidates for humanity are numerous and they are not those that the common herd would think of. Who knows, perhaps one day our descendants will find themselves faced by a rival in all the strength of his youth? Creation has not been idle since man first emerged: since this monster appeared, nature has gone on with its labor: the human chance can happen all over again tomorrow.[14]

The affinities then are obvious between some of Gourmont's theories and themes and Shaw's ideas as expressed in the Prefaces of *Man and Superman* (or *The Revolutionist's Handbook*), *Getting Married*, *Overruled*, and even *Androcles and the Lion*. But for several reasons this internal evidence is not sufficient to show anything more than convergent trends of thought. First, other influences, more important and acknowledged by Shaw, can be found and have often been demonstrated: those of Butler, Ibsen, Nietzsche, Schopenhauer, for instance, are the most obvious ones. Second, Shaw had other theories on moral responsibility and marriage and other explanations of current and modern morality. Third, Shaw was always very fond of giving lists of thinkers whose ideas and attitudes were akin to his own. There is one in the Epistle Dedicatory of *Man and Superman*:

> Bunyan, Blake, Hogarth and Turner. . . . Goethe, Shelley, Schopenhauer, Wagner, Ibsen, Morris, Tolstoy and Nietzsche are among the writers whose peculiar sense of the world I recognize as more or less akin to my own.[15]

Neither in Bevan's *Concordance*, nor in the index to the *Complete Prefaces*, nor in the index of the first two volumes of the *Collected Letters* is the name of Gourmont to be found. Shaw may well have known and read Gourmont's theories, perhaps through the instrumentality of Hamon and his circle of radical thinkers, but it has been impossible until now to ascertain the fact. This would tend to show that Shaw's and Gourmont's ideas were developing along similar or parallel lines, at least on a certain number of subjects, and this would explain why Gourmont was ready to welcome Shaw favorably as a thinker and as a dramatist. And, in this perspective, Augustin Hamon is an indisputable link between Shaw and Rémy de Gourmont.

Notes

1. Hamon had translated and published separately most of the pleasant and unpleasant plays in 1908, but they were published in 1913 in one volume, *Pièces plaisantes et déplaisantes*, "en la version française faite sur son [Shaw's] instance par Augustin et Henriette Hamon."

2. I am indebted to Professor Dan H. Laurence for drawing my attention to this letter and supplying me with a photocopy, and to Professor Wayne Bell, Assistant Dean of the Hofstra University Library, who generously granted me permission to reproduce it. Here is the French text as copied by Shaw:

Rémy de Gourmont

20/2/13   71, rue des Saints Pères

Mon cher Hamon

J'ai reçu le premier volume de votre Bernard Shaw. Cela m'a intéressé, amusé, enivré plus que je ne saurais dire. Quel mirroir [*sic*] des moeurs anglaises! Vous avez eu la meillure [*sic*] des idées en traduisant ces pièces si curieuses *qui n'ont pas l'air d'être tradiuts* [*sic*] *d'ailleurs, tant le style français parait naturel*. Faite [*sic*] partager mes compliments à votre collaboratrice.

Je me rappelle à votre souvenir. Le temps de Sarine, hein, comme cela remonte

deja dans le passé?
Bien cordialement
[signed] R. G. [Rémy de Gourmont—in Shaw's autograph longhand.]

3. Rémy de Gourmont, "Bernard Shaw" in "Les Idées du jour," *La France*, 27 Février 1913, p. 1, col. 4. Here is the text of the article:

> Je sais bien quel devrait être le successeur de M. Claretie. Ce devrait être un homme qui mît au répertoire le théâtre d'Ibsen et celui de Bernard Shaw. Pour ma part, je ne lui demanderais pas autre chose et je considèrerais qu'ayant fait cela, il aurait bien mérité, non pas sans doute des auteurs dramtiques français, mais de l'art dramatique, ce qui est assez différent. Le génie dramatique est le plus rare de tous les génies. On ne l'a pas revu en France depuis le dix-septième siècle. Peut-être se manifestera-t-il encore demain ou après-demain. C'est possible. On n'en sait rien. En tout cas, il est évident qu'il s'est manifesté en Norvège, avec Ibsen et qu'après un moment de vogue, nous sommes en train de le traiter comme s'il n'avait jamais existé et que c'est un crime contre les dons de l'esprit. La carrière française de Bernard Shaw s'annonce dans des conditions moins bonnes encore. Un courageux théâtre joue de temps en temps quelqu'une des ses pièces, mais Shaw ne bénéficie même pas de cette sorte d'enthousiasme momentané qui n'a pas réussi a maintenir Ibsen contre la vanité française. C'est pourtant le seul génie dramatique de la présente heure européenne et c'est le seul théâtre qui traduise une vie un peu élevée et une vie profondément originale. Son traducteur français l'a appelé "le Molière du XIXe [*sic*] siècle," ce qui n'est pas sans l'écraser un peu. Molière! Ibsen n'est pas Shakespeare et Shaw n'est pas Molière, mais il y a dans ses comédies des traits dignes de Molière, qui n'a pas fait un médecin plus comiquement médecin que le Dr. Paramore, ni des femmes plus femmes que celles de la même pièce (*L'Homme aimé des femmes*), qui se prétendent sans "féminité." Elles ont le bovarysme du *Bourgeois Gentilhomme* lui-même. C'est admirable. La vie a encore de belles surprises, quand on regarde au loin. Rémy de Gourmont.

4. The Sarine is a river in Switzerland, in the canton of Fribourg. Gourmont might have alluded to that place or region, but it is hardly likely. Besides, the phrase "le temps de Sarine," if referring to a river, is awkward. It would rather be applied to a village, a town, or a person, and not to a river (le temps de *la* Sarine). Another expression would be "outre-Sarine," meaning "in Switzerland," in the same way as "outre-Manche" means "in Britain" for French people.

5. A. Hamon, *La France sociale et politique en 1891* (Paris: Savine, 1892), 167–69.

6. For instance, Augustin Filon, "M. Bernard Shaw et son théâtre," *Revue des Deux Mondes*, 15 November 1905, pp. 405–33; Jean Blum, "George Bernard Shaw," *Revue Germanique* 5 (Nov./Dec. 1906), 634–55; Charles Cestre, *Bernard Shaw et son oeuvre* (Paris: Mercure de France, 1912). Augustin Hamon was to publish his *Le Molière du XXe siècle: Bernard Shaw* in 1913 (Paris: Figuière).

7. H. R. Lenormand, *Les Pitoeff* (Paris: Odette Lieutier, 1943), 84. [my translation]

8. L. Thomas, "A propos de la 'Jeanne d'Arc' de B. Shaw, M. Louis Thomas répond à M. Hamon," *Comoedia*, 22 Février 1924.

9. R. de Smet, "Les adaptateurs défigurent-ils les auteurs étrangers?" *Comoedia*, 4 Mars 1924.

10. "La 'Jeanne d'Arc' de Bernard Shaw. Une lettre originale du dramaturge irlandais," *Comoedia*, 16 Mars 1924. My translation of Shaw's text published in French.

11. A. Antoine, "Le Manifeste de Bernard Shaw," *Comoedia* 18 Mars 1924.

12. Martin Ellehauge, *The Position of Bernard Shaw in European Drama and Philosophy* (Copenhagen: Levin & Munksgaard, 1931), 362sq.

13. R. de Gourmont, *La Physique de l'Amour* (Paris: 1903; Paris: Le Club Français du Livre, 1962), 6–7.

14. Ibid., p. 299.

15. B. Shaw, *Man and Superman* in *The Bodley Head Bernard Shaw*, ed. Dan H. Laurence (London: Max Reinhardt, The Bodley Head, 1971), 2, 519–20.

Constance Cummings

PLAYING JOAN ON RADIO AND TELEVISION

Some years ago I had the rare experience of playing Shaw's Saint Joan on the stage and then on the radio and finally on television. This happy series started in 1939 when I was asked to join the Old Vic Theatre Company for a year—this was before it became the National Theatre— and Joan was to be one of my parts.

I was told by the Theatre that before Shaw would give consent for me to play the part, he would want to meet me. So it was arranged that I should go to Whitehall Court one afternoon at three o'clock. To meet Shaw was a great bonus for a young actress on top of playing Saint Joan, and of course I was thrilled. I arrived promptly and his secretary said to me firmly, "Before I take you in, I must tell you Mr. Shaw has another appointment at 3:30." I got her point, and said I would certainly keep my eye on my watch and not stay beyond that time. She then showed me into the drawing room.

Shaw was standing in the middle of it and he came towards me and took my hand and patted rather than shook it. He was very thin and his hair and beard quite white, and he looked so fragile that my first thought was one of concern for him as he moved across the room. I thought a breeze from the open window might blow him away like a dandelion top gone to feathery seed. But when he got close and looked down at me with his twinkly, aquamarine eyes, I saw in him enough vitality and strength for ten men, and I ceased worrying about him.

It was summer and the sunlight brightened the big Edwardian room. We sat down by the window. I do not remember how the conversation began, but after we had talked a bit, I asked him if he had ever seen me on the stage. He said "No." I asked him "How can you tell then if I will be what you want for Joan?" "I can tell, child, I can tell." The energy in his voice was tempered by the soft Irish accent. I said that whether or not I could achieve it, I was fairly sure that I knew how he wanted Joan to be played. He laughed delightedly and said "Oh, the impudence of it—the impudence." To elaborate I said that though I had never seen Sybil Thorndike play it (she was the original Saint Joan), I had seen her in other things, and I knew her well and I was sure she must have been one hundred percent right. And though I could not and would not have the boldness to think that I could compare with her, I would say that I was sensitive to her understanding of the part and hoped that I would play it in that spirit.

We then talked of other actors who played it, and I mentioned one well-known lady and said that I had not seen her either, but I was sure she must have been very wrong, and I *would not* play it that way. "Oh, she was bad, child," he replied. "She was bad, she came onto the stage in the first act half burned already."

I cannot remember what else was said, but before you could spell cat, the door opened and his secretary came in and said she was sorry to interrupt, but it was after 3:30 and Mr. Shaw was late for his next appointment! I could not believe half-an-hour had flown by. I did not believe either that Mr. Shaw had another appointment. I longed for more time, but thank God I had the manners to make apologies for staying too long, and I left.

I do not think he ever saw the play. Just before we opened at Buxton in Yorkshire, war was declared, and we did not even come to the Old Vic, although we did finally play at Golders Green and Streatham Hill. I wrote to him once during rehearsals to ask him why the Church was so censorious of Joan's leaving off her womanly clothes and wearing men's armor, as the latter was so much more suitable in the circumstances. He replied on one of his famous postcards which had his photo on one side. He was pictured with his chin dropped onto his fingers and a rather quizzical expression on his face. One could see from his face in the picture, he observed to me, that he wasn't at all sure why the Church frowned on idiosyncratic attire, since John the Baptist and St. Francis of Assisi had dispensed with conventional clothes and some of their followers had been known to disrobe completely.

In the stage production of the Old Vic we did the entire play. There was never any talk of cutting it. When later I did Saint Joan on the radio in 1941, we did the entire play. It lasted three and a quarter hours. I did not know till afterwards that I had frightened the life out of everyone by saying that I preferred to do it without a script. I had played it not long before on the stage and I knew it, and of course it is easier to give a performance if one has not one's nose buried in a script. So when rehearsals started I was without a book. If I had known how nervous the rest of the cast and the technical crew were (we were broadcasting live) I would have at least held the book in my hands as a gesture, but no one said anything. Val Gielgud, who directed, was game and let me do it, although I believe he had posted one or two prompters at strategic points to whisper the lines if I went astray. After the broadcast Shaw wrote Val the following letter:

> 4, Whitehall Court
> London, S.W. 1
> 24th September 1941

Dear Mr. Gielgud,

If you broadcast St. Joan again, you had better ask me to adapt it a little to an audience which cannot see it. I shall have to write a part for the announcer. In the second scene and in the church scene he must introduce the late comers, as the listeners are quite puzzled by hearing people speak of whose entry they have had no notice.

At the end of the court scene Tremouille must say to the Dauphin "Do you think you can snap your fingers in my face?" then the *DAUPHIN.* "I can. I will (popgun). *JOAN.* Thou art answered, old Gruffandgrum (rattle of her sword-hilt and tearing of a bit of calico to imitate the drawing of her sword) Who is for God and his maid? Who is for Orleans with me? *ALL.* (with a clash of swords) To Orleans! *ARCHBISHOP.* On your knees, all! God and his maid! (Thump of knees).

Winchester Cathedral should be cut out of the epilogue. It is impossible without vision and is quite unnecessary.

The organ should be used in the Rheims scene. There are several little things like that.

The meaning of the play got through perfectly. Miss Cummings has strength and great intelligence (or was the intelligence coached?): what she lacks is music and artistry in the touches of dialect; but if she has a good ear she will get that and go far. Warwick was all right; but Cauchon in the tent scene did not give contrast enough between the ecclesiastic and the courtier. Bluebeard and La Hire were not distinguishable. Bluebeard should exploit some peculiarity, say an effeminate lisp, or the speech of someone whom he likes to mimic; and La Hire should talk like a sheepdog. They both seemed determined to talk like English gentlemen—perhaps they were imitating Warwick. Dunois was good except in a few passages in the church scene, where he showed temper, like the Archbishop, and immediately lost his distinction. He should never lose his good natured pleasant selfpossession.

Faithfully,

George Bernard Shaw

P.S. The pages must not be played by girls. It turns the performance into a XIX century opera bouffe. If a boy is not available, a man will do. Joan in her last speech in the trial scene should not pause long enough to let the agitated court interrupt her. Impetuosity *con tutta la forza* is the secret of it. Except for this it was good.[1]

Obviously, Shaw was not averse to making cuts. Also, he showed himself sensitive to additions and interruptions which would enable the radio audience to know who—where—and what they were listening to. In a subsequent letter to Val Gielgud, Shaw discussed others of his plays and ideas for broadcasting, and he was cooperative and inventive and showed himself to be interested in the possibilities of the medium.

Perhaps the point that needs most attention in doing Joan on the radio is one that Shaw himself commented on. In the Court Scene, the Cathedral Scene, and also the Epilogue where you have many people speaking, it is important to establish and maintain the different characters by a variety of voices and accents. On the stage and on television one does not need to bother about that so much, for the costume of the character places him visually in his social context. In *Saint Joan* the various characters stand not only for themselves as individuals in society, but also for the Church, the Monarchy, the Aristocratic Officer Class, the Common Soldier, etc. So distinction is doubly important.

To appreciate and understand the play one must pay attention to what Shaw says in his preface. He is not writing about villains persecuting a heroine in a romantic play. His concern is to pursue and clarify the circumstances in which well-meaning people with the best intentions solemnly burn a young girl to death. To give point to this seeming paradox he quotes some South Sea islanders, who, when told the story of Saint Joan, did not believe it as they could not credit the fact that sane people would go to the trouble of roasting someone whom they did not intend to eat! There are no villains in *Saint Joan*. I would go so far as to say there are no villains in Shaw at all. Just as there are no bad parts. Long parts and small ones, but no bad ones.

To return to the establishment of individuality, in the marvellous tent scene, Cauchon and Warwick are urbane, educated gentlemen. The language both use is courtly and elegant, but there must be no moment when the audience has any doubt about which of them is speaking. For the radio this can best be assured by contrasting timbre and accent of the actors' voices. I think there is not a great deal of difference in studying the play for radio or the stage, except the latter of course requires more volume and projection, and this applies in ratio to the size of the theatre in use. Television has one advantage neither stage nor radio has. I will write of that in a moment.

The constant factor which supports all Shaw's plays, the bedrock on which they rest, is the intellectual idea that has caught his attention. Even in the delightful *You Never Can Tell*—at first glance the perfect drawing room comedy—there are serious threads that can be found in his other plays dealing with the position of women, the degradation that can attend on marriage, the Life Force, etc. See *Mrs Warren's Profession, The Philanderer, Man and Superman*. However deceptively playful plays by Shaw may seem, he is never really playing but is always in earnest. This, of course, is why his arrows of wit always hit the bull's eye. His pen is directed by a very clear head. The idea is what gives the truth and vitality to his plays. This has a relation to radio acting, for on the radio one has to have a sharp picture in one's mind of the setting of the play, the look of the other characters, the relationships which result. It is not done for the audience by the scene designer and costumier. And in some miraculous way, this effort of realization the actor makes, flies through the air to the listener's comprehension. The effort does help to get closer to Shaw because he is working in the realms of thoughts and ideas more than visual effects.

Let me say at once that I am not for a moment maintaining the error that people have made in saying that Shaw was all head and no heart. People who think that Joan should be played in blond curls with her eyes turned to heaven like the heroine on the cover of the Victorian ballad are apt to complain that Shaw had no religious feeling and was incapable of portraying a saint, that he was out of his depth in these waters. They are wrong. Shaw understood how close Joan felt to her God. She turned to him as to a father, and indeed, a great deal of what Joan says in his play the real, living Joan actually did say. Perhaps the words of no other figure of that time have been taken down with such accuracy and in such completeness. She was in the hands of the Church for eight months before she was excommunicated and turned over to the English for her destruction. During that time she was frequently examined as to her beliefs and her so-called heresy and all these investigations and enquiries were taken down faithfully in writing by the Church.

She was a true saint in that her inspiration and her courage came to her directly from God. She was untainted and unclouded by worldly considerations. They had no place in her understanding. She heard God and his angels speak in the ringing of the church bells, yet she was not a dreamy mystic with this. The Church accused her, "the voices you hear are the voices of your own imagination." "Of course," she replied, astonished by the obtuseness of the accusation, "that is how the words of God come to us."

Shaw himself must have been a man of religious sensitivity, however unorthodox, to be able to understand and portray with such sensitivity Joan's belief that she had a direct line to her God. Shaw must have had something of the sort himself. The play is a highly emotional one, not in the sense of melodrama which begs our tears, but from the fact that the purest, the most formidable, the most lasting emotions come from the unidentified wind that blows unbidden through our minds and demands our lifelong devotion. Shaw was acquainted with this wind, and by virtue of this he understood how it moved Joan to do everything she accomplished. It cannot be that she could have done so much by the age of eighteen or nineteen without being some kind of saint, that is to say a person of rare purity.

I said television has one advantage over stage and radio, and that is the close-up. The Loire scene, for instance, is always a difficult scene in the theatre—the river bank, the wind changing, the looking across the river at the English enemy. I have seen the play many times and have never believed in that river bank. I have accepted it because there is no alternative. On television it can be played very largely in close-ups with the river and country-side in the background. It can even be filmed on the bank of a real river. Not so much with us in feeling as it has to be in the theatre, and not so much to be imagined as it needs to be on the radio. A great deal of Shaw lends itself to close-up, as does Shakespeare.

One difficulty in Shaw for television can be some of the long speeches. The Inquisitor's speech in *Joan* lasts twelve minutes. That is really too long to keep the camera on one face when the virtue and the expectation of that medium is fluid movement. Moving the camera to the faces of those who are listening does not help a great deal, as the camera is then making the selection for the audience, and this can be a tyranny when the piece is not written for that to happen. In the theatre you are free to let your eyes wander over the whole stage and select what you will look at. When this is done in an arbitrary way on television as a refuge from "too long a view of one thing" it can be most distracting.

Whatever the medium, the main thing to concentrate on with Shaw is what he is saying, and that is not difficult to discover. Some actors and directors say "I never bother with the stage directions that an author puts in. They just get in the way." Shaw's stage directions are often delightful, often witty, and always very revealing. They should be read and followed as closely as his dialogue. They are signposts and clarifications. There is not one that has been put in carelessly, or without a definite purpose. I think to some extent Shaw meant them as a supplement to the lines, and to a great extent to protect himself from the misinterpretation and even stupidities that he knew he would be subject to in the hands of incompetent actors and directors. Take for example the first three pages of *Mrs Warren's Profession*. If the actors playing Praed and Vivie are in any doubt as to what their characters are or how the parts should be played, they will find blueprints in the stage directions accompanying the lines. If they say the stage directions are of no consequence and ignore them, two other actors should be playing the parts.

The prefaces also are a great help to understanding the plays and in any case make interesting and enjoyable reading without reference to the plays. An interesting point in connection with understanding Shaw's plays and characters comes from his use of language. The language he speaks is very direct and simple. The vocabulary he uses is comparatively small. I do not suggest this is because he knew fewer words than the next writer. I think he felt no need for long, difficult words. One never needs recourse to a dictionary when reading his work. Yet within this limitation he expresses many different points of view and characters.

Where one can trail behind his intentions is in the realms of his humanity and understanding and in the straightforward clarity with which he comprehends and portrays his people. He says in the preface to *Plays Unpleasant*: ". . . I got a clue to my real condition from a friend of mine, a physician who had devoted himself specifically to ophthalmic surgery. He tested my eyesight one evening and informed me that it was quite uninteresting to him because it was normal. I naturally took this to mean that it was like everyone else's; but he rejected this construction as paradoxical and hastened to explain to me that I was an exceptional and highly fortunate person optically, normal sight conveying the power of seeing things accurately, and being enjoyed by only about 10 percent of the population, the remaining 90 percent being abnormal. . . . All I had to do was to open my normal eyes, and with my utmost literary skill put the case exactly as it struck me or describe the thing exactly as I saw it, to be applauded as the most humorously extravagant paradoxer in London. The only reproach with which I became familiar was the everlasting 'Why can you not be serious?'"

This is still true. The epithets *crank, jester* and *buffoon* can still be heard against him, though these words condemn the user and not Shaw. Although Shaw's writing is seemingly so simple, it is almost impossible to cut his plays without getting into trouble. I do not mean trouble with his executors, I mean trouble on the next page! When we did the television *Saint Joan* we did discuss the feasibility of cutting some of the Inquisitor's twelve-minute speech and intended to ask Shaw if he would agree, but when we sat down to see whether we could make it shorter, we discovered that every cut left a wound and that what had been taken out was needed to clarify something that was to come later.

Neither can Shaw be paraphrased. Every actor with whom I have discussed Shaw's plays agrees with me that if you say the wrong word in a speech before long you will find that you have painted yourself into a corner. You need the precise words as he wrote them. So very exact and economical is he. What is more, if you do say the wrong words, you know it as soon as they are out of your mouth. I have never understood how this works, nor found it to be so unfailing with another author, but with Shaw, if you alter his lines ever so slightly, a bell rings in your mind and you know what you have done and before long you will know that you need the correct words. This makes a hazard for television performances that is not so easily dealt with as on the stage. If one is doing a play on the radio or one is reading it one should get the text absolutely correct. On the stage one can make a shot at covering the mistake, getting the key word in, be it ever so clumsily done. But in television if the camera is on the face of the actor, the moment of guilt and perhaps panic flashes its signal long enough for the concentration to be broken and probably for the director to call "Cut!"

There is another difference that I think comes into play with the three different media: Shaw's marvelous wit. His plays all sparkle with this, which can be at a slight disadvantage in radio. The physical attitude of an actor, his facial expression, the movements he makes, or indeed his lack of movement all help to deliver comedy lines neatly and economically to the audience. In radio the comedy survives through the voices alone. In television the camera can and usually does swoop upon the person who has the comedy line, which of course is a straight tip to the audience as to when the play is being funny. I prefer the stage where the audience makes its own change of focus and feels it has discovered the joke by itself.

My preference may be for the stage as the easiest form in which to deal with Shaw's comedy, but it does not always work out that way! I have seen Shaw presented on the stage with such lugubrious care and heavy undercurrents that the performance was almost unbearable. I recall a production of *Major Barbara* where the audience sat through the entire first act as well behaved and unsmiling as if they had found themselves at a slightly mystifying funeral service. In a way they had. The comedy in that first act, of which there is a great deal, was lying flat on the stage stone dead.

One final word about playing Shaw in whatever medium. It is advisable for the actor to make himself familiar with what Shaw intends in the play. If there is a conflict between Shaw and his interpreter, it is the actor who loses out. Shaw writes in a beautifully dove-tailed way. His grip on his subject is strong and clear, and the actor who thinks he knows better than what is written, or who thinks he can do something much more interesting than Shaw had thought of, is walking into quicksands and is in danger of disappearing. Somehow Shaw's plays cannot be made to look foolish as many other plays can.

The actor cannot dominate Shaw by ignoring the sense of the play and trying to present an interpretation which appeals to him as something he has invented from whole cloth. The play may be deadened a bit, not sparkle as it truly should, but it will keep its shape and its meaning will force its way through a bad interpretation.

A convention has grown up to dog the present-day theatre which insists that much artistry can be proven from finding a "new way" to do a play, that genius consists in throwing a light on the work from far out in left field, however arbitrary left field may be. This is a fairly tiresome approach at the best of times when it is based on a genuinely felt belief that all the richness of the work concerned has never before been mined. But it can be intolerable when the motive is to allow a director to stand the play on its head or an actor to "tear a passion to shreds." In any case it will not do for Shaw. He must be played straight, and the actors and producers must hold his hand all the way. This is no hardship! As I said earlier, all the parts in Shaw's plays are very good. It is a joy and a privilege to be able to spend three hours talking in language so much more exquisite than one's own. Whether we are on the radio, the television, or the stage, let us present Shaw honestly and simply and let him speak for himself. Well—he will anyway.

Notes

1. From a copy of the original in the collection of Mrs. Judy Gielgud. Copyright © 1984 The Trustees of the British Museum, the Governors and Guardians of the National Library of Ireland, and the Royal Academy of Dramatic Art.

Richard F. Dietrich

SHAVIAN PSYCHOLOGY

Shaw has been psychoanalyzed (see Daniel Dervin's *Bernard Shaw: A Psychological Study* and Arnold Silver's *Bernard Shaw: The Darker Side*); his works have been mined for psychological insights by many (see especially Arthur H. Nethercot's "Bernard Shaw and Psychoanalysis in *Modern Drama*, 1969, as qualified by Sidney P. Albert's "Reflections on Shaw and Psychoanalysis" in *Modern Drama*, 1971); he and Freud have even been paired as the two saviors of modern life (see Brigid Brophy's *Black Ship to Hell*). But no one has called attention to the fact that Shaw was apparently the inventor of a system of psychology that antedates Freud, Jung, Adler, et al. and that provides a unique and valuable understanding of the human mind. Shaw's Realist, Idealist, and Philistine are primarily psychological categories, providing the basis for an entire system of psychological analysis. For the most part Shaw's system is suggestively embodied in his art, the closest he came to a direct statement being in *The Quintessence of Ibsenism*, later buttressed and qualified by *The Sanity of Art* and *The Perfect Wagnerite*.[1] In her *Shavian Guide to the Intelligent Woman*, Barbara Bellow Watson writes that "it may some day become clear that Shaw created an early literary parallel of Freudian psychology."[2] In this article I propose to show that Shavian psychology *was* parallel in important respects but that ultimately it was an alternative to Freudian psychology.

In the *American Journal of Psychology* (XXI, 72), Ernest Jones, the English Freudian Shaw probably knew best, began an article on the Oedipus complex in *Hamlet* by citing Shaw's essays on Ibsen and Wagner as examples of the way great writers make the most penetrating generalizations in practical psychology without the world being the wiser until some elucidator like Shaw points them out. And the same could be said for Shaw's own writings. For example, in the process of elucidating Ibsen's plays in *The Quintessence of Ibsenism*, Shaw incurred misunderstandings about his own meanings, and scholars have been hard at work lately attempting to rescue Shaw from Shaw as much as Ibsen from Shaw. As scholars rediscover the worth of *The Quintessence* as philosophy and criticism and set the record straight as to what Shaw did and did not say about Ibsen, the result has been the reclamation of a document that had been denounced for crimes against Ibsen it didn't really commit, largely clearing Shaw of the charge that he made Ibsen into a purely social dramatist or a political ideologue. But if Shaw has been largely cleared of distorting Ibsen, he has not been entirely cleared of similar distortions that were partly self-inflicted and partly the result of misreading. These distortions frequently derive from doubts about whether Shaw's life and work have any psychological depth, or even any psychological dimension.

A way to dismiss Shaw as an artist has always been to declare him merely a speech-maker, pamphleteer, and propagandist, concerned with shallow and trivial matters. When Yeats, for instance, said that "we make out of the quarrel with others, rhetoric, but of the quarrel with ourselves, poetry,"[3] he might have been thinking of one of his favorite distinctions between Shaw and himself. On another occasion Yeats wrote explicitly: "Mr. Bernard Shaw . . . makes his comedies something less than life by never forgetting that he is a reformer."[4] Inasmuch as Ibsen too thought of writing more as warring with the trolls within than as a means of social reform, Ibsen would seem to be in league with Yeats. The true poet is psychological and soulful; Shaw was sociological and political and therefore no true poet. But blame Yeats less than Shaw himself for distorting matters, for Shaw all too often allowed narrow polemical purposes to mislead people about the nature of his art. When Shaw insisted that his writing was didactic, journalistic, and propagandistic, only the more semantically attuned reader realized that Shaw used such words in ways a Yeats would not understand.

Putting aside the question of whether Yeats' idea of poetry is adequate, a study of Shaw's art, including the polemics, reveals it to be a good deal more psychological and soulful than Yeats thought. To begin with, *The Quintessence of Ibsenism*, *The Sanity of Art*, and *The Perfect Wagnerite*, written in the 1890s, constitute a trilogy of "major critical essays" that provide theoretical underpinning for much of what Shaw put into practice in his plays, and among the accomplishments of this trilogy in philosophy, criticism, esthetics, and semantics is a formulation of Shaw's understanding of the human mind, of his psychology. But because they are polemics as well, directed at public concerns, these works mislead readers into assuming that Shaw was primarily interested in matters sociological. The sociological is an important dimension in Shaw's multi-dimensional writing, but his classical and dramatic art—his habit of externalizing—makes it seem more important than it is. Typically, of the writing of his first novel (1879), Shaw said, "I . . . cut out pages of analysis of character, because I think the dramatic method of *exhibiting* character the true one."[5] Even in his novels he was indirect. Thus we find little more direct psychological probing of character in Shaw than we do in, say, Homer. Shaw's polemics are also the result of projection. Originally shy and introverted, Shaw used art to extrovert himself.[6] To get at the psychological content of his works one must reverse the projection, translating the social and dramatic metaphors into their psychological sources. The extrovert must be re-introverted.

The Quintessence of Ibsenism is a case in point. Written by a young man who had failed in the private world of art as a novelist but who was beginning to succeed in the public world as a critic, pamphleteer, and gadfly, *The Quintessence* takes on the character of that Shaw who was struggling to extrovert himself. Having come to an understanding of his social alienation as more an evolutionary phenomenon than a family condition—i.e., he was separated from others not so much because his father's drunkenness had brought ostracism on the family as because he was more highly evolved—he proceeds to classify people according to how evolved they are. He divides the world into Realists, Idealists, and Philistines—seemingly objective, sociological categories—based on people's attitude toward evolutionary social change. Roughly 70% of humankind consists of easygoing, satisfied Philistines, willing to go along with things as they are, having no ambitions beyond living for the moment. Roughly 29% of humankind consists of the more highly evolved Idealists, secretly dissatisfied because things as they are don't measure up to ideals but afraid to face that truth and so committed to a policy of pretending that ideals are in effect and forcing everybody to live up to them. That leaves roughly 1% of humankind to the lonely Realists, the most highly evolved, those few who are strong enough to face the truth the Idealists are shirking and to point out the need for reform. When the Realist proposes a reform, such as abolishing the compulsory character of marriage, "The Philistines will simply think him mad. But the Idealists will be terrified beyond measure at the proclamation of their hidden thought—at the presence of the traitor among the conspirators of silence. . . . At his worst they will call [the Realist] cynic and paradoxer: at his best they do their utmost to ruin him if not to take his life"(*MCE*,28). This at least was the reaction to Ibsen. And so Shaw sets the stage for the Ibsenite drama, which he conceives of as portraying "a conflict of unsettled ideals"(*MCE*,139). Shaw sees Ibsen as dramatizing the evolution of the species in the clash among Idealists, Philistines, and incipient Realists.

The first thing to notice is that, despite appearances, Shaw's categories are not fundamentally sociological. They are not based primarily on group behavior patterns but rather on mind set. How Idealists, Philistines, and

Realists react to one another in social situations is important to Shaw because the conflict among them is the stuff of drama, but their social behavior is presented as effect, not cause. The cause of their behavior is psychological; their behavior is due to the kind of mind they have. Either the way they think is the way they behave, frequently to the point of obsession, or they behave opposite to the way they think, involved in unconscious hypocrisy. Shaw saw Ibsen as satirical of both fanaticism and hypocrisy, which are primarily mental states, capable of neurotic and psychotic development. At the very least, then, Shaw's categories fall under the rubric of "social psychology," not of sociology.

Going further, however, the balance between sociology and psychology is tipped to the latter when we discover Shaw's view of the source of human behavior. At first *The Quintessence* gives us the impression that the source is external—in social change—but we gradually discover that Shaw really believed the source to be internal—in the individual will. Believing that "the real slavery of today is slavery to ideals of goodness"(*MCE*,117), he analyzes the differences among human types according to their response to Will:

> The Realist at last loses patience with ideals, altogether, and sees in them only something to blind us, something to numb us, something to murder self in us, something whereby, instead of resisting death, we can disarm it by committing suicide. The Idealist, who has taken refuge with the ideals because he hates himself and is ashamed of himself, thinks that all this is so much for the better. The Realist, who has come to have a deep respect for himself and faith in the validity of his own will, thinks it so much the worse. To the [Idealist], human nature, naturally corrupt, is held back from ruinous excesses only by self-denying conformity to the ideals. To [the Realist] these ideals are only swaddling clothes which man has outgrown, and which insufferably impede his progress. No wonder the two cannot agree. The Idealist says, "Realism means egotism; and egotism means depravity." The realist declares that when a man abnegates the will to live and be free in a world of the living and the free, seeking only to conform to ideals for the sake of being, not himself, but "a good man," then he is morally dead and rotten, and must be left unheeded to abide his resurrection, if that by good luck arrive before his bodily death (*MCE*,31).

The essence of this is that Will operates in Shaw's system as *libido* does in Freud's. As Freud argued for a greater trust in *libido*, so Shaw argued for a greater trust in Will, although Freud's *libido* is entirely sexual while Shaw's Will is the Life Force in general. At any rate, Philistine-Idealist-Realist are more obviously psychological categories when we see that their base is internal; they are responses to the call of the Will within. The Philistine, tamed by convention, heeds the Will insofar as it is convenient and prudent; the Idealist, fearing the Will as a corrupting force, tries to deny the Will whenever its call contradicts established ideals; the Realist seeks to fufill Will, suffering repression from the Idealists and those Philistines who find it prudent to serve the Idealists. This presages Freud's psychology of repression, the Idealist operating as a Super-Ego to prevent the Realist from realizing the will of the Id.

The difficulty in reading *The Quintessence* as psychology is that Shaw, already thinking in character types, speaks mostly of conflict among and between groups of people rather than of inner conflict. And he too often makes it sound as though human beings were no more complicated than puppets. For this reason some critics have interpreted his plays as mere theorems, the working out of allegorical conflicts between bad guy Idealists and good guy Realists to prove his social theory. And when in *The Quintessence* Shaw calls for a doctrinal theatre, that sounds as though he is going to create his characters according to the propaganda needs of his socialist theory. But, as he also said, "there is no more reason for making a doctrinal theatre inartistic than for putting a cathedral organ out of tune"(*MCE*,149). Fortunately, Shaw was a true playwright and he allowed his characters to take on an artistic life of their own, independent of their author's political theories. Shaw recognized this when he once declared that creating characters was "a process over which I assure you I have no more real control than I have over my wife."[7] And of *Mrs Warren's Profession* he said, "It is no mere theorem, but a play of instincts and temperaments in conflict."[8]

Mrs Warren's Profession (1893) is the third of a trio of "Unpleasant Plays" Shaw wrote immediately after *The Quintessence*, and of the three it most completely embodies the theory of *The Quintessence* while revealing more obviously the primarily psychological nature of it. On its sociological level *Mrs Warren's Profession* attacks several different kinds of social idealism—marital, parental, religious, esthetic, romantic, and so on. But their social occurrence is effect, not cause, and the attack on them is not really the heart of the play. The principal action of this as well as many other Shaw plays is essentially psychological—one character, usually a younger person, a potential Realist, is taught a lesson by another character, usually an older person, who may or may not be aware of what is being taught, and the result is, first, disillusionment, second, enlightenment, and third, a growth in spirit that allows the evolving character to better realize his or her authentic self. Here Mrs. Warren, rather unawares, is the principal catalyst in the development of Vivie, as Vivie experiences a death of the old Idealist self and is reborn as an incipient Realist.

That is, the heart of the play is Vivie's *inner* conflict. Though possessed of originality, a dislike of humbug, and a stronger spirit than most of the others, Vivie is still weak in the head, so to speak. Psychologically unstable, she is at first still subject to idealism. She is susceptible to "love's young dream" in the form of Frank Gardner's irrepressible wooing, she strikes conventional poses (as when she turns the gun on herself after learning of the possible incest in her relation with Frank), she attitudinizes in the sentimental scene of mother-daughter reconciliation at the end of Act II, and she is flawed by sudden delicacies, as when she can't utter the two words that describe her mother's profession. Despite the many relapses to Victorian womanhood, Vivie's genuine Realist self emerges from the series of painful disillusionments that strengthen her for the final break with her mother. A test of the would-be Realist is in the ability to assert independence from parental authority and to escape the drug of romance. Vivie passes the test, but one wonders if the work of actuarial accountant is really appropriate to one who sees that prostitution is a universal, inescapable condition of modern employment. She seems curiously uncommitted, as cutting off parent and suitor only leaves her in a vacuum. Leaving Vivie with nothing very worthwhile to do with her new soul may, however, be expressive of the problematic nature of becoming a Realist. Unlike the Freudian system which posits personal adjustment as its goal, Shavian psychology seems to acknowledge maladjustment as a healthy condition, for it is the spur to further growth. Vivie will not be satisfied with accounting for long, any more than Shaw had been as a teenager back in Dublin.

Vivie's inner struggle testifies in another way to Shaw's categories being more psychological than they seem, for in practice Shaw's characters turn out to be not just sociological types but human beings torn by warring psychic principles. Shaw later wrote of his characterization of Caesar, "All men . . . possess all qualities in some degree."[9] That implies that Realist, Idealist, and Philistine are within us all and give rise to contradictory behavior. Some critics have commented on what they see as inconsistent characterization, some characters sounding like Realists but acting like Idealists, others sounding like Idealists but acting like Philistines, and so on, but in such "inconsistency" Shaw was simply accomplishing life-like characterization, portraying the psychological truth that we are all mixed in our beings. Note how several of the characters in Mrs Warren's Profession are very good at puncturing the illusions of others, as though they were Realists, and yet as Idealists seem to be cherishing illusions of their own, as, for example, the way Mrs. Warren debunks marriage idealism but is a hopeless addict of parental idealism. As Mrs. Warren is a woman in conflict, so are they all in conflict. They all escape absolute sociological typing by virtue of their wills, instincts, and temperaments contradicting their own thinking. The hung-over Rev. Gardner, for instance, gives voice to all the traditional Christian idealism but is by temperament a pleasure-loving Philistine. To the degree that they all love a bit of comfort and pleasure and just want to be let alone, they are all Philistines. But they have ideals as well, and they can be realistic at times when it is necessary to see through the ideals of others.

Shaw's characters escape absolute sociological typing for another reason. It is not just that Realist, Idealist, and Philistine principles struggle for dominance or balance within the mind, as Id, Ego, and Super-Ego do in the Freudian system and Persona, Anima, and Shadow do in the Jungian, but that their struggle acknowledges evolution. In varying degrees, their inner conflict is caused not just by a struggle for dominance or balance among psychic principles but by the reaching for growth—philistinism trying to be idealism, idealism trying to be realism, and realism trying to fully realize itself. In striving to go beyond their ordinary selves by realizing their best selves, these characters experience a confusion of personality that shows evolution consisting of ups and downs, false starts and strange turns, detours and delays. And mostly failures. At moments of crisis, most of the characters relapse to their lower selves. Only the strongest, psychologically, grow. In this play Vivie succeeds to a degree in realizing her Realist potential. But she has just begun; her future is by no means certain.

We can better understand Shaw's apparently sociological grouping of Realists, Idealists, and Philistines in *The Quintessence* if we acknowledge another psychological truth—that although we have warring factions within, the strongest faction tends to dominate the weaker factions over the long haul and in moments of crisis. Thus although Shaw portrays human beings as torn within, he can also justifiably classify them in his polemical writings according to their dominant principle. An Idealist he *should* have defined as someone who has Realist and Philistine moments but who tends to idealism, but he chose to simplify things by leaving out these important qualifiers, the swift-striking journalist tripping him up. Unlike Freud's categories, then, Shaw's are more serviceable by being both psychological *and* sociological. We don't speak sociologically of Idites or Super-egoists, but we can speak of Idealists and Realists.

It should also be noted that Shaw portrays each character type as having great variety, a point he makes in *The Quintessence* by showing the great variety of Ibsen's characters. Just as Ibsen individualizes his Idealists, for example, so too Shaw presents no two Idealists, no two Philistines, and no two Realists as exactly alike. We need only mention Vivie Warren, Bluntschli, Marchbanks, Caesar, Andrew Undershaft, John Tanner, Professor Higgins, Captain Shotover, Saint Joan, and King Magnus to realize how varied are Shaw's Realists or incipient Realists, and within a single play such as *Mrs Warren's Profession* one can easily see the variety and individualization among the idealisms of Mrs. Warren, Frank, Rev. Gardner, Praed, and Crofts.

But what is this all about? Even if *The Quintessence* and the "unpleasant plays" that embody its theory of character types *are* primarily psychological, what is the purpose of the psychologizing? Freud's system, as that of most psychologists, began in an effort to understand himself. Is that true also of Shaw? Is there soulfulness at the root of what seems a very public art?

The Sanity of Art (1908), published first in 1895 as a solicited letter to the editor of *Liberty* under the title of "A Degenerate's View of Nordau," makes plain in its two titles Shaw's increasing awareness that it is a particular psychological condition that is uppermost in his mind. *The Sanity of Art* suggests that Shaw's concern all along has been with the psychology of the creative mind and that his theory of character types in *The Quintessence* was at bottom a struggle to understand himself as an artist, an exercise in self-analysis disguised as sociological analysis. In the 1907 Preface to *The Sanity of Art*, which identifies "the genius," "the artist-philosopher," and "the Superman" with "the Realist," Shaw explains his 1895 defense of artists against Max Nordau's charge in *Degeneration* that modern artists are the diseased products of an exhausted society. Such explanation is needed because Shaw has gained a reputation for being as opposed to "artists" as Nordau was. Inasmuch as many of the artists under attack were, like Yeats, of an artistic school opposed to Shaw's journalistic school, and inasmuch as even Yeats thought that his generation of artists was uncommonly stricken with the ills of decadence, one might expect Shaw to side with Nordau against common antagonists. In some respects the 1907 Preface fulfills this expectation. Besides being willing to consider "how far genius is a morbid symptom," Shaw concedes that "the arts have their criminals and lunatics"(*MCE*,287). Further, the Preface begins with an *apologia* for journalistic art—"All the highest literature is journalism. . . . I too am a journalist, proud of it, deliberately cutting out of my works all that is not journalism, convinced that nothing that is not journalism will live long as literature, or be of any use whilst it does live"(*MCE*,283). This establishes Shaw's credibility with a public suspicious of art that is not useful, a favorite strategy, but his attacking style also covers a defensiveness about his artistic nature, the idea of an artist held by so many of his peers being inimical to who and what he was.

But largely *The Sanity of Art* defends all artists, even those whose theory of art was opposed to his. Despite superficial quarrels among artists, Shaw senses an underlying kinship with all true artists. He may be a journalist, but that does not mean that his journalism is not soulful or psychological. Here, for example, he tempers his journalism with admissions of autobiographical writing—after the passage just quoted above, he goes on to say, "I deal with all periods; but I never study any period but the present . . . , and as a dramatist I have no clue to any historical or other personage save that part of him which is also myself. . . . The man who writes about himself and his own time is the only man who writes about all people and about all time"(*MCE*,283–84). Shaw told Archibald Henderson at the age of ninety-one, "My imagination has always rearranged facts into stories."[10] In *Sixteen Self-Sketches* he wrote, "All my happenings have taken the form of books and plays," and "If a man is a deep writer all his works are confessions."[11] The point was well summed up by Eric Bentley when he wrote that "Shavian drama is didactic and public. But it is personal and expressive as well. . . . Shaw's drama expresses his nature much more than it champions particular doctrines. It even mirrors Shaw's life rather closely in a series of self-portraits."[12]

Yet these self-portraits add up to anything but a picture of either degeneracy or a conventional artist. So when he writes an article entitled "A Degenerate's View . . . ," thus identifying himself with the artists Nordau attacked, the obvious irony of this non-degenerate's stance is expressive of the struggle within for self-definition as well as the struggle without to establish a public identity. The rhetorical strategy, here as in so many other of his polemical works, is to combine and conquer. That is, his rhetorical strategy is also a psychological strategy—after disproving either degeneracy or mere estheticism in himself by virtue of being a journalist, Shaw looks for what he has in common with other artists and what all artists have in common with ordinary people, the purpose being to alleviate his two-fold alienation—from the public and from fellow artists. Contrary to the singling out of the Realist in *The Quintessence*, the argument of *The Sanity of Art* is that most artists are sane and healthy people like Shaw and that in most points geniuses are really harmless, likeable, and relatively undistinguishable from everybody else— "Your geniuses are for the most part keeping step and marking time with the rest, an occasional stumble forward being the utmost they can accomplish, often visibly against their own notions of propriety. The greatest possible difference in conduct between a genius and his contemporaries is so small that it is always difficult to persuade the people who are in daily contact with the gifted one that he is anybody in particular. . . . Your genius is ever 1 part genius and 99 parts Tory"(*MCE*,288–89). If one is publicly an artist and one's secret being is 99 parts Tory, psychological strife must surely prevail over social strife, the social bickering with Idealists and Philistines mild indeed compared to the holocaust within. Yet so many of Shaw's fellow artists allowed the 1% to define entirely who they were and the resultant social conflict to take precedence, reveling in the misery of their alienation from respectable society. In contrast, Shaw dramatized and fictionalized the special problems of genius in its attempt to adapt to a hostile environment, his craving for public participation in his private story an expression of his need for human communion. The remarkable thing about Shaw and his superman characters is their determined friendliness toward the society that disapproves of them and of which they disapprove. The Shavian hero is essentially characterized by his refusal to be alienated. Rather he argues for toleration and trust, for the sake of the evolution of the species.

The bulk of *The Sanity of Art* is devoted either to specific rebuttal of Nordau's charges or to a general rationalization of the career of the artist much like that given the Realist in *The Quintessence*. The artist, like the Realist, is to be tolerated as far as possible because his special gifts allow him to perceive the path of evolution and to work more directly towards its ends. As a pioneer, the artist cannot be held to the rules that regulate ordinary behavior; in fact, the artist's special charge is to experiment with new modes of perception and behavior in order to lead a more general development of the species. The thrust of this argument is moral. The artist-Realist does not need to be restrained by as many laws as the ordinary man because he contains within his more highly evolved being natural laws. Not reason or conscience restraining the passions, as conventional psychology would have it,[13] but "moral passion" directing the lower passions is what drives the artist-Realist towards "the good." Though the ordinary man "can neither make a morality for himself nor do without one"(*MCE*,305), the artist-Realist is compelled by his moral passion to create an original morality appropriate to himself and his existential context. As this newly created morality is generally in the direction of greater self-assertion and trust in the individual will, what the artist-Realist "is really doing is substituting his own will, bit by bit, for what he calls the will of God or the laws of Nature"(*MCE*,309).

In the midst of this Shaw declares an artistic *credo* that puts all artists in the service of this evolutionary growth:

> The claim of art to our respect must stand or fall with the validity of its pretension to cultivate and refine our senses and faculties until seeing, feeling, smelling, and tasting become highly conscious and critical acts with us. . . . Further, art should refine our sense of character and conduct, of justice and sympathy, greatly heightening our self-knowledge, self-control, precision of action, and considerateness, and making us intolerant of baseness, cruelty, injustice, and intellectual superficiality or vulgarity. The worthy artist or craftsman is he who serves the physical and moral senses by feeding them with pictures, musical compositions,

pleasant houses and gardens, good clothes and fine implements, poems, fictions, essays, and dramas which call the heightened senses and ennobled faculties into pleasurable activity. The great artist is he who goes a step beyond the demand and, by supplying works of a higher beauty and a higher interest than have yet been perceived, succeeds, after a brief struggle with its strangeness, in adding this fresh extension of sense to the heritage of the race. This is why we value art: this is why we feel that the iconoclast and the Philistine are attacking something made holier, by solid usefulness, than their own theories of purity and practicality: this is why art has won the privileges of religion. [*MCE*,315–16]

Uncommonly lofty and pious for Shaw, this *credo* is large enough to include both artists like himself and esthetes like Oscar Wilde, though of course the latter would find it all a bit too Fabian.

So Shaw's psychology takes him beyond the invention of a triad of psychic principles to the assertion of a moral and evolutionary purpose. The balancing of Id, Ego, and Super-ego in Freudian therapy serves only the amoral end of personal adjustment, as though there were some eternal ideal of rational adjustment which all therapy should aim for; Shavian psychology presupposes an evolutionary reality that is constantly growing and which is correctly perceived and responded to only by the maladjusted person. As John Tanner put it—"The reasonable man adapts himself to the world: the unreasonable one persists in trying to adapt the world to himself. Therefore all progress depends on the unreasonable man." [14] If the goal of life is not personal adjustment but growth, then a 1% aberration in the balance of one's personality would be a healthy thing, conducive to that creativity that makes it possible for humankind to grow in spirit. Healthier than thou, is Shaw's rejoinder to those like Nordau who put his character into doubt on the grounds of being an artist. For the question of whether the maladjustment of the artistic genius can be distinguished from that of the neurotic or the psychotic, Shaw had no answer. Neither had Freud, apparently, but Shaw at least liked to say, "By their fruits ye shall know them." At their roots all maladjustments may look alike; it is only in their consequences that they can be distinguished. And perhaps creative outlet, its realization or frustration of the will, is the key to success or failure in all cases, constituting the real sanity of art.

The Sanity of Art ends with a psychological pun—having filled more pages than necessary to destroy Nordau's argument, Shaw apologizes for his Agoraphobia, or Fear of Space (*MCE*,332). But Shaw's wordage is a feature of all his works and its source is perhaps less of a joke. "I am nothing if not explanatory," said Shaw. [15] So much explanation, however, takes on the character of a compulsion and may cover an inordinate need for self-justification. The waves of rhetoric that come at Shaw's dedicated reader pound always upon the same rocks—the possibility of being misunderstood. Well, we all like to explain ourselves, if only *to* ourselves. But seldom does our compulsion take on such rhetorical brilliance, vehemence, and variety as it did with Shaw and serve by the way to explain so many others to themselves.

Of the four "Pleasant Plays" that were written around the time of *The Sanity of Art*, the one that most explicitly develops the themes of the essay is *Candida* (1894), written just prior to *The Sanity of Art*. *Candida* also recapitulates the theory of *The Quintessence* and illustrates both its psychological and sociological aspects. Arthur Nethercot identifies the three main characters as Idealist (the Reverend James Mavor Morell), Philistine (Morell's wife, Candida), and incipient Realist (the poet Marchbanks).[16] Rather bored by poetry herself, Candida is the sort of woman young men like Marchbanks write poetry about. Immaturely succumbing to idealism, the poet transmutes Candida into something she is not. The critics, equally charmed by her, have done the same, so much so that Shaw ridiculed them as Candidamaniacs. For Candida, according to this view, is simply a more mature version of Anne Whitefield, what Anne will be after she's married for, say, fifteen years, still fascinating to men but dedicated to her maternal role. The clue to Candida's basic philistinism is in her name—*candida* is Latin for "yeast," that common element without which the bread of life is flat. Shaw may even have had the maternal condition in mind (as in "Metaphors" Sylvia Plath speaks of the "yeasty rising" of her pregnant self), all the more reason for connecting Candida with that other vital genius, Anne Whitefield. At any rate, the point of the play is that however essential to life bread is, poets like Marchbanks cannot live by bread alone. The hot baked bread of domestic bliss which is the husband's ideal of marriage and the illusion that the Philistine wife works hard to maintain is not sufficient food for the artist-Realist, whose real craving is for spiritual sustenance. Or so Shaw thought then. In a few more years Shaw would not only get married himself but submit John Tanner to marriage as well. It turned out that, properly conducted, marriage could serve the Realist too.

Although I agree with Nethercot's basic typing of the characters in *Candida*, I realize that other critics have taken exception to this typing, especially arguing that Candida is more Realist than Philistine.[17] A solution is to realize that, as in *Mrs Warren's Profession*, the characters of *Candida* are deliberately "inconsistent," torn by psychic principles in conflict.[18] The Idealist Morell has moments when he slips back to philistinism, needing his "castle of comfort and indulgence and love,"[19] and moments when he has a Realist's vision of things, as when he leaves Candida and Marchbanks alone or when he agrees with Marchbanks's vision of him as David dancing before the people. So too Candida has moments when she reaches beyond philistinism to idealism, as when she takes seriously (as opposed to naturally) the role of Madonna others project on her, treating both men as children, and to realism, as when she debunks Morell's sermonizing and identifies "Prossy's Complaint." As for Marchbanks, his philistinism is tempted by the bread of domesticity and his idealism romanticizes Candida into a domestic angel, but ultimately his Realist potential prevails, as, leaving Candida, he goes out into the night to search out his destiny. Not surprisingly, Shaw's next play, about Napoleon, is entitled *The Man of Destiny*, as Marchbanks transmutes into the most practical sort of artist—he who strives to shape life by mastering it.

Although Candida gives her name to the play and is the central figure, the play is not hers. The play is only *about* her. She is central only because the issue of the artist's relation to domestic reality is central. As in *The Sanity of Art*, the question is how much an artist is like ordinary people. The answer *Candida* gives is also similar—the artist is not so unlike others that he isn't tempted to live within "the castle of comfort, indulgence, and love;" in fact, later in the person of the older John Tanner he will succumb to it; but while young and vigorous he imagines himself compelled to leave the castle to live a harder life in the service of the Life Force. He is thought "mad" for doing so, as so many other Shaw characters are thought "mad" for trying to live beyond bourgeois notions of happiness. But the sanity of art consists in just such "madness," that 1% of genius unbalancing him just enough so that he can see life fresh, as it is and not as habit has decreed it is, and see as well into its purpose. Such "madness" is divine and saner than sane.

In *The Sanity of Art*, Shaw's prime example of the artist who possesses such vision is Richard Wagner, whose 1% of genius so unbalanced the music of his day, from the point of view of musical Idealists, that Shaw must argue long and hard that, after all, there is "sanity in the supposed Wagner chaos"(*MCE*,297). But not long enough apparently, for in 1898 Shaw devoted an entire book to Wagner, publishing the last of his three "major critical essays," *The Perfect Wagnerite*.

As with *The Quintessence* and *The Sanity of Art*, *The Perfect Wagnerite* misleads as to its objectivity. Written to explain Wagnerian ideas and music, it purports to present *The Ring of the Nibelungs* as "a first essay in political philosophy"(*MCE*,164), representing the sociological ideas germinating in the European atmosphere of the mid-nineteenth century (*MCE*,237). To explain *The Ring* as an allegory of "unregulated industrial capitalism"(*MCE*,163), Shaw arranges Wagner's characters in seemingly socio-political categories similar to *The Quintessence*. In evolutionary order, from lowest to highest, Wagner's giants correspond to Philistines—"the patient, toiling, stupid, respectful, money-worshipping people"(*MCE*,189); Wagner's gods correspond to the Idealists—"the intellectual, moral, talented people who devise and administer States and Churches"(*MCE*,189); and Wagner's Hero corresponds to the Realist, who sees how short godhead falls of its own ideals and "in whom the god's unavailing thought shall have become effective will and life, who shall make his way straight to truth and reality. . . ."(*MCE*,184). A fourth type, overlooked in *The Quintessence*, is Wagner's dwarfs, the lowest of all—"the instinctive, predatory, lustful, greedy people"(*MCE*,189). Since Shaw has no name for the dwarf in his own system, I would offer "Plutocrat" as corresponding to Realist, Idealist, and Philistine, appropriate because the plutocrat of *The Ring*, the dwarf Alberic, bends all his greedy energies to the establishment of the Plutonic empire of gold. The Hero is the only one truly human; the other three types are subhuman, though the gods (the Idealists) are at least capable of conceiving that higher thing (the Hero) which will replace them.[20]

The plot of *The Ring* is too complicated for summary, but basically it involves a struggle for Plutonic and Olympian power among dwarf (Alberic), giant (Fafnir), and gods (Wotan, Fricka, and others), a struggle that can be resolved only by the Hero's (Siegfried's) assertion of his fuller humanity. As a "freewiller of Necessity"(*MCE*,216) and a man "whose likes and dislikes are sane and healthy"(*MCE*,200), the Hero can be trusted to establish a republic based on natural feeling and free thought, replacing all the old tyrannies of artificial law that arose to disguise and control the power struggle at the root of things.

This power struggle certainly has its socio-political dimension, which as usual Shaw emphasizes for polemical reasons, but his implicit treatment of *The Ring* is heavily psychological. Although he speaks of a sociopolitical allegory, what in fact he mostly details is a psychological allegory, *The Ring* a kind of modern *psychomachia* in which most of the characters are figments of Wotan's imagination. Shaw presents the external power struggle among Alberic, Fafnir, Wotan, Fricka, Brynhild, Siegfried, and others as an emblem of a struggle within the mind of Wotan. Wotan's "assumed character of lawgiver is altogether false to his real passionate nature"(*MCE*,177), and out of that inner conflict comes most of the drama of *The Ring*.[21]

Wotan's inner conflict is exacerbated by Alberic's stealing of the Rhine gold and establishing a Plutonic empire that challenges the god's Olympian authority. Alberic's presence in the allegory implies that there is something largely external to the god that can disrupt his peace of mind. The thing largely external to all of us, disruptive to all, is the sheer brute nature of the universe. It is in how we respond to that, especially in its human form, especially in ourselves, that is the measure of our sanity. And because in its human form that sheer brute nature may have its own psychological complexity, Alberic is portrayed as coming to the Rhine maidens "with a fruitful impulse in him, in search of what he lacks in himself, beauty, lightness of heart, imagination, music"(*MCE*,172). Imbued with the universal evolutionary impulse, even the lowest aspires to higher things. But, unable to see the beauty and nobility of his aspiration (an inner, psychological reality), the Rhine maidens respond only to his ugly, dwarfish exterior, rejecting and humiliating him, and thereby poisoning his desire for love. Forswearing love, Alberic is able to grasp the gold and wield its Plutonic powers, soon enslaving everyone else to those powers. Brutishness and littleness are bad enough by themselves but when they command Plutonic powers they become forces of evil that challenge the highest of Olympian ideals and authority. Somehow Wotan must wrest the gold from Alberic, but Wotan is so compromised by his own laws and so corrupted by his own methods that nothing can save him and the world but the creation of heroic virtue, that is, natural, internal virtue as opposed to external, law-enforced virtue. And thus Wotan conceives of the heroic Siegfried, "an anticipation of the 'Overman' of Nietzsche"(*MCE*,200), as much a projection of Wotan's mind as Athena was of Zeus'.

In that regard, Shaw speaks directly of Brynhild, Siegfried's intended, as "the inner thought and will of Godhead"(*MCE*,196). And with Siegfried born of an incestuous relationship between two other conceptions of Wotan, Siegmund and Sieglinde, with the giant Fafnir metamorphosing into a Kafkaesque monster to guard the gold he steals from Alberic, with the wishing cap (the tarnhelm) allowing wish-fulfillment to its possessor, with the ring of fire around Brynhild being a mere illusion that vanishes before the heroic will, and so on, the wonder is that Shaw's interpretation could be taken for anything but psychoanalysis. And when the ultimate conflict of *The Ring* turns out to be between Wotan and his own conception, Siegfried, whose supplanting of himself Wotan both desires and fears, the theme of the Idealist's ambivalence is plainly psychological. *The Ring* is thus presented principally as an allegorizing of the European *state of mind* rather than of its socio-political realities. Shaw *says* he is talking about the external effects of that state of mind, and to a degree he does, but mainly he analyzes its inner drama.

The Ring obviously appealed to Shaw partly because it confirmed his psychological system and added new insights to it. But he was dissatisfied by its conclusion. Much of the last part of *The Perfect Wagnerite* is devoted to analyzing Wagner and explaining Wagner's failure to support the heroic characterization of Siegfried and Brynhild in *Götterdämmerung*. Not only do they not succeed in giving birth to a whole new race of heroes, but in this final music-drama they relapse to operatic posings and plottings, totally incongruous with what came before, ending in death and failure. As Siegfried is betrayed by Hagen, Alberic's son, so, Shaw believes, did Wagner betray Siegfried by not allowing him a triumphant demonstration of the new heroism. Like Ibsen, Wagner could theorize and prophesy the Hero of "the third empire," but he couldn't sustain a convincing characterization of it in human form. And thus the relevance of the play Shaw wrote in the same year as *The Perfect Wagnerite. Caesar and Cleopatra* (1898), one of "Three Plays for Puritans" written in the period of *The Perfect Wagnerite*, is Shaw's most successful attempt to embody the Hero-Realist-Artist, combining the prescriptions of Shaw's three "major critical essays." As Jorge Luis Borges put it, Shaw's Julius Caesar surpasses "any character imagined by the art of our time. To think of Monsieur Teste or the histrionic Zarathustra of Nietzsche alongside [him] is to apprehend, with surprise or even astonishment, the primacy of Shaw."[22]

In *The Perfect Wagnerite* Shaw accounts for certain inconsistencies in Wagner's characterizations by saying, "There is only one way of dramatizing an idea; and that is by putting on the stage a human possessed by that idea, yet none the less a human being with all the impulses which make him akin and therefore interesting to us," the impulses sometimes contradicting the ideas(*MCE*,188). This is what Shaw had in mind for his Caesar. He wanted to portray the heroic idea more convincingly than anyone had done before, and the secret to his success was in his humanizing the idea, in allowing the Hero to be a human being as well. Caesar's bald head, stringy physique, and rheumatism, as well as certain weaknesses of character such as his speechifying and occasional romantic posturing, make him more credible than anything found in Wagner, Ibsen, or anywhere else. Shaw did not go so far in his debunking of literary heroism that he annihilated heroism itself, as many modern writers have, for Caesar is still an impressive figure, but he tried to separate the heroic from the romantic, the real from the ideal. As he said,

> We want credible heroes. The old demand for the incredible, the impossible, the superhuman, which was supplied by bombast, inflation, and the piling of crimes on catastrophes and factitious raptures on artificial agonies, has fallen off; and the demand now is for heroes in whom we can recognize our own humanity, and who, instead of walking, talking, eating, drinking, making love, and fighting combats in a monotonous ecstasy of continuous heroism, are heroic in the true human fashion; that is, touching the summits only at rare moments, and finding the proper level on all occasions, condescending with humor and good sense to the prosaic ones as well as rising to the noble ones, instead of ridiculously persisting in rising to them all on the principle that a hero must always soar, in season or out of season.[23]

Adding to the credibility is the fact that although Caesar succeeds in establishing the *Pax Romana* in Egypt, he partially fails as a teacher of Cleopatra and the others. Wagner shows Siegfried himself as a failure; Shaw presents Caesar as a success in himself and only partially failing with others. But, again, the partial failure expresses the problematical nature of the Realist's career.

The principal method of characterizing Caesar is by contrast with Cleopatra. As Plutocrat, Philistine, Idealist, and Potential Realist, she contains the same mix in her psyche as does Caesar; but whereas Caesar gave up Plutocratic brutality and no longer justifies it (the murders of Vercingetorix and Pompey), Cleopatra is still dominated by it, even sending a symbolically brutish woman, Ftatateeta, to fulfill it in the murder of Pothinus; whereas Caesar saves his craving for Philistine relaxation for brief moments when he can afford a holiday, Cleopatra is rather more devoted to her creature comforts, which she maintains in a luxurious style, no doubt in anticipation of the arrival of her desired playmate, Mark Antony; whereas Caesar's idealistic posturing is confined mostly to fine speech-making and romancing at dinner about building a holy city at the source of the Nile, Cleopatra's imagination is largely possessed by the idealism of Queenliness and Heroic Honor—it is her dedication to this idealism that causes her vengefulness against the offending Pothinus and thus her failure to absorb the lessons of Caesar in realism. Caesar, in fact, stands alone in seeing the futility of vengeance, and it is his independence from the moral system of his day that chiefly characterizes him as the Hero-Realist. Such independence is further manifested, paradoxically, in his acceptance of Rufio's execution of Ftatateeta. In an anachronistic swipe at the categorical imperatives of Christian pacifism, Caesar does not ask Rufio to turn the other cheek to a beast who would kill him if he did not kill it first.

But perhaps Caesar's principal interest for Shaw is in his being the right kind of artist. Caesar's artistic nature is conveyed partly by his appreciation of Apollodorus but more by his transcending of Apollodorus' estheticism in asserting the usefulness of art. When Apollodorus chides Rome for producing no art, Caesar retorts, "What! Rome produce no art! is peace not an art? is war not an art? is government not an art? is civilization not an art? All these we give you in exchange for a few ornaments. You will have the best of the bargain."[24] For Shaw, the true artist, the artist of sanity, understands that art is not for art's sake but for life's sake. Caesar is the supreme artist in giving shape and meaning to the lives of the people he rules, making possible that higher, more refined sensibility Shaw cites in his artistic *credo* in *The Sanity of Art*.[25]

In being so fully an embodiment of the Hero-Realist-Artist, Caesar is a lonely figure. His loneliness is summed up in his anachronistic identification with the Christ who is not yet born as he speaks to Cleopatra after the murdering of Pothinus: "If one man in all the world can be found, now or forever, to know that you did wrong, that man will have either to conquer the world as I have, or be crucified by it."[26] This identification with Christ is gradually developed by demonstrations of Caesar's childlike nature (in contrast to Cleopatra's childish nature), of Caesar's lovingkindness, presaging the *filios* and *agapé* of the New Testament (in contrast to Cleopatra's possessive, erotic love), and of Caesar's selflessness (in contrast to Cleopatra's selfishness). Caesar paradoxically achieves his selflessness by selfishly pursuing his own ends because his ends happen to be those of the gods as well, unlike Cleopatra whose will is nothing but her own. Cleopatra too often allows the baser parts of her psyche to drive her will, whereas Caesar follows his will towards the realization of his god-like Realist potential.

In the address to the sphinx in which Caesar identifies with the will of the gods in their struggle to bring more light and more life, he adds a religious dimension to Shaw's portrayal of the Realist that was only suggested in the characterizations of Vivie Warren and Marchbanks. And the identification between Caesar and Christ that builds throughout the play contributes further to that religious dimension. Yet Shaw cuts off the play before Caesar returns to Rome for his "crucifixion," thus undermining the identification. In the Preface to *Androcles and the Lion* Shaw later explained his abhorrence of the death-worshipping scapegoatism so characteristic of what he called "Crosstianity." The example of the Hero's life, not his death, was what mattered to Shaw. In this affirmation of life through avoidance of martyrdom, and in his acceptance of the execution of Ftatateeta and of his general role as instituter of the *Pax Romana*, Caesar is clearly distinguished from Christ, the difference being that between a full-fledged Realist and a Realist, half in love with martyrdom, who relapsed to Idealism. Psychologically, this play projects both Shaw's own frequently-referred-to martyr complex and his customary evasion of it. He was most explicit when he said, "Mark Twain and I . . . have to put things in such a way as to make people who would otherwise hang us think we are joking."[27] Shaw lived on the gallows much of his public life, but escaped the noose time after time with quip after quip. For this reason Eric Bentley called Shaw, "The Fool in Christ."[28]

The climactic point about Shaw's psychology is that it is fundamentally religious, inevitably referring to the Christian ethos that nurtures it. As a teenager Shaw declared his intent to establish a new religion. His first play was a passion play featuring Christ, and his last novel focuses on a character who says he "is fit for no calling but that of saviour of mankind."[29] But in drawing Mephistopheles on his bedroom wall as a child and in contriving a devilish appearance as a young adult, Shaw made it clear that his new religion was going to give "the devil" his due. "The devil" we now understand as expressive of that part of humanity victimized by psychological repression. To make the liberation of "the devil" the cornerstone of his religion, Shaw ironically inverted Victorian values. In celebrating the willfulness of the "immoral," "unreasonable," "selfish," "maladjusted" Realist, he exposed the evil of repressive Christian idealism which suicidally killed self and sacrificed others to dead gods. From *The Quintessence* on, Shaw sees the Realist's quest for self-expression as a holy mission in the service of the most divine purpose of the universe—growth and transcendence. He speaks of Ibsen and Wagner as prophets of this purpose, their works as scripture and gospel, their attack on Idealism as akin to the biblical attack on idolatry, an attack that is a "symptom of the revival of religion, not of its extinction"(*MCE*,121). And in these three "major critical essays" he speaks more often of "souls" than of "psyches," believing that our centers are not just some neurological mechanism needing only to be "adjusted" but are abodes of living Will that can be saved or damned according to the Will's realization or perversion.

It was, in fact, in pursuit of his salvation that Shaw strove for the domination of the Realist in himself. The small amount of Plutocrat in him he allowed out in relatively beneficial ways; finding that "money is the root of all good," he preached from the Fabian pulpit the socially healthful use of money and in private generally made good use of his own and his wife's wealth. The larger amount of Philistine in him, rather repressed during his years as a ragged young journalist and would-be artist, he gave vent to in his marriage to Charlotte, that candid "cabbage" of a wife who made of his Ayot St. Lawrence home and his London apartments "a castle of comfort and indulgence and love." The considerable amount of Idealist in him, that he thought he had exhausted in youthful romancing, never really left him, expressing itself in numerous ways—in post-midnight letter writing to pretty ladies, in his cosmic optimism and faith in the goodness of man (which the Nazi horror camps gave a jolt to), and especially in his characteristic way of dealing with reality by making a romance of the real. If the Realist prevailed in him, it was because he was able to channel Plutocratic, Philistine, and Idealist energies to Realist ends, the warring with the trolls within and the quarreling with oneself not generally a matter of repressing the lower parts of his nature but of making them serve higher purposes. Because he resolved inner conflict not by repression but by synthesizing his energies, he gave the impression of a man so self-assured and untroubled by doubt that there was nothing soulful going on in him—thus the famous irrepressible and imperturbable GBS. But Shaw himself told us that was a mask, devised to deal with a public dedicated to illusion. At any rate, if being psychological and soulful make a writer a poet, then Shaw was a poet.

Shaw reports in *The Sanity of Art* that his family crest bears the motto, in Latin, "Know Thyself"(*MCE*,311). Shaw's way of knowing himself was to see himself in action, as Fabian and public figure, and to work out his personal development through projection into art. As he understood his own nature, Shaw believed that there was no saving himself unless he saved the world as well. Thus his need for public participation and his habit of disguising his soulful art as journalism.

One test of a psychological system is whether it explains human behavior in general. Shavian psychology is obviously operating in Shaw's life and work, from beginning to end; Shaw himself convincingly shows it at work in the art of Ibsen and Wagner as well. But can we say in looking at the everyday world that Realist, Idealist, Philistine, and Plutocrat explain things as well as Id, Ego, and Super-Ego do, or as Persona, Anima, and Shadow do, or as any other system does? Well, as we've watched the murderous antics of the Ayatollahs and of the Belfast Boyos and IRA terrorists; as we've observed the British, true to Shaw's portrayal of them, sailing comically off to a tragic war in the Falklands, where Argentine idealism matched British idealism in the depth of its insanity; as we've seen the bloody effect of Zionism and PLO fanaticism; as we've witnessed the book-censoring and witch-hunting of the Falwellian moral Idealists; as we've suffered the consequences of an economy sacrificed to political theory; as we've seen urban and environmental despoliation illustrate the madness of *laisser-faire* idealism; as we've watched our children being victimized by educational theorists; and, yes, even as we've seen in our own departments the unending, genteel cutthroatery of academic idealism, *ad infinitum*, certainly it is not Freudian or Jungian categories that best explain such behavior. In the wake of World War I, Shaw added a Preface to a new edition of *The Quintessence* in which he spoke of the war as a war of ideals—"Men with empty phrases in their mouths and foolish fables *in their heads* have seen each other, not as fellow creatures but as dragons and devils, and have slaughtered each other accordingly. . . . We still cannot bring ourselves to criticize our ideals, because that would be a form of *self*-criticism"(*MCE*,3; italics mine).

Another test of a psychological system is whether it serves the cause of achieving personal and social health. The quote just above implies that Shaw found self-criticism therapeutic and liberating. But in view of his intense dislike of Prufrockian self-analysis and his preference for projection, it appears that any sort of therapeutic use of Shavian psychology would have to involve an indirect method. As Shaw criticized self by criticizing what he saw of himself in the world, and as he worked out personal problems by projection into art, so the Shavian method of therapy might be equally objective and creative. There might be wisdom in this, for how many psychoanalyzed people do we know who seem to have been maimed in the process of inward probing?

To end on a personal note, when I first read Shaw, seriously, I had just graduated with an A.B. in psychology, my interest being focused on the psychology of the creative mind. Coming to Shaw, as I did then, completely unspoiled by reading critics, I reacted spontaneously to him as a kindred spirit. When I later read what so many critics had been saying about Shaw for the last seventy years—that he was principally sociological and political in his thinking—I couldn't believe my eyes. This was obviously a case of idealistic critics reading into Shaw their own picture of him. Somewhat more tolerant these days, I now see the usefulness of multiple perspectives. Shaw's writing was itself multi-dimensional, and there's no point in denying the socio-political as one dimension. But neither is there any point in denying the psychological, the root of all the dimensions, and so I have written in behalf of restoring to Shaw a dimension so often missing in the world's speaking of him. Whether that amounts to the discovery of a valuable system of psychology and therapy, as I've argued here, is debatable of course, but at the very least, as Shaw himself said in summation of his art, "Every man who records his illusions is providing data for the genuinely scientific psychology which the world still waits for."[30]

Notes

1. These three essays are published as a collection entitled *Major Critical Essays* in the *Standard Edition of the Works of Bernard Shaw* (London: Constable & Co., 1932). Hereafter cited as *MCE* in the text.

2. Barbara Bellow Watson, *A Shavian Guide to the Intelligent Woman* (London: Chatto & Windus, 1964), 132.

3. William Butler Yeats, *Mythologies* (New York: Macmillan, 1969), 331.

4. William Butler Yeats, *Explorations* (New York: Macmillan, 1962), 198.

5. Dan H. Laurence, ed., *Bernard Shaw: Collected Letters 1874–1897* (New York: Dodd, Mead, 1965), 27.

6. For an example of the attempt to trace the way Shaw used art to extrovert himself, see my book, *Portrait of the Artist as a Young Superman: A Study of Shaw's Novels* (Gainesville: U. of Florida Press, 1969).

7. "Epistle Dedicatory" to *Man and Superman*, *The Bodley Head Bernard Shaw*, vol. 2 (London: Max Reinhardt, 1971), 507.

8. "Preface" to *Mrs Warren's Profession, The Bodley Head Bernard Shaw*, vol. 1 (London: Max Reinhardt, 1970), 251–52.

9. "Afterword" to *Caesar and Cleopatra, The Bodley Head*, vol. 2, 304.

10. Archibald Henderson, *George Bernard Shaw: Man of the Century* (New York: Appleton-Century-Crofts, 1956), 946.

11. Bernard Shaw, *Sixteen Self-Sketches* (London: Constable, 1949), 6.

12. Eric Bentley, *Bernard Shaw* (New York: New Directions, 1957), 203–4.

13. Much of Shaw's psychological commentary is a critique of conventional psychology, debunking such clichés as warm hearts, dark passion, cold reason, reason as restraint, etc. For Shaw, thought was a passion, as morality was a passion, and the seat of the emotions, conventionally located in the heart, was really located in the head. In this Shaw was much closer to modern physiology than were those contemporaries who used such clichés. For further elucidation, see my article "Shaw and the Passionate Mind," *The Shaw Review* (May, 1961), 2–11.

14. "Maxims for Revolutionists," *The Bodley Head*, vol. 2, 792.

15. "Preface" to *Three Plays for Puritans, The Bodley Head*, vol. 2, 33.

16. Arthur H. Nethercot, *Men and Supermen: The Shavian Portrait Gallery*, 2nd. ed., corrected (New York: Benjamin Blom, 1966), 7–17.

17. See Charles A. Carpenter's *Bernard Shaw and the Art of Destroying Ideals* (U. of Wisconsin Press, 1969), 106–123.

18. Alfred Turco, Jr. offers another solution in *Shaw's Moral Vision: The Self and Salvation* (Cornell U. Press, 1976), 103–4. He argues that Candida is ambiguously characterized because the pragmatism she embodies, although the chief quality of the Realist as Shaw defined it in *The Quintessence* in 1891, is inadequate to Shaw's 1895 vision of what it takes to be a Realist, as exemplified by Marchbanks at the end of the play. Perhaps, but Shaw's original examples of Realists were Plato and Shelley, neither of whom could be called pragmatists. Critics are always being tripped up by Shaw's journalistic habit of "slanting both ways," exaggerating two sides of the question to get at a truth that can't be formulated except as between two extremes, as in one part of *The Quintessence* he creates the impression that his Realist is essentially pragmatic and in another part that the Realist is essentially "impractical" or Shelleyan. Shaw's truth, as Eric Bentley pointed out, was always in the "Both/And." The reader must synthesize opposite hyperboles. However, Turco acknowledges elsewhere that "Shaw's definition of the *Quintessence*'s ethical categories does not preclude a person's being an 'idealist' in one respect and a 'realist' in another"(p.72), and this view coincides with mine, except that here I emphasize "psychic principles in conflict" rather than ethical principles in conflict.

19. *Candida, The Bodley Head*, vol. 1, 593.

20. Shaw's Realist-Hero has been misunderstood on another point. The realism of the Realist is not to be identified with cynicism, skepticism, or materialism. Citing Shelley and Plato as examples of Realists, Shaw in *The Quintessence* strives to regain the initiative for art against science in the pursuit of truth and reality by making that pursuit a matter of seeing as the visionary sees, looking through the veil of illusion to the reality behind apparent reality. Later, Shaw qualified the visionary's realism by distinguishing not between reality and illusion but between different degrees and kinds of illusion, for, as he said in "The Illusions of Socialism," "Take from the activity of mankind that part of it which consists in the pursuit of illusions, and you take out the world's mainspring." Illusions were better or worse, harmful or not, healthy or not, closer or less close to reality. Reality could be approached by mortals only through illusion, the illusion itself becoming a kind and degree of reality.

21. See Turco's *Shaw's Moral Vision: The Self and Salvation* for a development of the idea that Wotan is central to Shaw's concern at the writing of *The Perfect Wagnerite*. See also

Robert F. Whitman's *Shaw and the Play of Ideas* (Cornell U. Press, 1977) and J. L. Wisenthal's *Shaw and Ibsen* (U. of Toronto Press, 1979) for other interesting treatments of *The Perfect Wagnerite*.

22. Jorge Luis Borges, *Other Inquisitions* (New York: Washington Square Press, 1966), 174.

23. "Bernard Shaw and the Heroic Actor," *The Bodley Head*, vol. 2, 307.

24. *Caesar and Cleopatra, The Bodley Head*, vol. 2, 288.

25. For a similar treatment, emphasizing Caesar as poet, see Charles H. Berst's "In the Beginning: The Poetic Genesis of Shaw's God," *The Annual of Bernard Shaw Studies*, vol. 1 (1981), 35–38. A lengthier version of my treatment of *Caesar and Cleopatra* appeared in the Instructor's Manual for *The Art of Drama* (New York: Holt, Rinehart & Winston, 1969, Revised, 1975).

26. Ibid., 277.

27. Henderson, *George Bernard Shaw: Man of the Century*, 831.

28. See the chapter entitled "The Fool in Christ" in Eric Bentley's *Bernard Shaw*, 183–219.

29. *An Unsocial Socialist* (London: Constable, 1932), 104.

30. "Epistle Dedicatory" to *Man and Superman, The Bodley Head*, vol. 2, 517.

REVIEWS

G.B.S. as a Bishop

Warren Sylvester Smith. *Bishop of Everywhere: Bernard Shaw and the Life Force*. University Park: The Pennsylvania State University Press, 1982. 191 pp. $16.95.

This is an engaging book partly because of its paradoxical nature: it is unpretentious and ambitious, simple and complex, digressive and well-focused. Several other studies have explored the origins of Shaw's Life Force philosophy but they have failed to follow through adequately the development of his concepts. In contrast, this study only sketches its origins and then concentrates on its later evolution and implications. As the book spans almost fifty years of Shaw's art, religion, and politics in only 191 pages, it is audacious. Covering much familiar Shavian territory so briefly, it inevitably teeters on the edge of being a generalized study for non-specialists. Some of its arguments and many of its critical details suffer from *déjà vu*. But ultimately it transcends generality in the very clarity of its exposition of complex matters and in the episodic, anecdotal, specialized nature of its development. This latter no doubt occurs because much of the material has appeared as articles and in Smith's introduction to his edition of Shaw's religious speeches. Rough joints and abrupt shifts in subject matter produce a piecemeal effect. However the pieces relate in stimulating ways. They comprise a lively collage, not exhaustive but unified by a general theme and a cohesive authorial presence. The end result is that Smith gives Shaw's later years a concise yet varied and luminous perspective.

The book starts vigorously with a brief analysis of *John Bull's Other Island* as "the play which most clearly gives us the three dominant compass-points of Bernard Shaw's personality." These points are personified in Broadbent—the robust, optimistic, political Englishman; Doyle—

the sensitive, cynical, critical Irishman; and Keegan—the artistic, mystic, unfrocked priest. Like Keegan's unique trinitarian gospel, these three indeed provide an apt metaphoric touchstone for the ambiguities of G.B.S., all of them emerging in varying degrees as Shaw wrestles with his Life Force ideas.

Smith is least original when he backtracks and surveys the origins of Shaw's religious impulses, from his creative childhood prayers and youthful *Passion Play* to those early plays which suggest a force guiding human destinies. A chapter on *Man and Superman* offers a clear but largely familiar analysis of the Life Force in that play, and there is nothing new in a citation of Shaw's Life Force sources. One fresh spark comes from Smith's treatment of the climactic scene of Tanner and Ann as orgasmic. Most important, he agrees with others that Shaw's dramatic talents in *Man and Superman* obscure rather than delineate his Life Force thesis. As with Napoleon in *The Man of Destiny* and Undershaft in *Major Barbara*, the Devil gets almost more than his due. For this reason, the author suggests, Shaw sought to express his religious views more directly, from the lecture platform.

Those who desire to explore these views in depth must refer to Smith's invaluable edition of *The Religious Speeches of Bernard Shaw*, since he skips over most of the speeches here. Instead he probes new materials, presenting extracts of an important, previously unpublished item: a paper on Darwin and Darwinism which Shaw delivered to the Fabian Society in 1906. In this, Smith discovers the basic pattern of the Preface to *Back to Methuselah* and the clearest available evidence of Shaw linking his religious views to socialism, a connection he also made to education, science, and art. Yet, Smith observes, much as art obscured Shaw's Life Force ideas in *Man and Superman*, his attempt to convey such ideas too directly through drama, as in *The Shewing-up of Blanco Posnet* and *Androcles and the Lion*, compromised his art. Consequently Shaw's exegesis of Christianity in the Preface to *Androcles* is more satisfactory than the play, and, added to the speeches, constitutes the most effective expression of his religious position up to 1914. Perceptively summarizing and analyzing this preface, Smith gives particular credence to the general conclusion that "Shaw, like many another, took from the Bible what he wanted to take from it."

The two chapters which follow might at first appear to be digressive, but each offers special rewards. The first deals with a contentious epistolary exchange between Shaw, the Bishop of Kensington and others, which was published for a week by *The Times* in November 1913 under the heading, "MR. SHAW ON MORALS." The letters were provoked by a complaint the Bishop had registered with the Lord Chamberlain over a slightly racy revue performed by a French variety artiste, Gaby

Deslys. As might be expected, Shaw criticizes the Bishop for presuming to be a spokesman for morality above the individual sensibilities Shaw or anyone else might possess, and goes on to stress the ambiguity of morality on the stage, in art, and, for that matter, in religion. Thus he spins around the Bishop's own guns, and the chapter presents an emphatic, pertinent view of his special status. Here is Shaw at the crest of his religious speech-making, about to write the Preface to *Androcles*, a Life Force advocate who was later to call himself "a sort of Unofficial Bishop of Everywhere," challenging the province of the Establishment. Implicitly the exchange constitutes morality against Morality, bishop against Bishop, with the Establishment diminished under the very title of the dispute: *Mr. Shaw* on Morals.

The next apparently digressive chapter springs from Shaw's defense of conscientious objectors during World War I, a position that brought him into contact with the Quakers. Shaw later stated that if he had to denominate himself, Quakerism would be his choice. Smith analyzes this position by observing that Shaw actually had an ambivalent attitude toward pacificism, and finds that his admiration of the Society of Friends was based more on a stereotyped historical view than on the contemporary denomination. Shaw's portrayal of George Fox in *"In Good King Charles's Golden Days"* indicates that he had read Fox's *Journal*, but while he characterizes Fox with considerable fidelity, the founder of Quakerism was less typical of the sect than were others. No doubt Shaw was attracted more by Fox's irascible personality, his iconoclasm and stress on an Inner Light, than on his being strictly representative. Much as he had interpreted the Bible, Shaw viewed Quakerism according to the inner light of his own Life Force.

However parenthetical such matters may at first seem, Smith's definition of Shaw as the antagonist of a bishop, an ambivalent pacifist, and an instinctive Quaker produces fresher insights than his subsequent and more conventional analysis of *Heartbreak House* as a play reflecting its author's struggle against cynicism. The setback which World War I effected on Shaw's Life Force meliorism, a setback echoed in the despair and nihilism of this play, is a subject necessary for Smith's thesis but one which others have covered thoroughly. More stimulating is his next section, seven short chapters comprising Part II of the book, in which the Life Force reemerges front and center.

At this point Smith's treatment of Shaw's Life Force "religion" is especially ingenious. Instead of directly tackling it in the important preface and five parts of *Back to Methuselah*, which would seem logical since the play not only follows *Heartbreak House* chronologically but is, in Shaw's words, his "contribution to the modern Bible," he engages it via illuminating touchstones. The primary ones are Julian Huxley and Teilhard de Chardin, complemented by Lamarck, Bergson, and highly selective citations of the play. The disadvantage of this approach is that much of the play and preface are bypassed. The compensating advantage is that these touchstones offer fascinating perspectives which not only clarify the subject in themselves but move it into a contemporary context, avoiding the tunnel vision and tedium which can result from tracing the discursive development of Shaw's ideas in both the preface and the play.

Since a major portion of Shaw's argument for the Life Force involves a Lamarckian attack on neo-Darwinism, the selection of the views of Julian Huxley, a leading neo-Darwinian, gives the opposition an articulate response. Conversely, Teilhard de Chardin was both a Jesuit and a paleontologist, and his views introduce an orthodox Christian framework, thoughtfully modified by science and a personal mysticism—so personal that the Church forbade the publication of his major works during his lifetime. Set against Shaw's Life Force philosophy, these two perspectives sharply reveal its strengths and idiosyncrasies.

Briefly abstracted, Smith's findings are that Shaw, Huxley, and Teilhard have a number of common denominators. All three are evolutionists. They agree that since the advent of man (which is the point at which *Back to Methuselah* begins) human consciousness has exercised choice and responsibility over the evolutionary process, superseding the theretofore relatively unconscious evolution of life. All believe that with his exceptional powers man must strive toward making the human community functional, and that eugenics are a key means of speeding up civilization. The three differ markedly, however, regarding other factors—the most notable ones being the nature of the impetus behind evolution, the nature of pre-human evolution, and the nature of ultimate ends. Shaw and Teilhard (along with Bergson) conceive these factors according to a metaphysical impetus and end, while Huxley conceives them according to Darwin's theory of natural selection. Smith quite soundly observes that this difference is more than academic. It is immediate and strategic because as mankind works toward civilization there is a profound difference between aiming at success according to a context of moral principle and aiming at it according to values improvised in a context of the law of the jungle. In such matters mysticism and naturalism can translate into very practical differences of means, and as means involve the quality of life, they are linked to ends.

Beyond this the distinction between Teilhard and Shaw is even more telling. As a Jesuit, Teilhard's ultimate context is God, manifest in Christ. On the other hand, Shaw is a more secular mystic, his ultimate context being an evolutionary impetus driving toward a "vortex of pure thought." Touched on but not fully explored by Smith is that Shaw thus conceives divinity more as a dynamic process moving from unconsciousness to supernal consciousness, a process capable of making mistakes along the way, while Teilhard's view must accommodate the underlying stasis of his religion in which the perfect Godhead at the end also existed in the beginning. One important result of this difference is that Shaw's theory overcomes the problem of an omnipotent divinity allowing evil, while Teilhard is haunted by that age-old theological dilemma.

In other aspects, however, Shaw's metaphysical assumptions, especially as they are given form in *Back to Methuselah*, seem less credible than Teilhard's. Offsetting Teilhard's orthodox theological burden was his expertise as a scientist, an expertise he applied to his metaphysical projections. In contrast, Shaw's adaptation of Lamarck's theories is based more on his personal instincts than on evidence. He is eccentric in proposing that rapid genetic change may be effected by human will and that acquired characteristics, including will, may be transmitted by heredity. Scientifically speaking, the theme of the evolution of longlivers—a theme central to the main action of *Back to Methuselah*—stretches hypothesis to fancy and fancy to a never-never land. Hence while the play's beginning and final visions of a "vortex" are fancy set in an adventuresomely plausible metaphysical framework, much in the central bulk of the play goes awry. A few of its details have become dated in just the last sixty years.

Nonetheless time is, with an almost metaphysical irony, catching up with certain key aspects of Shaw's hypotheses. Recent scientific research has at least in part confirmed Shaw and Samuel Butler's early view that the Darwinian script must be modified if not rewritten. Evidence accumulated since then has shown that Shaw was probing important evolutionary factors which were ignored or denied by scientific dogmatists of his day. Smith mentions a few good examples of modern research, and the interested reader can dig up many that are even more up to date. David B. Wake, former editor of the *Journal of Evolution* and a zoologist at the University of California at Berkeley comments, "I think there is little question the 1980s will be the most dynamic period ever in the study of evolution." Molecular biologists and biochemists have speeded up the evolutionary clock, finding that the split between apes and humans occurred five million years ago, not twenty-five million as was previously supposed. Paul MacLean has distinguished man's neocortex— the intellectual, symbol-making, calculating part of the brain—as having developed a mere 40,000 years ago. After 120 years, Darwin's missing links are still missing. A number of evolutionists have found no examples of a major species evolving gradually into another. However, genetic engineering is now distinctly possible. Consequently, many issues that Shaw raised and Smith defines are far from dead. Indeed, they seem more alive than ever, indicating that Shaw, far from being obsolete, was intuitively prescient. Specifics of *Back to Methuselah* may be farfetched, but Shaw's skepticism of doctrinaire Darwinism is just now being echoed with a considerable stir in scientific circles.

Smith titles his concluding section "Ambiguity and Anguish," indicating that *Back to Methuselah* largely overreached the more immediate, nagging problems of *Heartbreak House*. In surveying the ambiguity of Shavian drama, his argument continues to be clear, but he probes this element with less rigor than other recent critics. He is at his best in a chapter on the late political plays—*The Apple Cart, On the Rocks*, and *Geneva*. Here he briefly but convincingly etches Shaw's disillusionment with democracy, his attraction to dictators, and his ultimate failure to propose a satisfactory form of government which would combine broad-based representation with administrative efficiency. In politics Shaw's Life Force creed weighed against the mediocre masses and toward strong leaders, but, since history shows that corruption commonly accompanies the power of autocrats, practical answers eluded him.

The last chapter is the most graceful in a book filled with graceful touches. Shavians may object that its subject—Shaw's twenty-six year correspondence and relationship with Sister Laurentia McLachlan—has been adequately developed by *In a Great Tradition*; others may feel that this is strange material with which to end a section on "ambiguity and anguish." But Smith's rendition is lively, charming, and includes hitherto unpublished extracts from Laurentia's letters to Shaw. Further, the juxtaposition of this material with the anguish of Shaw's concurrent political concerns poignantly emphasizes the ambiguity of his later years. Here he is sensitively adaptive to the psyche of a cloistered nun, practicing, as Smith says, a "protective duplicity," substituting "God" and "Holy Ghost" for "Life Force" and otherwise going to great lengths to please, but nonetheless sticking by his opinions in essential spiritual matters. His most compelling motive for the prolonged correspondence appears to lie in his comment to her: "I mean well, and find great solace in writing to you instead of to all the worldly people whose letters are howling to be answered." Here was a breath of pure spiritual air away from the press of mundane affairs. And here was a strong character. When Laurentia was elected Abbess he wrote: "you would boss the establishment if you were only the scullery maid." To Shavians this may seem precognitive of the "born boss" of *The Millionairess*; all the more so as Laurentia, like a habited Epifania, took fire over blasphemy in *The Black Girl*, forcing the heretic in Shaw to be adroitly defensive.

Two of Smith's most appealing observations come at the end of the book. He likens the Shaw-Laurentia correspondence to love letters, and defines Shaw's spiritual rarity by calling him a reasonable mystic and "laughing prophet." The love-letter analogy rings true. Shaw was drawn to women of distinctive character, most of whom, as Smith comments, were or proved to be inaccessible. Sister Laurentia is a worthy addition to the list.

In distinguishing Shaw as a laughing prophet, Smith sees the humor which interpenetrated his mysticism as "the mark of determination not to get too involved in the world, a sort of emotional declaration of independence." Yet as the humor came from one who was obviously very much involved with the world, one should stretch this definition to include the temperament of the activist whose very seriousness demanded ultimate perspectives, and these included detachment via a light spirit, a Sister Laurentia, and a personal philosophy. Thus, humor is an aspect of spiritual equilibrium, a method of both engaging the world and putting worldly illusions in their proper place. Through it Shaw could immerse himself in such diverse interests as politics, religion, and art with the coherent power of his own Life Force. This combination of attachment, detachment, and mediating laughter produced, as Smith rightly observes, a personality rarely found in major religious figures. Early Christianity suppressed laughter from the Gospels. Only in recent times has a study of the newly discovered Gnostic texts of Nag Hammadi emboldened one writer to characterize Jesus much as Smith does Shaw, in a book entitled *The Laughing Savior*.

In sum, Shaw was hardly a savior but Warren Smith has made a provocative case for his exceptional role as "a sort of Unofficial Bishop of Everywhere."

Charles A. Berst

Surprising Shaw

Stanley Weintraub. *The Unexpected Shaw: Biographical Approaches to G.B.S. and His Work*. New York: Frederick Ungar Publishing Co., 1983. 254 pp. Illustrated. $22.50.

Numerous "unexpecteds" pop up in reading Stanley Weintraub's new volume. One is purely personal. Of the nineteen articles and prefaces that he has gathered and revised for this work, I missed seven over the years in which they first appeared—1958 through 1982. I thought I was doing a reasonably good job of keeping abreast of the constant flow of articles on Shaw but my oversights conjure up the unexpected vision of a simpleton of the Shavian idles. Since what Professor Weintraub has to say about Shaw is always important, the likelihood that other Shavians

missed any of these pieces is excellent reason for presenting them in
readily available book form.

After a brief preface, the volume begins with a comprehensive
biographical-critical essay, "Everybody's Shaw," and then proceeds chapter by chapter chronologically through the life of the developing Shaw,
focusing on the novelist, the art critic, the literary critic, the boxer, the
friend, the dramatist, and the circumstances attending the writing of a
number of his major plays. The final chapter (originally, a Shaw Semi-
nar paper at Niagara-on-the-Lake which I had been trying to get a copy
of for years) on "The Avant-Garde Shaw: *Too True to Be Good* and Its
Predecessors" takes a level-headed look at Shaw's Theater of the Absurd. The unexpected here is that these pieces, written now and again
over a quarter of a century and prepared for such diverse publications
as *Modern Drama*, the *Times Literary Supplement*, and a *Dictionary of Literary Biography*, weave into a unified work stylistically as well as in content.
Occasionally there are overlappings as the same facts and insights are
used in different contexts. But, although there are a few changes of
tone—as in "Bernard Shaw, Actor," which first appeared in the popular
journal, *Theatre Arts*—the voice is consistent, authoritative, clear, seemingly as informed in 1958 as in 1982. Of course, things did not just fall
into place. The author explains in his preface that "no part of this book
appears in its original form. Some of these essays are extensively revised, rewritten, and augmented, and others coalesce several related
pieces." One has only to look at the dates of footnote citations and compare them with the original dates of publication to see how thorough
the revisions have been.

How unexpected are the Shaws that Weintraub presents? He acknowledges that "Much of what was the unexpected Shaw when first published is now everybody's Shaw." Yet the surprises are there even for one
well acquainted with Shaw lore. It is one thing to refer in passing to
Shaw's being an amateur boxer; it is another to read a chapter about his
involvement in the sport and discover Shaw at ninety-two writing to Gene
Tunney about then-champion Joe Louis. I had always dismissed Shaw's
fisticuffs as a minor issue, a typical bit of Shavian press-agentry, but when
I focused on the matter, I found myself asking questions about this Fabian in boxing gloves, questions that ranged from Cashel Byron, through
Andrew Undershaft to the Shav who knocked Shakes down in what was,
I know, a Punch and Judy but has the stage direction: "At the count of
nine Shav springs up and knocks Shakes down with a right to the chin."
I guess when you get to a certain age, you've got to settle these things
once and for all! The chapter, "Shaw's *Lear*" (*Heartbreak House*, of course),
leaves no doubt that Shaw's rivalry with Shakespeare was more than a
pose. Pugilism is not a minor issue after all.

Shaw, the acute and witty art-critic, is not unexpected, but I found myself once again amazed at the account of his use of art as presented in "Exploiting Art: Shaw in the Picture Galleries and the Picture Galleries in Shaw's Plays." This article had first appeared in *Modern Drama* and then was revised for Michael Holroyd's *The Genius of Shaw*. In its present re-revised and expanded form it is an absolute model of exact, clear, seemingly effortless presentation. The amazement is two-fold: our eyes are opened as we see how open-eyed Shaw was when he chose specific pictures for the walls of his sets; and our appreciation of these non-verbal techniques opens us to greater awareness of how rich the plays are. Critics focusing on the non-verbal elements in Shaw's drama *must* start with a reading of this chapter.

This seems the logical place to call attention to another unexpected since it relates specifically to this "Exploiting Art" piece, though it actually applies to the book as a whole, a book whose open, uncrowded pages reveal unusual taste and care in design. Twenty-four illustrations accompany "Exploiting Art," many of them three-quarter and full-page pictures—more than were used in the beautifully produced *The Genius of Shaw* and many that are more relevant to the course of the article's argument. One grows so accustomed to high-priced, shoddily-produced books that this handsome volume comes as a genuine surprise.

With many of us curious as to how Michael Holroyd is approaching his authorized biography of Shaw, this volume's subtitle is intriguing: "Biographical Approaches to G.B.S. and His Work." Some of the unexpected pugilist in Shaw surfaces in Weintraub's accounts of how G.B.S. sparred with biographers and would-be biographers: Archibald Henderson, a shadow boxer doing it by the numbers—the shadow supplied by Shaw; Hesketh Pearson, a spirited light-weight who found the champ's foot-work too much for his energetic thrusts that sometimes missed their mark and left him sprawled on the canvas; Thomas Denis O'Bolger, a fellow Irishman who was knocked out by the possible *ménage à trois* that Shaw alluded to in discussing Vandeleur Lee's presence in his parents' home, a hint Shaw would never let him use; Frank Harris, Shaw's editor at *The Saturday Review*, whose biography of him Shaw assumed the editorship of and ended writing himself. In all of those bouts, Shaw not only outweighed the contenders but refereed them as well. In two of his chapters, Weintraub observes these departures from Queensberry rules, reports them, and with cool eyes speculates about their significance. Of the Harris relationship he writes:

> Shaw['s] teasing the hard-up and ailing Harris with the prospect of making his book from Shaw's letters and then alternately withdrawing and restoring permission to quote; censoring the mildly objectionable—and

> hardly Harrisian—parts after tantalizing the pathetic Harris with them
> . . . and finally (in an excess of guilt or self-protectiveness, or both) re-
> writing the book as well as seeing it through the press for Harris's widow,
> suggests an unsatisfactory side of Shaw. . . . That for years he had been
> toying with his old friend while making efforts to help him suggests an
> element of unrecognized cruelty in the underside of benevolence.

Shaw's behavior here is not quite unexpected: Harris apparently was
such a venal, unprincipled "pirate" that justice cried out for balance.
The case of Thomas Denis O'Bolger is another matter. When I first
came upon it, totally unprepared, I was sickened by what seemed to me
Shaw's deliberate breaking of a talented man. Holroyd is fortunate in
not having Shaw's active "cooperation" in his endeavor.

I modify that remark with the adjective "active" because there is yet
another contradiction involved in the case of Shaw and his biographers.
Just when we have concluded that Shaw wanted to tell his story in his
own way and that way included the distancing device of a malleable
biographer, we are reminded that Shaw told his own story in his own
voice and at considerable length. Professor Weintraub is well aware of
this since he arranged material from Shaw's *Sixteen Self Sketches* and various prefaces and autobiographical pieces into a two-volume "autobiography" a dozen years ago. In the present volume, in a chapter titled
"Sketches for a Self-Portrait," one of Shaw's letters to Henderson is quoted:

> It is quite true that the best authority on Shaw is Shaw. My activities have
> lain in so many watertight compartments that nobody has yet given any-
> thing but a sectional and inaccurate account of me except when they have
> tried to piece me out of my own confessions.

Weintraub concludes the passage with the observation that Shaw "continued to produce pages of additional 'confessions,' the raw material for
what is very likely one of the great biographies in the English language."

Another biographical approach that arises in the course of this book
is less unexpected perhaps but is unusual if not unique. Shaw may have
misled, blocked, or destroyed biographers who came too close to his
center for fear they would find what the theoretical physicists speculate
is at the heart of a black hole—a nothing or, as they put it, a "singularity"
that absorbs all in preparation, perhaps, for the next creative bang.
Everything was grist for Shaw's singularity mill. The plays are a kind of
epic myth—his *Nibelungenlied*—in which dwarfs, giants, gods, everything has to be sacrificed for the coming of the hero. This is what Weintraub is getting at, I think, when he writes of Shaw's heroes in whom
"selflessness could exist . . . in the form of complete selfishness. . . . Shaw
described the quality as 'originality' in his notes to *Caesar*." Originality,
singularity, whatever it is called, it is a nothingness. At heart the opin-

ionated Shaw did not have opinions; he had a desire for totality. Weintraub makes a central point in parentheses when he refers to "Shavian dialogue (based so much on debating technique)." Chesterton wrote that the only way to win a debate with Shaw was to present your own side so inadequately that Shaw began to present it for you. As playwright, as critic, as human being, Shaw instinctively tried to see the other side, and it is a theme that runs through the various chapters of this book: Desmond MacCarthy is quoted as saying of *Major Barbara* "that it was the first play he had ever experienced in which the conflict was 'between two religions in one mind'"; Shaw admits that to counterbalance the influence of Academic painting, he backed Impressionists "who could not draw a nose differently from an elbow"; Frank Harris's attempt to be a playwright countered by Shaw's pose as a pirate sets the pattern for a series of alter-ego friendships. The book might well have been subtitled "The Compensating Mind."

The mind of Shaw. Those of us who have spent decades grappling with it and its products could not help but sympathize with Stanley Weintraub when at an MLA meeting a few years ago, he began a talk by announcing that he did not think of himself as a Shaw man. The range of figures covered in his many publications bear him out and almost cancel the delicious irony of that remark, but I suspect the real reason for that announcement was self-preservation. One can know too much and be sucked into that singularity. Consider this passage dealing with Shaw's unfinished sixth novel:

> On January 23, 1888, Shaw added two pages to it and then added one more page on each of the two days that followed. He also wrote a leader for the *Star*, self-taught himself some algebra and German, lectured at the Lee and Lewisham Radical Club on "Practical Socialism," visited several friends, went at his arrears of correspondence, wrote two additional pieces for the *Star*, attended the Hampstead Historical Club and the Bedford Debating Society and a meeting of the Fabian Executive, and had himself fitted for two pairs of trousers at his favorite (and only) clothing supplier, Jaeger's.

I see Weintraub teetering on the edge. He knows so much about Shaw that he cannot prevent himself from toppling into that mind. In writing about *Saint Joan*, he tells us that Shaw "often let works simmer in his mind for considerable periods before composing them" and then falls into the cauldron himself as he traces references to Joan through the years, concluding that "a great deal of it was in Shaw's mind before the first date on the first known draft of the play. . . . When Joan had found her time, she could spring from Shaw's head fully armed, like Pallas Athene from the brow of Zeus. Only such gestation as this can explain the composition of a masterpiece in what seems an inspirationally brief span." Again, in establishing the "Four Fathers for Barbara," Weintraub marvels at what "Shaw's capacious subconscious stored" after having given us a remarkable tour of those simmering depths.

If my tone in the preceding paragraph is not clear, I can only confess it is not clear to me either. Perhaps uneasy envy sums it up. The fall into the cauldron is a danger and a challenge. One of these days, a far-ranging Shaw man—and I fear I must include Professor Weintraub in that select group—is going to perform a John Livingston Lowes on Shaw, is going to take one major play and demonstrate how it has drawn from, been shaped by, become a comment on the world of art, drama, literature, music, politics, religion, science, economics that Shaw was drawing from, shaping, and commenting on. The chapter on "Exploiting Art" is a forty-page example of what can be produced by absorbing all the relevant material on one facet of Shaw's world of interests and meditating—I use the word precisely here—meditating on that material's impact on the plays.

In the meantime, while we wait for "The Road to Rouen," the present volume offers a number of questions for the less than far-ranging Shavian to take on, many of them in asides, such as whether "'The Religion of the Pianoforte' [is] perhaps Shaw's finest musical essay," whether Shaw's own plays attest to the truth of his claim that "the prose of very great dramatic writers . . . acquires a rhythmic majesty and energy to which actual versification could add nothing," whether "it still remains for criticism to apply itself to Shaw's deliberate dramatic ambiguities in character and situation."

That last question returns us to what the book under discussion is all about. Unexpectedly, I find the subtitle is the right one after all: *Biographical Approaches to G.B.S. and His Work* with, however, the emphasis on *G.B.S.* Most of these nineteen approaches confront ambiguities in Shaw, the man. Biographical fallacy not withstanding, the thrust of this study is to uncover the contradiction, paradoxes, dialectical tensions of Shaw's life and catch their reflection in his work. But, reflection is the wrong word. We are not dealing with a simplistic reductionism that would explain the plays through isolated incidents in Shaw's life. It is the habits of thought, the directions of psychic movement that are being charted. When those patterns are better understood, the plays become clearer and—paradox again—more complex. Stanley Weintraub points the way, asks the right questions, and gives a half-dozen model answers. Even if you caught all of the articles and prefaces first time round, this revision and reordering of them all in one place is likely to leave you with a radically revised view of G.B.S.

                                                              Daniel Leary

Attila, Adolf, and George

Arnold Silver. *Bernard Shaw: The Darker Side*. Stanford: Stanford University Press, 1982. xii + 348 pp. + index. $25.00

This book is an example of a good idea gone madly awry. Mr. Silver's psychogenetic approach to drama, while not new in itself, is certainly promising as applied to Shaw. In the case of a dramatist such as Strindberg, everyone realizes that the man projected personal problems and obsessions into his art, while Shaw's plays do not on the surface seem to display the same tendency. But the playwright's own statement to the effect that "if a man is a deep writer, all his works are confessions" (p. 2) serves as the author's point of departure for arguing that Shaw *can* be treated like Strindberg in this regard: "the characters, rather than serving merely as mouthpieces through which he expounded his philosophy, were the means by which he released the pressure of his own inner conflicts and explored them" (p. 9). To support this thesis, the critic provides what he believes to be the pertinent biographical facts and attempts to peel away the defensive strategies Shaw used to conceal (perhaps even from himself) the hidden relation between his life and his art. More specifically, *The Darker Side* argues for a connection between the strong anti-human element in the later Shaw—as evidenced by his embarrassing support of Mussolini, Hitler, and Stalin—and deep sexual frustrations involving four women in the dramatist's life: his mother (Lucinda Elizabeth Gurly), an early flame (Alice Lockett), his wife (Charlotte Payne-Townshend), and a famous actress (Mrs. Patrick Campbell). Attention is also paid to the effect of unresolved Oedipal feelings involving his father (George Carr Shaw) and the music teacher (George John Vandeleur Lee) who supplanted Mr. Shaw as the dominant male in the Dublin household. Ultimately Mr. Silver wishes to enrich and deepen (rather than to denigrate) our appreciation of Shaw's plays, however dim a view he may sometimes take toward the man who wrote them.

Some sense of both the potential and problems of this critical approach can be gained from the book's opening chapter dealing with Shaw's late play, *The Simpleton of the Unexpected Isles*. There Mr. Silver begins by noting accurately that this work "takes place in a kind of limbo and floats in and out of allegory, farce, fable, and tract" (p. 27). At the end of the play, Shaw presents a parable in which a comical Angel arrives to announce the Day of Judgment—followed by reports that whole hosts of earthly worthies have disappeared into thin air: "Indescribable panic. Stock Exchange closes: only two members left. House of Commons decimated: only fourteen members to be found: none of Cabinet rank. . . .

the most unquestionably useful and popular professions . . . are most
heavily attacked, the medical profession having disappeared almost en
bloc. . . . More than a million persons have disappeared in the act of
reading novels" (pp. 29–30). Shaw's satirical purpose here, not surprisingly, is to exhort and berate his audience by saying in effect, "Look
here, you self-satisfied fools who imagine that you are so modern and
enlightened! If an old-fashioned Day of Judgment were held just now,
how well do you suppose you would fare? Start living your lives as if
every day were a Day of Judgment." If there is a fault to be found in the
scene, it lies not in this unexceptionable moral, but in a quality of wit
and invention that falls noticeably below Shaw's best.

It is fair to say that Mr. Silver takes a much darker view of these pro-
ceedings. Putting aside his own earlier description of the play's ambi-
ance of unreality, he now claims that the allegory is "at best decorative"
(p. 49), a defensive dodge utilized by Shaw to avoid admitting a "homicidal longing" (p. 36) against doctors, members of Parliament, novel
readers, and just about everyone else. *The Simpleton*'s humor serves the
end of "annulling the significance of murder" (p. 46); the work is "a
death-filled fantasy" which contains "the most numerous killings in all
of Shaw's work" (p. 50). In its "advocacy of execution chambers and
wars," the play is "sadistic and homicidal" (p. 51); its apocalyptic conclusion is a plea for "supposedly justified deeds of mass extermination . . .
with the giggles of its architect rebounding from the walls" (p. 46).

Having no memory of these giggles, I returned to the text of *The
Simpleton* to find near the beginning a scene to which Mr. Silver alludes
(without actually quoting it) as an instance of how "Shaw gives vent in
comic guise to destructive impulses" (pp. 30–31):

> THE E[MIGRATION] O[FFICER] (*planting himself on the edge and facing
> the abyss*) I am going to do it: see? Nobody shall say that I lived a dog's
> life because I was afraid to make an end of it. (*He bends his knees to spring,
> but cannot*). I WILL. (*He makes another effort, bending almost to his haunches,
> but again fails to make the spring-up a spring-over*).
> THE PRIEST. Poor fellow! Let me assist you. (*He shoots his foot against the
> E. O.'s posterior and sends him over the cliff*).
> THE E.O. (*in a tone of the strongest remonstrance as he is catapulted into the
> void*) Oh! (*A prodigious splash*).
> THE Y[OUNG] W[OMAN]. Murderer!
> THE PRIEST. Not quite. There are nets below, and a palisade to keep
> out the sharks. The shock will do him good.
> THE Y.W. Well I never!

It rapidly becomes clear that, for Mr. Silver, taking something seriously
means taking it *literally*. He admits that the priestess Prola, the character
in the play who most closely approximates an authorial voice, condemns

murder as a way of solving problems; nonetheless—Mr. Silver can hardly believe it—"*shortly afterwards [Shaw] brings on the Angel to begin the killing!*" (p. 48; my italics). The critic even hears Shaw emitting "grunts of delight as he vicariously wipes out vast numbers of Englishmen" (p. 44), presumably as a prelude to doing away with humanity altogether. This thought has occurred to satirists before.

The same critical literalism disfigures the interpretation of the four offspring of the eugenic experiment in Act I of the play. The futuristic progeny of a union of East and West, these two young men and two young women are physically beautiful but lack a moral sense. That they only mouth jingoistic and romantic shibboleths of modern civilization is a typically Shavian way of commenting on the unpredictable outcome of neatly planned utopian schemes. Despite the fact that it is this quartet (not the more sympathetic Pra or Prola) who glorify death and extol killing in their speeches, Mr. Silver apparently finds these four mutants to be quite winsome: incredibly, he attributes the play's barbs against them to Shaw's "septuagenarian envy of youth" (p. 31). He becomes especially exercised regarding "Shaw's annihilation of the beautiful girl [called Maya] who represents love" (p. 282). One of the failed foursome, Maya represents in fact less the spirit of love than that of vapid amorism. (In calling her a "ravishing blonde" (p. 32), the critic comes closer to the truth than he realizes.) As the Judgment Day proceeds, the play's susceptible clergyman hero (Iddy) reaches out to embrace the girl only to find that she simply isn't *there*. The reason is that Maya embodies an erotic ideal that was only a figment to begin with: her very name *means* illusion. Predictably immune to allegory, Mr. Silver reports this incident as another "killing" and comments that "[With] youth and potency . . . destroyed, . . . Shaw thereby betrays his animus against the human race itself" (pp. 32–33).

The critic's feelings would doubtless do him credit if they were a reaction to Bernard Shaw's having actually murdered a young woman in real life; but as a response to Shavian satirical fantasy, the tone of moral outrage becomes rather trying once its novelty wears off. This is not to deny that there is a valid subject to explore here. Several of Shaw's later prose writings—in particular the notorious preface to *On the Rocks*—do appear seriously to advocate elimination of the incorrigibly unfit; and a study might explore the possible pathological source of Shaw's plunge off the deep end in this regard. But this opportunity to gain insight into a Shavian "homicidal impulse" is vitiated by the unique brand of critical overkill which is the main hallmark of *The Darker Side*.

The treatment of *Man and Superman* typifies again the book's lack of balance. Mr. Silver sees the play as the product of Shaw's response to his unconsummated marriage. Stung by the (presumed) "defeat in his battle

with Charlotte over sexual relations" (p. 153), the dramatist in "Don
Juan in Hell" attempts spitefully to "wrap himself in the philosopher's
cloak and to glorify contemplation as man's highest activity" (p. 154). As
for the insistence in the work that the Life Force is amoral and that the
Superman will be generated outside marriage, these claims are held to
be nothing but disguised "schemes for extramarital sex!" which Shaw
presumably sought as solace from the recalcitrant Charlotte (p. 156).
Moreover, the pursuit of the Superman gratifies Shaw's "quite pervasive
destructive misanthropy" (p. 161) by depending on an eugenics program that "would in effect sterilize huge numbers of the population and
deny existence to as yet unborn generations" (p. 163): such an ideal
expresses Shaw's "homicidal impulses" in "publicly acceptable" form
(p. 164).

One must not imagine that Don Juan is really the humane, high-
minded, life-affirming fellow he pretends to be. Replying to Satan's charge
that man is self-destructive, Juan maintains that humanity's willingness
to die for an idea may be viewed positively: Mr. Silver views this argument as revealing a "lust for killing [that] is Shaw's very own" (p. 162)
and suspects that, by offering the Superman as an instance of an idea
worth dying for, the dramatist is luring his fellow creatures into collec-
tive suicide (p. 169). When Juan claims that he must ever be "striving to
bring [something better than himself] into existence or clearing the way
for it" (p. 166), the phrase *clearing the way* is construed speciously (on
the basis of problematical evidence from outside the play) to mean murdering the unfit (pp. 167–68): the Life Force is really a Death Force
since "it must quite literally seek to wipe out people" (p. 168). Shaw's
frustration seems boundless indeed: not content with merely "venting
his resentment toward all males who happen to have less forbidding
wives," he in fact "yearned for the extinction of the whole human race"
(p. 172). Thus the vision of the Superman is "a sadomasochistic and
homicidal fantasy . . . hidden with cunning beneath a seemingly re-
splendent idealism" (p. 168); and Don Juan himself is a "moral monster"
(p. 169), a "minister of Death . . . far more evil than the devil himself"
(p. 164), who in contrast impresses the author as a quite commendable
Bloomsbury Christian (pp. 150, 170).

Given the severity of this indictment of Juan, it may seem a piddling
matter that he is accused as well of having "a grievously confused mind"
(p. 151) and displaying "an awesome talent for self-contradiction" (p.
152). Nonetheless, some examples of these allegations are worth examining for what they reveal about Mr. Silver's grasp of Shavian ideas. He
objects first that Juan on the one hand glorifies contemplation and reason yet on the other maintains that the Life Force proceeds by instinct
and intuition (p. 326). But at least from the time of *The Quintessence of*

Ibsenism (1891), Shaw had held that reason, while undeniably a valuable tool for implementing the will, cannot itself be a prime motor in human action: the instrumental intellect serves an anterior evolutionary appetite of which we can give no rational account. One must *recognize* this Shavian position in order to challenge it effectively: the critic does neither. Mr. Silver is also unhappy that Juan "condemns Hell as the home of 'the seekers for happiness' . . . yet elsewhere he boasts that the philosopher is the one 'sort of man [who] has ever been happy'" (p. 152). Here it might help to recall an aphorism from "The Revolutionist's Handbook" appended to the play: "Folly is the direct pursuit of Happiness and Beauty." Shaw's point is that the harder one strives to be happy, the less happy one is likely to be: felicity is not the result of sybaritic self-indulgence but the *by-product* of commitment of one's being to a meaningful goal. This insight, one of Shaw's most psychologically acute paradoxes, the critic obtusely converts into a contradiction. Mr. Silver charges too that Frederick P.W. McDowell "slides over all the difficult questions we might put to [this play]," especially when "he finds that Shaw is not really condemning music nor beauty nor patriotism but only their sham forms" (p. 326). But McDowell's position exactly reflects Shaw's own emphasis: Juan clearly distinguishes between "great ideas" and their "illusory forms." Indeed, the famous peroration he unleashes against Satan near the dream's end—"Your friends are . . . not beautiful . . . only decorated . . . not moral . . . only conventional . . . not kind . . . only sentimental [etc.]"—is nothing more than a systematic pairing of noble qualities with their debased counterparts. Mr. Silver would not have dismissed this climax of Juan's argument as "glibly rhetorical" (p. 152) and consisting of "embarrassingly mechanical antitheses about men" (p. 161) if he had understood the critique of idealism developed throughout the Shavian corpus. Does not Juan introduce his indictment in terms which make explicit that he means it as a description of Satan's cohorts and "friends," *not* as a misanthropic denunciation of all of humanity? What radically flaws Mr. Silver's approach is not these errors of judgment concerning particular points, but the tacit arrogance of a critical attitude which assumes that Shaw's thoughts on any subject whatever are of interest only as symptoms of underlying sexual pathology.

No one who has noted the stern justice *The Darker Side* metes out to Don Juan will be so naive as to expect Henry Higgins to escape with a slap on the wrist. To be sure, there is much evidence in *Pygmalion* to support the critic's view that Higgins can be insensitive and callous; the character at times "expresses a dehumanizing impulse within the very heart of the artist-creator" (p. 188). Not content with this claim against Higgins, Mr. Silver holds that the man's behavior "often goes quite beyond the malicious" (p. 201); he exhibits "pronounced sexual perversities" (p. 195) and is "extremely cruel" (p. 206); in his climactic confrontation with Eliza he experiences—what else?—"a blend of sadomasochistic pleasures" (209). Foremost among the latter is Higgins's desire "to punish himself for being a masochist!" (p. 210): he has a "perverse desire to be spanked" (p. 212) by Eliza (albeit verbally), as chastisement for desiring a mother-surrogate sexually. As if this indictment were not enough, Higgins's words and deeds "show him to be nothing less than diabolically evil" (p. 214) and the play exposes "the savage destructiveness in the heart of a supposed idealist" (p. 222). *It does?*

In the opening scene at Covent Garden, Higgins stands to one side jotting down notes on people's accents. When Eliza becomes alarmed by a bystander's suggestion that the notetaker is a detective, he curtly disabuses her of this notion: "Oh, shut up, shut up. Do I look like a policeman?" Stalwartly text-proof, Mr. Silver finds evidence here for Higgins's cruelty: "in the first act . . . he terrifies [Eliza] by seeming to be a police spy" (p. 201). Next the professor makes a bet with Pickering that he can pass Eliza off as a duchess at an ambassador's garden party in just three months; what sort of rigid moralism would condemn this whimsy as an attempt to "deceiv[e] . . . the public" (p. 216)? Instances of preposterous Higginsian rhodomontade in addressing Eliza—"Throw her out of the window" or "Throw her into the gutter" or "[Her] head will be cut off"— are taken, virtually, as real sadistic threats (p. 215). There is also Higgins's profanity (he is "infinitely more foulmouthed than [his] pupil"— [p. 215]), which includes such dreadful expressions as damn! blast! and bloody! That Satan is the man's presiding deity is revealed by such lines to Eliza as "How the devil do I know what's to become of you?" (p. 216). An annoyed Higgins complains to her, "I waste the treasures of my Miltonic mind by spreading them before you." Are we not meant to sense a degree of self-conscious comic hyperbole behind his outrageous remark? Mr. Silver thinks not (p. 219).

Early on, *The Darker Side* identified an obsessive tendency called "the Unattended Admonition—that moment when [Shaw] states the case against killing and then simply ignores it" (p. 171; also p. 48). Mr. Silver reveals an analogous compulsion in his own treatment of Shaw's characters and plays: to wit, he first credits Higgins with several humane and attractive qualities, then disregards them in his zeal to turn the character into a horrendous ogre. Taken together, the foregoing summaries of his chapters on *Pygmalion, Man and Superman,* and *The Simpleton* should give some sense of the ultimately stupefying impact of the author's indulgence in his monomania for 348 relentless pages.

A critic cannot "read" Shaw if he is tonedeaf to Shavian irony. *The Darker Side* recounts the famous anecdote in which Shaw appeared before the curtain after a successful early performance of *Arms and the*

Man. When the applause was interrupted by a lone dissenting boo, the dramatist replied, "My dear fellow, I quite agree with you, but what are we two against so many?" Did Shaw expect his audience to suppose that he ridiculed his own play? According to Mr. Silver, the famous quip "in truth reflected something of what he really felt" (p. 87). Analogously, a line from a youthful letter to the uncooperative Alice Lockett—"Beware. When all the love has gone out of me I am remorseless: I hurl the truth about like destroying lightning"—is invoked three times in the book as an example of how dangerously destructive Shaw could become when disappointed (pp. 72, 173, 282). In the "Epistle Dedicatory" to *Man and Superman*, Shaw comments wryly to Arthur Bingham Walkley that "*I first prove that anything I write on the relation of the sexes is sure to be misleading*; and then I proceed to write a Don Juan play" (p. 297; Silver's italics). Missing both the point and wit of the paradox (which the context clarifies), Mr. Silver concludes from the statement that "Shaw has in effect dismissed his own pretensions as a reliable philosopher" (p. 289). When Eliza is described in a stage direction as "*a piteous spectacle of abject terror*" anticipating her first bath, Mr. Silver treats this "manifestly sadistic" scene much as if it were an excerpt from *The One Hundred and Twenty Days of Sodom* (pp. 271–72). What is one to do with a critic who takes a sentence from the conclusion to *The Intelligent Woman's Guide to Socialism*—"For my part I hate the poor and look forward eagerly to their extermination"—as expressing an urge to alleviate poverty by offing the indigent (p. 41)? "Why should a dog, a horse, a rat, have life / And thou no breath at all?" asks King Lear, looking down at Cordelia dead. Had he been there on opening night, Mr. Silver would have reported Shakespeare to the R.S.P.C.A.

Now the critic's response to these objections would most likely be that they prove all too well how Shaw succeeded in using wit and satire to disguise his destructive and homicidal tendencies from unsuspecting readers. But such fundamentalist certitude concerning Shaw's darker side can be sustained only by placing the most ungenerous interpretation on even the very limited evidence Mr. Silver chooses to consider.* As the motto for his "Afterword," the author selects a Shavian quotation

---

*While I have tried to avoid faulting the author for not doing what he has not set out to do, some of *The Darker Side*'s omissions are nonetheless surprising. The book offers only parenthetical remarks on *Major Barbara* and *Heartbreak House*, the two plays in which Shaw most definitively argues the possible justification for killing on a large scale. It also seems odd that a work in which the term *sadomasochism* and its variants appear on virtually every page contains no discussion of Shaw's own references to de Sade and sadism—two examples of which appear in the very preface to *On the Rocks* which Mr. Silver excoriates as an expression of Shaw's cruelty and bloodlust.

dating from 1927: "I am a man of the most extraordinary hardness of heart" (p. 281). No further allusion to this remark is made, its source and context are not supplied, and the reader seems invited to conclude that in an honest lapse Shaw blurted out the truth about himself. In fact, the line comes from a speech ("Woman—Man in Petticoats") Shaw delivered to a charitable group seeking to improve the plight of indigent women. Printed by Dan H. Laurence in *Platform and Pulpit* (pp. 172–78), the concluding paragraph contains the offending sentence:

> If I were to pretend to be deeply moved by the lot of all these homeless women, I should be a mere hypocrite. I am more than seventy years of age; and so much human suffering has been crowded into those seventy years that I am in the condition of Macbeth in his last Act: "I have supped full with horrors: direness, familiar to my slaughterous thoughts, cannot once start me." Another million of starving children has become as nothing to me. I am acquiring the curious callousness of old age. At first, when I was beginning to get on in years, I used to feel sad when my old friends and even enemies began dropping round me. Nowadays I have got over that: I exult every time another goes down. I am a man of the most extraordinary hardness of heart; and I suggest to you that this is an undesirable condition for an old man to be in. I suggest to you that it is a frightful thought that if you are not careful, if you are not more thoughtful and humane than my generation was, there may be, seventy years hence, another old man looking on at horrible preventable evils with a heart as hard as mine. That is clearly an undesirable thing; and so I will sit down and leave the appeal to younger people who have still some sensibilities left.

Either Mr. Silver has engaged in disingenuous management of evidence, or else he simply cannot *hear* Shaw's voice.

Another serious limitation of *The Darker Side* lies in its neglect of relevant secondary literature on Shaw. This defect is not immediately apparent, since 45 pages of footnotes are appended to the study and give the impression of thorough scholarly apparatus. But the most recent reference in this book published in 1982 is to Robert Whitman's *Shaw and the Play of Ideas* (1977), and Mr. Silver's citations are for the most part cosmetic in character. He praises Elsie Adams for her "pioneering study" (p. 307), recognizes Martin Meisel's volume as "excellent" (p. 328), and credits J. L. Wisenthal with having written "the best single book on Shaw as playwright" (p. 304). But such perfunctory accolades do not suggest how any aspect of *The Darker Side* would have been different if these justly praised critics had never written a word. With the exception of books by St. John Ervine, B. C. Rosset, and Philip Weissman (published in 1956, 1964, and 1965 respectively), *The Darker Side* seems to have been produced in a critical vacuum. When not resorting to generalized praise, Mr. Silver tends to agree or disagree on points of detail with mid-1970s scholars such as Bernard Dukore, Maurice Valency, and Charles Berst—only to ignore these writers completely when their arguments intersect significantly with his own. Moreover, the author has been preceded in his Freudian approach by Daniel Dervin, whose *Bernard Shaw: A Psychological Study* (1975) made a promising start in this direction. One would expect at key junctures for Mr. Silver to be initiating lively dialogue with Dervin. Instead, one finds a lone footnote in which the latter's book is faulted as well as blurbily praised as "well worth reading for its provocative insights" (pp. 305–6). In his attempt to explain Shaw's infatuation for totalitarian dictators, Mr. Silver has an important forerunner in Julian Kaye's standard work, whose last chapter ("Bernard Shaw in the Twentieth Century") was devoted to this very question. Yet the sole reference to *Bernard Shaw and the Nineteenth-Century Tradition* (1958) is found in a footnote where Kaye is cited for drawing "some useful distinctions [between Shaw and Nietzsche] in his valuable study" (p. 334). There is good cause to suspect the sort of originality that on the one hand declines to engage previous critics, but on the other insists that virtually all of them have missed the essence of Shaw's character as well as the "real" meaning of some of his major works. From Eric Bentley to the present, has any respected writer on Shaw in fact touted him as "a humane and rational fellow, sensibly leftist, and wholly devoted to the true, the good, and the beautiful" (p. 286)? *The Darker Side* is not a book for Shavians to take to the proverbial desert island, but much of it appears to have been written on one.

While granting that Shaw was "always alert to the cultural and political currents of his time," Mr. Silver feels scholars have been so preoccupied with the wider social context of Shavian writings that they have neglected the part played in them by "obsessive personal problems" (p. 21). His book rights this imbalance with a vengeance. What are the sources of Shaw's political thought? "Because Shaw's manhood was under assault during the affair with Alice [Lockett] . . . he was especially susceptible to the appeal of Karl Marx, who, as he said, 'made a man of me'" (p. 73). The preface to *Getting Married* and other essays attacking repressive Victorian sexual mores are contorted by the critic into oblique expressions of Shaw's (supposed) wrath over enforced marital abstinence (p. 141). And having warned us against accepting ingenuously what Shaw says in his own person, Mr. Silver proceeds to assume that the most whimsically polemical pronouncements of John Tanner, M.I.R.C.—i.e., Member of the Idle Rich Class and author of "The Revolutionist's Handbook"—are safe guides to what "Shaw" the social thinker believes. Thus, the critic zeroes in on the pamphlet's peroration, in which Tanner proposes that "we must establish a State Department of Evolution, with a seat in the

Cabinet for its chief . . . and provide inducements to private persons to achieve successful results . . . for the improvement of human live stock. . . . Even a joint stock human stud farm (piously disguised as a reformed Foundling Hospital or something of that sort) might well, under proper inspection and regulation, produce better results than our present reliance on promiscuous marriage." Ignoring the fictional authorial persona entirely, Mr. Silver maintains that "our author" is engaging in "an elaborate private fantasy. We can easily imagine Shaw graciously volunteering to put in an appearance now and then at the stud farm" (p. 158) to slake his lust under the pretense of social service. Regarding Tanner's concluding proposal for "a conference on the subject [of eugenics]" (p. 158), Mr. Silver assures us that, while the intellectual purpose of such a gathering must remain murky, we can be "relatively certain that Shaw would be there, and available to any of the women delegates seeking a father for the Superman" (p. 159). These suggestions are really quite delightful until one realizes they are meant to be taken seriously. Given the availability of sufficient biographical material, the same immutably psychogenetic method could doubtless be applied to the work of any creative artist or thinker with equally impoverishing results.

Finally *The Darker Side* sinks beneath the weight of its author's fanatically reductionist loyalty to Oedipal and sadomasochistic premises that could have been illuminating had they been handled more flexibly. "In . . . *Arms and the Man*, [Shaw] had allowed himself to kill, offstage, the first person to be killed until then in any of his plays, a father, the innocent old father of Captain Bluntschli, the hero with whom he had been identifying himself . . ." (p. 113). From such a statement, one might suppose old Bluntschli to be a loveable geezer who is gratuitously zapped in the course of the action. In fact the hero's father is not even a character in the play, but an absent relative to whom a very few slight passing references are made. There might be some point in referring to "innocent old *Duncan*" in order to underscore the horror of his murder by Macbeth; but the moral character of Bluntschli senior (concerning which the play tells us nothing at all) is obviously irrelevant to his death— unless we are to believe that an author is responsible for the "murder" of fictional personages who die in his works. Even if one overlooks the critic's peculiar refusal to distinguish between real life and a represented action, there remains the puzzle of why Shaw is deemed an especially apt subject for this exercise in imaginary scholarship. Are there not individual plays by Shakespeare (*Titus Andronicus, King Lear*) which contain more sadistically honed violence than all of Shaw's works put together? Surely every prominent dramatist from Aeschylus to Sam Shepard must plead guilty to capital crimes. Even *Arms and the Man* itself offers a more defensible example of sadism in its account of the fate of Bluntschli's companion, a soldier who roasted to death after being shot in a wood-pile; but since *this* absent character is apparently no one's father, he does not warrant a mention in *The Darker Side*. The alternative to such tunnel vision need not involve subscribing to the prettified image of a sunlit Shavian personality: I take Shaw's darker side much *too* seriously to be willing to have his later political aberrations "explained" by a theory that the totalitarian dictators he romanticized were the fathers he really wanted, while the helpless millions they slaughtered were all surrogates for George Carr Shaw (pp. 283–284).

Bemused, Mr. Silver notes that "other men, after all, suffer defeats in love and recover" (p. 276). This thought might have given him pause. Throughout *The Darker Side* there is an absurd disproportion between the vast scale of effects and the smallness of the causes claimed to have produced them. Shaw's allegedly cruel humiliation of a fine actress and sensitive human being by a vendetta sustained for twenty years; his en-thusiasm for Mussolini's bombing of Abyssinia, Hitler's atrocities, and Stalin's bloodthirsty liquidations; finally, the urge to obliterate the hu-man race from the planet and life from the universe—and all because Stella Campbell told him she'd rather not? (p. 282). Surely this great lady of the English stage would have reconsidered her decision had she understood the enormity of the consequences that were to follow from it. Even the implacably unbeddable Charlotte might have preferred to emulate the behavior of Wedekind's Lulu rather than encourage by so neat a scruple the perpetration of some of the worst human disasters of the twentieth century. Freud properly grasped that sometimes a cigar is just a cigar; what's more, sometimes a penis is just a penis. The one thing *The Darker Side* proves for sure is that plotting the putative ups and downs of this appendage does not constitute an adequate basis for understand-ing the life and works of its possessor.

What both mitigates and intensifies one's judgment of this book is the sense that its author is by no means a fool, but a resourceful mind hoist with the petard of his own monomania. The rare occasions when Mr. Silver is able to relax his obsession show him capable of real discovery. His reinterpretation of *Candida* in terms of an Oedipal instead of a ro-mantic triangle does help explain the strange ambivalence of the abor-tive love scene between Marchbanks and the heroine in Act III (p. 106). The observation that "on a psychic level Shaw was recreating Don Juan as Tanner's successor, not his ancestor" (p. 148), straightens out in one sentence the confusions of a dozen critical articles on *Man and Superman*. The superiority of the original version of *Pygmalion* (alas no longer con-veniently available) and the extent to which Shaw's later tinkerings and accretions marred the play, are ably argued. And Mr. Silver's hypothesis concerning why Shaw habitually misstated that he married Charlotte at

the age of 43 (Lee's age when Lucinda Shaw fled her home to join him
in London) is a brilliant conjecture—one supported by a sufficient number of biographical parallels between Shaw and Lee to leave one in-
trigued (pp. 136–138). Yet such redeeming insights—and there are more
of them—cannot redeem fully a work whose essential tone is so unbalanced that even those who agree with the critic's points are likely to want
to fight to the death against his right to make them in such an extreme
and aberrant way. I can only hope that somewhere out there breathes a
scholar in search of a promising approach to Shaw, who by returning to
The Darker Side's seminal starting point—"If a man is a deep writer, all
his works are confessions"—may yet make the most of Mr. Silver's for-
saken opportunities.

                                                              Alfred Turco, Jr.

The Origins of *Joan*

Brian Tyson. *The Story of Shaw's "Saint Joan."* Kingston and Montreal:
McGill-Queen's University Press, 1982. 142 pp.

In writing his "story" of Bernard Shaw's most famous play, Professor
Tyson has examined the sources of *Saint Joan* and closely compared them
with the original shorthand manuscript. He has also followed through
with the subsequent revisions. This evidence is supplemented by his
consulting not only the resources of the British Library but also Shaw's
correspondence, the accounts of his friends at the time of the play's composition, and much if not all of what has been written about the play
since it first appeared in 1923.

    The author found Bernard Shaw's Pitman shorthand quite clear and,
with skilled assistance, was able to decipher even heavily deleted passages since the manuscript was without contractions and contained only
occasional errors. Sometimes, as between speakers where Shaw had simply
inserted a paragraph sign, Professor Tyson found it necessary for his
reading to set out the speakers in dramatic fashion. Sometimes, he had
to clarify stage directions. He also consulted the supplements to the
original shorthand: a few sheets of corrected typescript in the British
Library Additional Manuscripts collection, Shaw having claimed that he
destroyed the rest. The printed text Tyson used was that of the first
edition published by Constable in 1924. Shaw claimed county Kerry in
Ireland as the scene of his composition of *Saint Joan* and was in this claim
supported by Blanche Patch, his secretary for thirty years. This is con-

tested by the author, who presents evidence for at least the inception and perhaps the conclusion of the play being written at Great Malvern and even at Stratford-on-Avon, despite Shaw's assertion that should he pen even a line in the place of Shakespeare's demeaning of The Maid, she would rise from her resting place and punch his head.

Professor Tyson examines several models for Shaw's Joan: Dame Sybil Thorndike of the stage; T. E. Lawrence, suggested by Professor Stanley Weintraub; and one least known, Mary Hankinson, who managed summer schools for the Fabian Society and received a copy of the play from its creator, Shaw alleging that she was indeed his model for Joan. Whatever the facts of the matter, for Bernard Shaw, Joan's "real attraction is that she is a fact." In his pursuit of her, Shaw followed with great fidelity the facts of those documents dealing with the process and the rehabilitation of Joan, as found in his major source for the play, the translation by T. Douglas Murray of J.E.J. Quicherat's *Procès de Jeanne d'Arc*. Murray was indeed essential, as the dramatist did not have access to the records of the Roman Catholic Church regarding Joan's then-recent canonization. There were other sources consulted by Shaw, but none was as vital as Murray. Tyson finds in his study that Shaw seldom departed from Murray, and then only when the needs of dramatization or the concept of character dictated it. Occasionally, language forced the issue, some passages demanding in Shaw's view an added rhetorical force or more poetic expression. Professor Tyson has built a generally superior study: being himself no slave to the text, he has been willing to interpret and to critically appraise without substituting his own for the Shavian intent. He has borne in mind that "the play's the thing" while respecting the occasion and facts of the composition.

The author correctly views conversion, the theme so vital to Shaw, as essential to an understanding of *Saint Joan*. He credits Stanley Weintraub with the thesis that Shaw pushed Joan into greater militancy because his own personal and dramatic needs demanded it. Weintraub—author of a significant commentary on this play—is correct: Joan is highlighted in contrast to the male characters, who are by turns too passive (the Dauphin), overreactive (the clergyman de Stogumber), or strong for the wrong reasons (Warwick and Cauchon). Not in vain, however, did Eva LeGallienne protest against Shaw's concept of what he termed "a role play" and one she called "Saint Bernard Shaw."

What emerges here is, by contrast, a rather charming Inquisitor. Here again, Shaw is pushing his thesis that in the modern world, "justice" is likely to be rendered by those acting wrongly from a desire to do the right thing. In his Preface, more truculent than the play, Shaw argued that this indeed is the tragic note. Professor Tyson sees *Saint Joan* as part of the Shavian process that will not simply despair with a "How long, O Lord," since Shaw also recognizes Joan as part of human progress.

In addressing the play, Brian Tyson is critically aware: he sees, for instance, the humor of the opening scene in which Shaw uses miracle not for orthodoxy but for believability. Why not a Maid from rural France who brings about the renewed ability of the hens to lay eggs? Miracles exist for the credulous, after all. Joan needs to be earth-rooted because, with such roots, she can better oppose both the clerics and the courtiers, if not the British. Her militancy, a victory over obdurate nature, has begun.

We see that Shaw builds credibility for Joan in such dramatic needs and in historical context. Each scene contributes to the portrait of the victorious fighter, first against the occupying forces and later against the French clerics and regional powers. These early scenes dramatically document Joan's rise to authority and power. For example, Tyson points out Shaw's careful delaying of Joan's arrival in the fourth scene, even before revisions he made in Ireland. He had determined to develop by then not only the nature of the Inquisitor but of the Inquisition. Delaying Joan's entrance offers Shaw the opportunity to thrust her into contrast with her judges and prosecutors already introduced. However reasonable such figures of authority are shown to be, they are also clearly wrong—wrong then and wrong now, just as their like, even now, so frequently are. Joan is punished not only because she represents a nationalist threat to the hegemony of the church and to the feudal barons, but also in part because she is too far ahead of her time. She has something of a romantic's trust in her intuition, something she shares with her creator. The time was far from ripe; Bernard Shaw nearing seventy was still searching. Though sometimes in despair over his advancing years, Shaw did not lose his nerve. He felt in *Saint Joan* he had written a fine drama; most who have seen or read the play agree.

Professor Tyson does not overlook the operatic element, always important to a Shaw play. The plays are not only cast in a rational and even a disquisitory mode, but are often sung in parts for voices that may chorus or point and counterpoint. The lonely, lovely aria which follows Dunois's warning, "That is the truth, Joan. Heed it," in the Cathedral Scene (V), is printed entire by Tyson, in parallel passages of original shorthand and revised (published) text. Side by side, the lines in revision appear more eloquent, yet less complex. The meaning is unaltered, and Shaw's fidelity to the Murray transcript remains close.

Tyson's furnishing such opportunities to examine Shaw's working methods, especially his uses of Murray, contributes to the interest and value of his study. Murray, for example, had found in his sources that the number of articles used in the act of accusation against Joan were reduced from seventy to twelve for the trial. Shaw uses such elements to point to the comic solemnities of the clerics; even some of the Shavian-styled jokes are from the contemporary transcript of Joan's remarks, which evidence a naive and charming wit. In the Trial Scene (VI), said Shaw, "I have used Joan's very words." Tyson demonstrates from Murray, and from the original manuscript, that "the brilliance of Shaw in this scene lies not in the creation but the selection of dialogue from his principal source." Some commentators have found, however, considerable poetic license in Joan's speech when, for example, she calls for the fire rather than suffer perpetual banishment.

Bernard Shaw's dramatic skill is most fully revealed in such passages as those near the end of *Saint Joan* in which the character of the executioner is developed and in the incident of the English soldier's fashioning a cross from two sticks tied together that he gives to Joan when in her suffering she cries for such an emblem. At least three witnesses to the execution collapsed, according to eyewitness testimony, including the executioner, who was overcome by the enormity of his deed. Shaw makes of him not the abject figure of the various depositions but a dignified man who objects to being called "a fellow" by the Earl of Warwick and whose trade is perceived as similar to a medieval mystery.

Shaw utilized, in the "common" soldier's proffering of the crude cross of two sticks, a tradition if not a fact which points to English national embarrassment. For example, the jingoistic chaplain, de Stogumber, after the shock of Joan's burning has somewhat cleared his mind (paradoxically leaving him to appear unhinged), comments that the bystanders laughing at the execution must indeed have been French. Even Shaw would observe that the soldier's gesture was an act of charity "so redemptive of the otherwise unrelieved ferocity of our share in the tragedy, that I innocently supposed my feeling about it to be a general possession."

Changes made by Shaw in the Epilogue were actually minor: much had been written in Ireland, Shaw leaving here and there blank spaces for Blanche Patch to type in from his shorthand. Tyson, in examining the manuscript, found that Shaw had "worked hard to improve each speech poetically" and that the cadences were more Biblical. He viewed this "inspiration" as an aspect of the Life Force—a superpersonal need, a creative imagination. Shaw believed his Epilogue was essential to *Saint Joan*: Tyson finds that it is indeed Shaw's part of the play, and he (Shaw) argues that the power of the imagination forms the future in the same way the Will does in the process of creative evolution.

Professor Tyson concludes that Shaw's voice is speaking in his evolutionary mode when at the end of the play, he asks "How long, O Lord, how long?" Some see in this the dramatist's despair at a world of Yahoos and the inhumanity of men; but we may also see in this Shaw's impatience at the length of the process. Joan has made a contribution but a gap yawns.

Two briefer chapters sum up: "First Performances" and "Lasting Impressions." In one, the author details the interesting history of the struggles over the roles in what Shaw had dubbed a "star play." From its initial performance by New York's Theatre Guild in 1923 through its suffering a melodramatic style in France, to the present, the play has survived well. In his final glimpse of impressions made by *Saint Joan*, Tyson cogently points to Bertolt Brecht, who shared the 1920s with Shaw and who also was developing, in defiance of the then current deterministic fatalism, a world of becoming rather than that of being.

Sam A. Yorks

Shaw and Lord Alfred Douglas

Bernard Shaw and Alfred Douglas: A Correspondence. Edited by Mary Hyde. New Haven and New York: Ticknor & Fields, 1982. 237 pp. Illustrated. $25.

The dust jacket of Mary Hyde's edition of the Shaw/Douglas correspondence quotes Richard Ellmann as saying that the "tragic shadow of Oscar Wilde broods over" this epistolary exchange. While Wilde is indeed a major topic of contention and discussion in these letters, Frank Harris is equally important—to Douglas a *bête noire*; to Shaw "a sensitive child" and "buccaneer." "The truth [Shaw told Douglas] is that Harris had the supreme virtue of knowing good literary work from bad and preferring the good. For that I forgave him all his sins, and have always defended him as far as he could be defended." Harris may have frightened people, said Shaw, "with his voice and his trenchant articulation," but Harris didn't frighten Shaw.

Shaw's first and only meeting with Douglas occurred in March 1895, when Wilde (and later Douglas) joined Shaw and Harris at the Café Royal. Having obtained a warrant for the Marquess of Queensberry's arrest on a charge of libel, Wilde urged Harris to testify on his behalf at the forthcoming trial that *The Picture of Dorian Gray* was not an immoral book. Harris declined, insisting that Wilde's case was hopeless; Shaw later stated that he "hardly" spoke, but Douglas (later writing to Harris) insisted that Shaw had agreed with Harris's evaluation. As Hyde states, "No one present forgot the scene in the Café Royal"; indeed, it looms as a pivotal scene in the Wilde tragedy.

Thirteen years later, Shaw and Douglas exchanged some angry letters (included as an appendix in Hyde's edition), when Douglas, editor of

The Academy, wrote a wounding notice of *Getting Married*. The correspondence proper in this edition, however, begins in 1931, when Douglas was sixty and Shaw was seventy-four; it ends in December, 1944, a few months before Douglas' death.

This extraordinary exchange of letters (most of which are in Hyde's private collection) brings together two of Wilde's friends (Shaw might have said "acquaintance" on his part, for, he said, he saw Wilde no more than half a dozen times); the result is a series of confrontations at once revealing and entertaining. Shaw became directly involved in the Harris/Douglas argument over the former's celebrated (but certainly, in part, fabricated) biography of Wilde, which had been published in America in 1916 but which could not be published in Britain for fear of Douglas's threatened libel suit. Wishing to help Mrs. Harris, who was reduced to poverty after the death of her husband in 1931, Shaw agreed to edit the biography of Wilde with the approval of Douglas and to write a preface to the volume. Predictably, Douglas remained dissatisfied because Shaw, he contended, had not followed all of his suggestions. The biography, Douglas told Shaw, was an "imbecile work, redeemed, of course, by your brilliant preface," but Shaw insisted that it had "very considerable literary merit in its Plutarchian way."

At times, the correspondence grows embarrassingly acrimonious on both sides, despite the fact that Douglas preferred to address Shaw as "St. Christopher" (the saintly ferryman), and Shaw decided to address him as "Childe Alfred" (after Browning's Childe Rowland), a quaint recognition of his aristocratic lineage and his "infantile complex," as Shaw called it (a complex that Douglas found in all true poets and the means of entering the Kingdom of Heaven). One of these intemperate exchanges occurred after Douglas had sent Shaw the manuscript of his *Oscar Wilde: The Summing Up* in 1939. He characterized Shaw's reaction as a "brilliant skit. It is *exactly* the sort of driveling idiocy that the average reader to a publisher . . . does write about a good book." Shaw returned: "You BLASTED idiot, who has asked you to change your views?" He insisted that Douglas could not bear criticism and that his "self-love" was "extraordinary"; Shaw, on the other hand, commended himself as one who was always grateful for any criticism, adding: "I have never liked myself very much." Douglas returned: "You are the most conceited man who ever lived (whereas I am fundamentally humble) and you are a hopeless case because you are cut off from the fountain of wisdom (God and the Catholic church) as I was myself before my conversion." Cut off or not, Shaw recommended Creative Evolution; Douglas, however, lit candles for his "St. Christopher" in the hope that Shaw might see the light. When Douglas persisted in urging him to consider conversion, Shaw responded: "As to becoming a Christian and letting Jesus suffer for my sins, damn it, Childe, I have still some instincts of a gentleman left."

Despite the occasional acrimony, Douglas had great admiration for Shaw's genius as a playwright, though he thought *St. Joan* a "flippant treatment of a martyr and saint," albeit "brilliant and original." Douglas's capacity for self-evaluation was always flawed by an almost pathological narcissism. When he inquired of Shaw about the possibility of a civil list pension, he stated that "after all, I am the best living English poet." To Shaw's praise of T. S. Eliot's poetic achievement in *Murder in the Cathedral*, he responded that "Pound, Eliot, Auden and Company" were not poets at all and therefore "incapable of writing even bad verse."

Hyde's editing of this correspondence is generally efficient, though sometimes unnecessarily minimal or non-existent. Birth and death dates in annotations are sporadic, and occasionally, allusions in letters remain unannotated. In one note, Hyde states that Robert Sherard, in his *Bernard Shaw, Frank Harris and Oscar Wilde* (1937), "disproved Harris's claim that he had had a yacht waiting at Erith for Wilde's escape to France." Sherard's "proof," however, is a piecing together of rather dubious evidence. Douglas himself (after having read Sherard's book) told Shaw that he had been "led to doubt" Harris' story about the yacht: thus, the impetuous Douglas is more cautious than the editor.

Hyde's general introduction is helpful for the general reader who does not know the details of Wilde's downfall, and her selection of photographs is excellent; many are unfamiliar, particularly those of the aging Douglas. When Shaw turned eighty-five, he ended one of his letters to Childe Alfred: "Time for me to die, Childe, time for me to die. But I can still saw logs. I am really proud of the pile of them in the garden, though nobody will ever call them immortal works." Hyde includes two photographs of Shaw engaged in his heroic endeavor.

Karl Beckson

Shaw's Intrepidity as Letter Writer: The Correspondence with Frank Harris

The Playwright and the Pirate, Bernard Shaw and Frank Harris: A Correspondence. Edited with an introduction by Stanley Weintraub. University Park, Pennsylvania: State University Press, 1982. 273 pages. Illustrated.

The Playwright and the Pirate is of great interest to Shavians and to students of late nineteenth century and early twentieth century literature, in filling out one corner of the literary scene and in casting light upon an important writer and personality and upon an assuredly major one. For everyone concerned with Shaw and his milieu, the reprinting of his letters in more complete and accurate form than in Frank Harris's *Bernard Shaw: An Unauthorized Biography Based upon First-Hand Information* (New York: Simon and Schuster, 1931) is welcome; and there are letters of major importance that appear in Weintraub's volume for the first time. I had the intimation when reading through the correspondence that I had read some of it before; and so I had. Many of the most important passages from Shaw's letters are in the biography; and, in fact, Harris's book has been in the past an indispensable source for scholars because of Shaw's own words reprinted therein. Now that we have the letters in their entirety and in unexpurgated form, Weintraub's book can be said virtually to supersede the Harris biography.

Perhaps not entirely, since Harris's biography did have Shaw's final blessing and, what is more significant, his imprimatur. To what degree Shaw was happy to give his complete blessing to the enterprise is not easy to ascertain. From the first Shaw had discouraged Harris in his attempts to write a biography of him when Harris needed the money that such a book might bring in. Shaw maintained, with discernment, that Harris's critical ability and intellectual capacity would be inadequate for the task that he had set himself. Harris, Shaw maintained, would never be willing to read the thirty volumes of the collected works in order to master his subject. In the upshot Harris was not willing to do so, and his biography has little to contribute of critical importance to the understanding of Shaw's work. Beyond an indication of a preference for *Candida, Caesar and Cleopatra*, and *Man and Superman*, there is little evidence that Harris read much Shaw—*Saint Joan*, perhaps to derogate it since he had just written a play on Joan, but certainly not *Our Theatres in the Nineties* or *Essays in Fabian Socialism*, let alone *The Intelligent Woman's Guide to Socialism and Capitalism*. The value of the biography lies in the insights that it gives into Shaw the man, and these emanate, for the most part, from Shaw's own letters. One function Harris consistently did perform was to bring out his greater compatriot: first, as drama critic for the *Saturday Review*, a position which was to establish Shaw as a voice in the destiny of the British theater even before his own plays became *de rigueur* with the Vedrenne-Barker seasons of 1904–1907; and then later, through the stimulus provided by Harris's letters, as commentator, in his replies, upon himself, his milieu, his ideas, and his work. Shaw never forgot the boost that Harris gave his career in the nineties and so tolerated much from Harris that he might have found tiresome from another. As for the biography, we can assume that Shaw must have almost completely rewritten the manuscript after Harris's death. Considering the fact that it is a longish book, Shaw can be regarded, I think, as having more than paid his debt to Harris. The proceeds from the book were considerable, and Harris's impoverished wife Nellie was the person who benefited most from the sales.

In view of these eventualities, some of Shaw's protests and prohibitions made in the letters are truly ironic. Shaw absolutely proscribed at various times the use of his correspondence in the Harris biography, though Harris always seemed to count on being able to publish it. Simon and Schuster in their advertisement boasted that Harris's book would contain 15,000 words by Shaw (ostensibly in the form of letters), and Shaw threatened to sue unless this advertising was withdrawn—as it apparently was. When Shaw called in the manuscript after Harris's death, he not only published many of his letters in it but reworked the text. The extent to which Shaw revised the work can never be known, for Shaw covered his tracks by destroying the manuscript. Shaw's contribution must have been large since the book is engagingly written and is most interesting. Even the minimal discussion of Shaw's works would argue not only Harris's unfamiliarity with them but an author's reluctance to discuss his own work critically. Finally, Shaw did write more than the 15,000 words mentioned in the publisher's announcement to which he had reacted so violently. One could argue that Shaw may also have been conscious of the publicity value of his own letters to Harris and so may have been doing more than repaying a debt in taking over the writing of the book from Frank Scully, Harris's ghost-writer.

Harris was, if nothing else, well aware of the commercial value of literary property. With Shaw's permission he had published a number of his letters and discussions in the magazines that he edited in Europe and America. After the success of the Shaw-Ellen Terry correspondence, he even proposed, in addition to the biography of Shaw, a book of Shaw-Harris letters. Shaw vetoed the project, sensing correctly that, from the standpoint of literary excellence, Harris's letters could scarcely qualify for such a book. The collection could not have had the great success of the Shaw-Terry collection, since Ellen Terry was a far more colorful figure in the popular imagination than Harris and a far more ingratiating personality.

Stanley Weintraub has in effect carried out, with knowledge and care, this project of a joint correspondence that Harris had originally proposed to Shaw. While the letters from Harris pale beside those from Shaw, they do provide the context out of which Shaw's can be best understood; and the context provided in Weintraub's book is fuller, certainly, than that offered in Harris's *Bernard Shaw*. Harris's letters have residual value, moreover, in revealing just the kind of person he was: an opportunist, a paranoiac, and a drifter of no great intellectual power but still a man who had strong convictions, even if he lacked the discipline to give them their inevitable and precise expression. Harris's letters do not qualify as literature if for no other reason than the fact that the person who wrote them is so peevish and unattractive. Not wishing to break with him out of gratitude for what Harris had done for him in the past, Shaw kept in epistolary touch with Harris and let himself be drawn out by him.

The Playwright and the Pirate is of considerable interest to Shavians in allowing us to see how Harris and Shaw utilized these letters in the Harris biography, now that we have the complete texts. Parts of the letters having to do with Harris's immediate personal situation or with matters in detail concerning the writing of the biography, Shaw omitted when he incorporated the letters into the text of the biography or edited it. Harris or Shaw would often break up one long letter into two shorter ones and print them in different parts of the book as if they were separate letters, generally using the same date for each. The letter of 20 June 1930 appears on pages 43–44 and 227 of the biography, whereas the first two paragraphs in the original, in which Shaw lectures Harris on how to write his book, and the postscript are not present there. As Weintraub notes, Shaw added to this letter "after the fact" when he changed the wording of the section that appears on page 227 from "You, as biographer will have to face the very unHarrisian fact that I escaped seduction until I was 29" to the more gratulatory and self-approving "You as a biographer will have to face the very unHarrisian fact that I lived on pictures and music, opera and fiction, and thus escaped seduction until I was 29." One important long letter of 5 June 1930, having to do with Shaw's Irish origins, does not appear in the biography, though phrasing from parts of it Harris (or Shaw) used in Chapters 4 and 5 of the biography (not, I think, Chapters 3 and 4 as Weintraub states in his introductory note). In this letter as he quoted from it on page 42 of the biography Shaw added a revealing sentence, in order to make sure apparently that the George Carr Shaw-Lucinda Shaw-Vandeleur Lee relationship be regarded in a Platonic light: "I do not want my mother to be the heroine of another Wagner-Geyer lie." Shaw, in short, did not wish to be seen in a situation parallel to that of Richard Wagner, who was perplexed as to whether Geyer or Wagner was his father since both men were parts of the household in which he grew up, just as Shaw was part of a household containing two grown men: George Carr Shaw and Vandeleur Lee. Concerning the letter of 18 September 1930, part is reprinted on pages xvii–xviii of the biography and the rest on pages 221– 223, with a paragraph being added on page 222: "All the great actresses I have known could have talked Dr. Johnson's head off and written it off too. Some of them were greater off the stage than on it. But I mustn't chatter about them in public." The postscript was omitted, and an interesting change in wording occurs from "you may count the women who have conquered me physically on less than the fingers of one hand" to the more decorous "you may count the women who have left me nothing to desire on less than the fingers of one hand." Some mistakes in dating occur in the Harris biography: a letter dated January 1917 on page 361 should be 20 October 1916, a letter dated 14 July 1918 on page 285 of the biography should be 5 March 1918, and a few other such discrepancies are present.

It is good to have letters in complete form such as the one of 5 March 1918: the parts on Harris's "ruffianism" and Shaw's pro-Boer stance have been printed but not the paragraphs in which Shaw castigates him most directly. The remarks on Wilson in the letter of 24 May 1919 are present in Harris's *Bernard Shaw*, but not, I think, Shaw's instructions to Harris as to how to write a short biography of him (for Harris's *Contemporary Portraits*). The letter of 15 September 1920 Shaw diagnoses acutely Harris's failings as a writer, pointing out that his limitations inhere in his "adoration" of literature as such which interferes with his direct apprehension of experience and with his creative vitality. One is grateful to have in its full form the letter of 5 June 1930, which is quoted and paraphrased in Chapters 4 and 5 of *Bernard Shaw* but given now for the first time in its original draft. It is a service, too, to have Shaw's sketch of Oscar Wilde (reprinted in the Harrisian edited text in *Pen Portraits and Reviews*) given in its original form, though it was a disappointment to find that "How Frank Ought to Have Done It" was not given in the original version of Harris's *Contemporary Portraits* series (though it is listed as being reprinted therefrom) but rather from the text that appears, in considerably revised form, in Shaw's *Sixteen Self-Sketches*. Since Weintraub does not reprint them or allude to them in *The Playwright and the Pirate*, I am led to wonder whether Shaw's letter of August 1928 (quoted on page 4 of Harris), in which he gives his reasons for being unable to fix a luncheon time with the Harrises, and Harris's letter (from 1916 apparently, on pages 365–70 in Harris), in which he criticizes Shaw's views of Christ, are fabrications on Harris's or Shaw's part or whether they are genuine as given in Harris. Some letters Shaw bowdlerized when he allowed them to be printed, notably the one containing Shaw's sex-credo from 24 June 1930, wherein "copulations" became "gallantries" and "whore" became "mistress." Shaw wished to preserve a more decorous public image than did Frank Harris, and it is noteworthy that Shaw revised his words further away from the bluntness and directness of the original text when he reprinted a version of it in *Sixteen Self-Sketches*.

This volume contains some of Shaw's best letters. Many of Shaw's letters, in whole or in part, have been available in Harris's *Bernard Shaw* since 1931, but Weintraub's collection is important in giving us several striking letters or parts thereof that have not appeared previously, in printing the full texts of the letters, and in setting the ambience in which they were written (provided mostly by Frank Harris's letters and by Weintraub's own judicious and informative headnotes, the results of much painstaking research). On the basis of this collection Shaw again emerges as an engaging, always interesting, and often memorable letter writer. The *Collected Letters* and the several compilations of Shaw's letters to one correspondent establish his eminence in the realm of letter writing, a position as high in this domain as in that of drama and that of non-fiction.

Perhaps I can now indicate some of the more arresting contents of these letters, most of them previously unpublished as far as I can ascertain by a careful though not exhaustive scrutiny of the Frank Harris biography. In a letter of 16 October 1916, Shaw comments on the relationship between his parents and the man who lived with them in Dublin, the musician, Vandeleur Lee. Shaw defends the lack of interest in sex characterizing his mother in words that make me believe him: "A man who could have done that [seduced his mother] could have seduced the wooden Virgin in the museum in Nuremberg." In this letter Shaw maintains that his plays are not deficient in passion but full of sexuality and that the characteristic modern man in love is a philanderer. In words that bring to mind one of the ruling ideas for Shaw since *Man and Superman*, he asserts that sex is not the only passion nor the most important one: "The infatuated Amorism of the nineteenth century, like its Bardolatry, made it necessary for me to say with emphasis that Life and not Love is the supreme good; that the restriction of the word passion to sexual appetite and its denial to science and philosophy is a modern abuse of the most sickening vulgarity and ignorance; that a man or woman who is preoccupied with sex to more than, say, one twentieth part of the extent (measured in time) during which he is preoccupied with hunger or business or art or science or education or dry living generally is a neurotic degenerate or a pampered idler; that there is no instinct or appetite which can be starved so easily or deflected so whimsically or trivially as the sex instinct in spite of its pretences to be the most imperative of all instincts; and that the people who talk and write most about it betray to the really experienced people that their romance is mere green sickness, and that they have either had no experience or have no capacity for experience and therefore did not notice what they really felt." Another letter, dated 5 March 1918, contains in a previously unpublished section the judgment that Strindberg's plays provide the greatest sex literature we now have by virtue of his protests against sexual tyranny, whereas Cervantes and Shakespeare show "what a curse this miserable preoccupation of literature with sexual infatuation is. The greatest sex literature we have, that of Strindberg, is really a fierce protest against this tyranny, which is only a reaction from the sexual and emotional starvation of the respectable middle class." In an apparently formerly unpublished letter of 15 January 1917, Shaw lectures Harris on his patronizing other people whom he claims to have discovered. Shaw rightly insists that these individuals resent such pretensions and Shaw is suspicious, moreover, of Harris's desire to order the inner lives of others with the view toward making them consistent.

In other letters Shaw comments on literature, art and the artist, and his own plays, and the opinions advanced are full of zest, weight, and relevance. In a letter of 27 September 1918 Shaw chides Harris for his lack of knowledge of Dickens, records his own judgment (to be found elsewhere also in Shaw's writings) as to the superiority of the late works, and so anticipates modern revaluations of the novelist: "Read Little Dorrit, Our Mutual Friend, and Great Expectations. Until you do you will not have the very faintest notion of what the name of Dickens means. Barnaby Rudge is mere boy's work in comparison. He did not come of age until Ruskin and Carlyle probed his social conscience to the depth, and he made a beginning of his great period with Hard Times. But when it came, it *was* great." In the same letter that contains his comment on Strindberg, Shaw indicates his own indebtedness to Mozart in a succinct statement: "it was from him that I learned how art work could reach the highest degree of strength, refinement, beauty and seriousness without being heavy and portentous." As an artist Shaw regards himself, in a letter of 18 January 1930, as having the same objective sympathy that Shakespeare possessed: Shaw says that, like Shakespeare, he has understanding but is impersonal and so reveals, if we can accept his analysis, a kind of Keatsian "negative capability" with respect to the experiences that he dramatizes in his plays. Harris in his biography, he says, tries, mistakenly, to endow him with a "soul": "Have you not yet found out that people like me and Shakespear *et hoc genus omne* have no souls? We understand all the souls and all the faiths and can dramatize them because they are to us wholly objective: we hold none of them." Similarly in a letter of 20 June 1930 he declares, "I am of the true Shakespearean type: I understand everything and everyone, and am nobody and nothing." As for his own plays he asserts in a letter of 15 September 1920 that fifty plays could be written on the theme set forth in *Back to Methuselah* and that in five plays and prefaces he has hardly touched his subject; and in a letter of 25 March 1924 he avers that Joan's lack of sexual attractiveness in *Saint Joan* makes her appear divine to her military comrades (both these letters appear in Harris). In the letter of 20

October 1916, also reproduced in Harris, Shaw writes a footnote to his large preface to *Androcles and the Lion*, describing the characteristics of each of the four gospel writers and emphasizing the elusive nature of Christ, and in another previously printed letter, dated 10 March 1919, he defends the superior military strategy of the British Army in World War I: "When everyone has owned up, England remains the most formidable single fighting Power in the world." There is a delightful skit on the international politicians' handling of the war indemnities in the letter of 22 March 1921; the skit has also been reprinted in Volume 7 of the Bodley Head *Bernard Shaw*, although its allusions, unexplained there, are clarified in *Pirate*.

The foregoing two paragraphs comprise only a sampling of the riches to be found in these letters. Like all other collections of Shaw's letters, these make fascinating browsing for the Shavian and general reader alike. We are grateful for the time and patience that bringing them together, along with Harris's letters, must have entailed.

Frederick P. W. McDowell

John R. Pfeiffer*

A CONTINUING CHECKLIST OF SHAVIANA

I. Works by Shaw

Shaw, Bernard. *Arms and the Man* in *College English*. Edited by Alton C. Morris, et al. Eighth edition. New York: Harcourt Brace Jovanovich, 1983. Not seen.

———. *Arms and the Man* in *Imaginative Literature*. Edited by Alton C. Morris, et al. Fourth edition. New York: Harcourt Brace Jovanovich, 1983. Not seen.

———. *Bernard Shaw and Alfred Douglas; A Correspondence*. Edited by Mary Hyde. New Haven and New York: Ticknor and Fields, 1982. Spans years from 1931 to 1944. GBS was 74; Douglas was 60. See reviews by Holroyd and Hyde in "Periodicals" below. Reviewed also in this volume.

———. "Bernard Shaw Meets Mark Twain." *Mark Twain Journal*, XX, no. 1 (Winter 1979–80), back cover. A GBS letter to Cyril Clemens describing two meetings with Mark Twain, from 4 Whitehall Court, on 1 April 1937.

———. "Bernard Shaw's Reflections on Being a City Councilman." *Public Administration Review*, XL, no. 4 (July/August 1980), 317–20. Published as "by" Randy H. Hamilton, but actually Hamilton's presentation of excerpts from Shaw's *The Common Sense of Municipal Trading* (Westminster: Archibald Constable and Co., 1904). Hamilton creates fourteen headings including the first, "On Innovation, Technology Transfer, and Undergrounding," and the last, "Summing up on Public Administrators." About administrators GBS wrote, ". . . the ratepayers, in spite of their stinginess in the matter of salaries on the professional scale, get so much better than they deserve."

———. "Bunyan and Shakespeare" in *Readings for Writers*. Edited by Jo Ray McCuen and Anthony C. Winkler. Fourth edition. New York: Harcourt Brace Jovanovich, 1983 pp. 514–18. Review of G. G. Collingham's play based on *Pilgrim's Progress*, at Olympic Theatre 24 December 1896. Original publication data not supplied.

———. Excerpts about doctors from works by GBS in *The Physician in Literature*. Edited by Norman Cousins. Philadelphia, London and Toronto: The Saunders Press, 1982.

---

*Professor Pfeiffer, *SHAW* Bibliographer, welcomes information about new or forthcoming Shaviana: books, articles, pamphlets, monographs, dissertations, reprints, etc. His address is Department of English, Central Michigan University, Mount Pleasant, Michigan 48859.

Three samples from *Methuselah, Doctor's Dilemma*, and "An Improbable Fiction," *Time and Tide* (22 February 1929).

————. *The Playwright and the Pirate. Bernard Shaw and Frank Harris: A Correspondence.* Edited by Stanley Weintraub. See under Weintraub, S.

————. Ten snippets, mostly from *Saint Joan* materials, in *The Oxford Guide to Writing*, by Thomas S. Kane. New York and Oxford: Oxford University Press, 1983. Emerson and Thoreau get eight extracts apiece. Nine for Bertrand Russell. Ten for E.B. White. Fifteen for Lawrence Durrell. Sixteen for Barbara Tuchman and Orwell. Eighteen for Mark Twain and Aldous Huxley. Nineteen for Joan Didion and James Baldwin. Twenty-eight for G.K. Chesterton!

II. Books and Pamphlets

Aldington, Richard. See MacNiven, Ian S., below.

Atkins, John. *J. B. Priestley. The Last of the Sages.* London: John Calder, 1981. Many references to GBS as if he is an important touchstone to the lesser career of Priestley.

Auerbach, Nina. *Woman and the Demon. The Life of a Victorian Myth.* Cambridge: Harvard University Press, 1982. "By virtue of her public identity, her self-transforming power, and her association with myths of fallen women and with literary character, the actress unleashes divine-demonic womanhood. George Bernard Shaw's worship of actresses was more unwavering, if no less impassioned, than Wilkie Collins'. Shaw's intimately reverential correspondence with Ellen Terry, whom he fled from meeting offstage, are the outpourings of a Victorian acolyte, though this fiercely modern iconoclast would no doubt have bristled at the suggestion." "The 'curse' of acting is the double face of a Faustian pact: the actress; transcendence of time and circumstance is manifest in the brilliant worship of Shaw's prose, while the off-stage woman is stripped of her characters' magic immunity." This single comment on Shaw in the book refers to the GBS-Ellen Terry correspondence.

Beauman, Sally. *The Royal Shakespeare Company. A History of Ten Decades.* Oxford, New York, Toronto, and Melbourne: Oxford University Press, 1982. Shaw's participation in the progress of events involving the Company and Shakespearean culture in general is substantially represented.

Bermel, Albert. *Farce. A History from Aristophanes to Woody Allen.* New York: Simon and Schuster, 1982. Many references to GBS including a chapter, "Stage Realism after Chekhov and Shaw," a comparison of Chaplin and GBS, and the following growing out of a discussion of Shaw's dislike of Oscar Wilde's *Importance of Being Earnest*:

> Wilde had pulled off what he himself had been reluctant to attempt: an altogether facetious play untrammeled by weighty themes, sustained speeches, or psychologizing. Shaw did indulge his clown (who had haggled him from the beginning), to the delight of his audiences, and allowed the tormentor to take charge of whole scenes at a time in the full-length plays *Arms and the Man* (1894), *You Never Can Tell* (1896), *The Devil's Disciple* (1897), *Caesar and Cleopatra* and *Captain Brassbound's Conversion* (both 1899), *Man and Superman* (1903), *John Bull's Other Island* (1904), *Major Barbara* (1905), *Androcles and the Lion* (1911), *Pygmalion* (1912), *Back to Methuselah* (1921), *The Apple Cart* (1929), and thenceforward as far as *Buoyant Billions*, written in 1947, when the playwright was ninety-one. Shaw's saddest work, *Heartbreak House* (1916), tingles with farce throughout; and that story of martyrdom *Saint Joan* (1923) opens with a farcical scene in which Robert de Baudricourt is intimidated by Joan's

apparently supernatural powers. But only in his one-acts did this mighty intellect of the theater let rip and give his clown the freedom of the house—in [names *Bashville, How He Lied, Dark Lady, Overruled, Augustus, O'Flaherty, Calais* and] most rampantly of all in *Passion, Poison and Petrifaction.*

Blamires, Harry. *Twentieth Century English Literature.* New York: Schocken Books, 1982. A number of references including a three-page summary and assessment of Shaw's achievement. "Paradox is powerful when it illuminates hidden truth at the expense of established prejudice: but it is only mildly entertaining when it projects the obvious at the expense of the generally discredited. What always redeems Shaw's comedies from the vapidity inherent in ideological shadow-boxing is the fluent and fertile argumentativeness, the comic topsy-turvydoms, and the unfailing Irish wit." "Any survey of Shaw's work will leave the impression of literary versatility and prodigality of a rare degree, and yet to search for a masterpiece comprehensively representative of his genius is vain, for the lasting comic qualities seem to emerge as by-products of energetic attempts to pose as social reformer or artist—sage."

Booth, Michael R. *Victorian Spectacular Theatre 1850–1910.* Boston, London and Henley: Routledge and Kegan Paul, 1981. Booth quotes GBS: "'The modern pantomime, as purveyed by the late Sir Augustus Harris, is neither visible nor audible. It is a glittering, noisy void, horribly wearisome and enervating like all performances which worry the physical senses without any recreative appeal to the emotions and through them to the intellect.' This was an extreme expression of the critical and intellectual hostility felt not only toward spectacle in pantomime but also to the place of spectacle in all forms of Victorian theatre."

Britain, Ian. *Fabianism and Culture. A Study in British Socialism and the Arts c. 1884–1918.* Cambridge, etc.: Cambridge University Press, 1982. Numerous references to GBS and most of the major plays, including a chapter on "Bernard Shaw," in which Britain describes Shaw's participation in the Fabian movement, noting among other matters that GBS didn't really want to "destroy art," but thought that "the death of traditional forms of art, as of traditional forms of economic organization, may be a part of the process by which art would find wider audiences and new practitioners throughout society."

Bruccoli, Matthew J. *Some Sort of Epic Grandeur, The Life of F. Scott Fitzgerald.* New York and London: Harcourt, Brace, Jovanovich, 1981. Fitzgerald and his friends admired Wells and GBS. There are only a few references here, including the following quotation of Fitzgerald: "'By style, I mean color,' he said. 'I want to be able to do anything with words: handle slashing, flaming descriptions like Wells, and use the paradox with the clarity of Samuel Butler, the breadth of Bernard Shaw and the wit of Oscar Wilde. . . . Conrad . . . Hichens . . . Kipling . . . Chesterton. . . .'"

Coale, Samuel. *Anthony Burgess.* New York: Ungar, 1981. Burgess praised the experimentalism in language of Whitman, Pound, Joyce, and Lawrence and "regarded the social significance of the language in Shaw's 'Pygmalion' as far-reaching and 'incredible.'"

Cockburn, Claud. *Cockburn Sums Up. An Autobiography.* New York, London, Melbourne: Quartet Books, 1981. Graham Greene called Cockburn, with G.K. Chesterton, one of the two greatest journalists of the century. Cockburn: "And at sixteen I read and profoundly appreciated Bernard Shaw's invaluable advice to 'get what you like, or you'll grow to like what you get.'"

Courtney, Richard. *Outline History of British Drama.* Totowa, New Jersey: Littlefield, Adams and Co., 1982. The entry for Shaw provides sixteen pages with headings, "Life, Early Plays: 1885–1900," "Mature Plays: 1900–1917," "Major Plays: 1918–1923," "The Malvern Years," and "Last Plays." Any single one of GBS's plays "would have made the reputation of a lesser dramatist." The selected secondary bibliography has no entry later than 1970. The index indicates numerous additional references to Shaw.

Coward, Noel. *The Noel Coward Diaries*. Edited by Graham Payn and Sheridan Morley. Boston and Toronto: Little, Brown, 1982. Index notes three references to Shaw, though there are actually at least a dozen, including a valuable one on speaking Shavian dialogue.

Dale, Alzina Stone. *The Outline of Sanity. A Biography of G. K. Chesterton*. Grand Rapids, Michigan: William B. Eerdmans Publishing Company, 1982. Many many references to Shaw, the plays, and Chesterton's relationship with G.B.S.

De Vitis, A. A., and Kalson, Albert E. *J. B. Priestley*. Boston: Twayne, 1980. There is little direct influence upon Priestley by Shaw, but Priestley thought about Shaw very carefully: "He held many beliefs but he did not hold them as most of us do. He never appeared to be emotionally committed to them. He could advance or defend them without anger. . . . Because he could hold his beliefs in his own peculiar fashion, keeping them free of negative emotions, he was able to create his own kind of comedy, good enough to put him among the world's great dramatists. This comedy of his has light without heat. The superbly theatrical wit crackles and dazzles and strikes without wounding. Behind the cut-and-thrust of the talk, like some smiling landscape behind a battle scene, is a vast golden good humour." "As for his assorted kittens, from Cleopatra to Orinthia, they are hygienic toys with never a gland in working order between them. No wonder that his greatest part for an actress is Joan of Arc."

Douglas, Helen Gahagan. *A Full Life*. Garden City, New York: Doubleday, 1982. Douglas, a Hollywood actress, opera singer, U.S. congresswoman, wife and mother, devotes several paragraphs to Arnold Daly's role in bringing Shaw's plays to New York, and the significance of Shavian drama in America.

Drakakis, John. See Lewis, Peter, ed., below.

Durrell, Lawrence. See MacNiven, Ian S., below.

Elborn, Geoffrey. *Edith Sitwell. A Biography*. Garden City, New York: Doubleday, 1981. One reference to GBS: Sitwell remembered she had made a film reading poetry with her brothers, that the technicians told her was very funny. But Bernard Shaw had not agreed, saying, "They are the biggest fools I have ever seen, you don't know what you are looking at." "That," said Edith, laughing, "was meant as a great compliment."

Ford, Colin, and Harrison, Brian. *A Hundred Years Ago. Britain in the 1880s in Words and Photographs*. Cambridge, Mass.: Harvard University Press, 1983. Although there are only four specific references to Shaw in the volume, it is nevertheless a valuable adjunct to Shaw studies, representing vividly what England, especially London, was like in his first full decade of residence after leaving Ireland (in 1876). The texture of English life is evoked graphically, and the chapter on "Social Tensions" is particularly valuable.

Gibbs, A. M. See Kosok, Heinz, below.

Goebbels, Joseph. *The Goebbels Diaries 1939–1941*. Translated and edited by Fred Taylor. New York: G. P. Putnam's Sons, 1983 (1982). There are at least seven references to Shaw, beginning on 11 October 1939. The last is 12 February 1940. GBS had written an article Hitler found very agreeable and Goebbels's entries record his own and Hitler's satisfaction with it. Sample: "With the Fuhrer. His is also amused, and laughs until the tears come when I read Shaw's article aloud to him. We can exploit this."

Goode, John. "Margaret Harkness and the Socialist Novel" in *The Socialist Novel in Britain: Towards the Recovery of a Tradition*. Edited by H. Gustav Klaus. New York: St. Martin's Press, 1982. A couple of references to *An Unsocial Socialist* and the remark that Morris and Shaw could not be realistic novelists because "realism" assumes reality is perceived and not constructed.

Grawe, Paul H. *Comedy in Space, Time and the Imagination.* Chicago: Nelson-Hall Publishers, 1982. Not seen. Flyer describes "Part Two. . . . 9. Romantic Comedy in Perspective: Shaw."

Grierson, John. *Grierson on the Movies.* Edited by Forsyth Hardy. London and Boston: Faber and Faber, 1981. A number of thoughtful references to GBS, including notice of *Arms and the Man, Androcles,* and *How He Lied to Her Husband,* in addition to the story of how Chaplin went to visit Shaw but got cold feet and left without seeing him.

Hamilton, Iain. *Koestler. A Biography.* New York: Macmillan, 1982. From an entry in Koestler's diary for July 30, 1949: "Bernard Shaw on his 93rd birthday called Stalin 'mainstay of peace.' Clowning through three-quarters of a century, never tiring of it. Still the naughty, naughty little boy. The most over-estimated writer of his time—"

Jeffares, A. Norman. *Anglo-Irish Literature.* New York: Schocken Books, 1982. A number of references to Shaw in addition to a five-page section, "II. George Bernard Shaw." Samples: "The difficulties affecting so many Anglo-Irish writers recur in the youth of . . . Shaw: lack of financial stability recorded with that self-conscious combination of pride and self-mockery, the result of being in a middle state neither Irish nor English, and hence detached observers of the human scene." "And he was a more orthodox dramatist than he sometimes appeared to be in his own time." "His claim [that comedy's 'terrible castigation' in GBS's versions was a higher form of dramatic art than tragedy], though backed by the superb dramatic skills which make so many of his plays still challenging and pleasurable, has not been received without some reserve: he was perhaps more in the grip of the comedy of manners than he realised. . . ."

Kilroy, Thomas. *"The Moon in the Yellow River*: Denis Johnston's Shavianism" in *Denis Johnston: A Retrospective.* Edited by Joseph Ronsley. Gerrards Cross: Colin Smythe, 1981; Totowa, New Jersey: Barnes and Noble, 1982. "The Shavianism of *The Moon in the Yellow River,* then, is a remarkable exercise, but one of the major reservations which one must have of the play is that Shaw does the same thing better in *Heartbreak House* and on a more ambitious scale." "As with Shaw, Johnston's specific concern is the dangerous absurdity of a situation where 'power and culture are in separate compartments.' The England of 1913 (and Shaw would claim it represented Europe) and the Ireland of the late twenties had this, at least, in common: both were threatened by violence and this violence was associated by both playwrights with a progressive materialism. The principal victim of this inhumane force in both plays is romanticism. It is typical of both Shaw and Johnston that while they see this fate as deserved, the romantic as an obsolete figure, it nevertheless allows them to concede a degree of guarded affection towards the romantic, however absurd he, Hector Hushabye or Darrell Blake, may be. What survives in both plays is a little community of inspired lunacy, people with a marvelous capacity to simply ignore or deflate the movement of power across their path. Observers of all this are Shotover and Dobelle, masters of the central rhetoric of the plays which is made up of scepticism, even misanthropy, plain-speaking and paradox and a vision which transcends the squalid present. It is an important part of the action of both plays that each man is reached, touched, restored by a figure of virginal girlhood."

Kosok, Heinz, ed. *Studies in Anglo-Irish Literature.* Bonn: Bouvier Verlag Herbert Grundmann, 1982. Includes the following three essays: A. M. Gibbs, "Bernard Shaw's Politics," proposes that Shaw's politics are a consistent Fabian socialism in *Intelligent Woman's Guide* (1928) and *Everybody's Political What's What?* (1944) and the other non-dramatic writings; but in the plays "Shaw comes close to a position of complete despair about man as a political animal." Rodelle Weintraub's "Captain Brassbound's Roots: The Ancestry of a Play" is a general analysis of the sources of the play. Stanley Weintraub's

"The Irish Playwright and the Irish Pirate: Bernard Shaw and Frank Harris, 1895–1931" is aptly described by this title, and is a version of the section in Weintraub's book, *The Unexpected Shaw* (1982).

Krause, David. *The Profane Book of Irish Comedy*. Ithaca, New York: Cornell University Press, 1982. Includes a section, "The Barbarous Morals of Shaw and Carroll," that discusses *John Bull's Other Island* as "one of those rare instances when Shaw allowed the poetry of drama to take precedence over propaganda, and so he concentrates on the comedy of defeat as the isolated Keegan remains magnificently mad and mockingly untriumphant at the end. Keegan has the saintly vision of Shaw's Joan without the vindicating glory of her beatitude." "The saintly Keegan's mad dream of a divine humanity has significant parallels to the heretical dreams of Shaw's St. Joan. They are both holy fools whose private visions are aimed at the salvation of their people. They are both essentially comic characters in a state of grace, wise fools who are so free from sin they cannot be seen as tragic. Joan especially has been mistakenly interpreted as a tragic heroine by most critics. On the contrary, I would go so far as to suggest that she is a comic-rogue heroine, a barbarous peasant girl who must profane all that passes for sacred belief in a corrupted world in order to reveal her divinely inspired and liberating faith in God through the individual conscience." In a different connection, "I sometimes think of Larry Doyle as an original for O'Neill's Larry Slade in *The Iceman Cometh*."

Lazarus, A. L., and Jones, Victor H. *Beyond Graustark: George Barr McCutcheon, Playwright Discovered*. London and Port Washington, New York: Kennikat, 1981. McCutcheon had the distinction of having works rejected by the Frohman Syndicate along with Ibsen and GBS. This account of McCutcheon's essentially failed career is loosely laced with the milepost notices of GBS's successful one.

Leary, Daniel, ed. *Shaw's Plays in Performance*. University Park: The Pennsylvania State University Press, 1983. Volume 3 of *Shaw. The Annual of Bernard Shaw Studies*, under the general editorship of Stanley Weintraub. For individual essays, see the volume's table of contents.

Lee, Hermione. *Elizabeth Bowen: An Estimation*. Totowa, New Jersey: Barnes and Noble, 1981. Bowen feels she belongs in the tradition stretching from "Swift to Bernard Shaw."

Lewis, Peter, ed. *Radio Drama*. London and New York: Longman, 1981. Two essays have GBS references: John Tydeman's "The Producer and Radio Drama: A Personal View" observes that *Doctor's Dilemma* took five days to prepare for radio, but would require as many weeks to prepare for television. John Drakakis's "The Essence That's not Seen: Radio Adaptations of Stage Plays" mentions *Doctor's Dilemma, Heartbreak, Mrs Warren* and *Saint Joan*, and finds "whereas Shaw's method is that of heightened naturalism, which allows his plays to adapt well to radio, the diffuseness of response and the constant adjustments of critical distance demanded by Brecht's make them intractable."

MacNiven, Ian S., and Moore, Harry T., eds. *Literary Lifelines, The Richard Aldington-Lawrence Durrell Correspondence*. New York: Viking, 1981. Aldington helped Ford Madox Ford write *When Blood is Their Argument*, an attempt to answer GBS's anti-war propaganda. Durrell, the major modern British novelist, in a December 1959 letter says, "I also have a wonderful insulting letter from Bernard Shaw written in a trembling hand which warns me against peddling pornography." An Aldington letter of 10 October 1961 reveals a glimpse of contemporary interaction among scholars, critics, and living writers and associates who have become subjects of the scholars' research. Aldington quotes a letter to him from Stanley Weintraub, written while Weintraub was working on a study of T.E. Lawrence and GBS, noticing that the allegation that Aldington had concocted a letter to Mrs. GBS was certainly false, and that Weintraub had attempted to say so in a letter to the *Times*.

Martin, Stoddard. *Wagner to "The Waste Land." A Study of the Relationship of Wagner to English Literature*. London and Basingstoke: Macmillan Press, Ltd., 1982. Included is a twenty-page chapter on "Shaw," along with chapters on Swinburne, Wilde, Symons, Moore, Yeats, Joyce, Lawrence, and T.S.Eliot. None of the Shaw/Wagner matter is new. "That he was a political Wagnerian is open to question, and a philosophical Wagnerian to serious debate. Still, to the extent that he was these things, and a literary Wagnerian after an idiosyncratic style, we might call him a Wagnerian of a second type: one who much like Nietzsche eschewed decadent Romanticism, and claimed Wagner as his 'sound Shavian' precursor in a tradition of 'heroic vitalist' art and idea."

Muggeridge, Malcolm. *Like it Was. The Diaries of Malcolm Muggeridge*. Edited by John Bright-Holmes. New York: Morrow, 1982. A number of references to GBS, mostly uncomplimentary, from the early 1930s to the middle 1950s. In April 1957, "Saw *My Fair Lady*, fantastically successful musical here. Not really very good, and in so far as Shaw's *Pygmalion* comes through, Abhorrent. How Shaw despised the poor and hated them. What a fabulous snob!"

Murray, Christopher. *"The Golden Cuckoo*: 'A Very Remarkable Bird'" in *Denis Johnston: A Retrospective*. Edited by Joseph Ronsley. Gerrards Cross: Colin Smythe, 1981; Totowa, New Jersey: Barnes and Noble Books, 1982. In *Golden Cuckoo* Johnston must move the play to a level of meaning above the trivial. "The point is akin to the moment in Shaw's *Major Barbara* when Barbara sees herself as betrayed by God (in that scene in the West Ham shelter when the Salvation Army accepts her father's cheque in spite of its origins). Dotheright, having learned that he is regarded judicially as insane, cries out: 'I am betrayed. Oh Heaven—betrayed! . . . But my voices—my voices? Do they not want my—my services? (*He grows very calm as he gazes upwards.*) Is there nobody up there?' . . . Whereas in Shaw this is the point of a new departure for Barbara, who comes eventually to a new concept of salvation by social revolution, according to the 'gospel' of Undershaft, in Johnston this is the moment of tragic awareness."

Nightingale, Benedict. *A Reader's Guide to Fifty Modern British Plays*. London: Heinemann; Totowa, New Jersey: Barnes & Noble, 1982. He chooses five plays by GBS, noting in his introduction "If the criterion was merit alone, I might end up with fifty plays by Shaw, Synge, O'Casey, Beckett, Pinter, and perhaps five or six others." The commentaries avoid plot summary and move quickly to intelligent analysis. On *Superman*: "A man's ideals have been dented, yet so have his myopia, complacency and folly; he has lost himself, he has the opportunity to find himself in a new and perhaps profounder way; marriage may mar him, marriage may make him. There is reason to feel pessimistic about his future, reason to feel optimistic, and reason to respect a play that ends by making us feel both at the same time." On *Major Barbara*: "So here we have Shaw the armchair revolutionary, with his intellectual bloodthirstiness; but also Shaw the intellectual provocateur, inciting debate and disagreement on a considerable range of subjects. Not many English plays have managed to be simultaneously serious about politics and religion." On *Pygmalion*: "This, perhaps, is the play's basic stance. . . . It is . . . a defence of a person's right to own and develop his or her soul." On *Heartbreak House*: Shaw may have considered this his greatest play. He acknowledged his debt to Chekhov. "The difference is that Chekhov's characters are more realistic, richer and more resonant, Shaw's the representatives of ideas, points of view, that shift and alter during the play, but do not become more credible as sentient, suffering people. Perhaps he should have subtitled it, 'a fantasia in the Shavian manner on Chekhovian themes.'" On *Saint Joan*: "Some have found the speech that ends the play mawkish, but it is surely inevitable: 'O God, that madest this beautiful earth, when will it be ready to receive Thy saints? How long, O God, how long?' The struggle between the Joans and the world will, *must*, continue: Shavian philosophy in a nutshell."

Nixon, Richard. *Leaders*. New York: Warner Books, 1982. Nixon remembers, "When GBS sent him [Churchill] two theatre tickets and a note reading, 'Come to my play and bring a friend, if you have a friend.' Churchill sent a reply that read, 'I am busy for the opening, but I will come the second night, if there is a second night,'" illustrating Churchill's capacity for being acerbic. Such second hand stuff doesn't distinguish Nixon's account.

O'Neill, Eugene, and Macgowan, Kenneth. *The Theatre We Worked For: The Letters of Eugene O'Neill and Kenneth Macgowan*. Edited by Jackson R. Bryer. New Haven and London: Yale University Press, 1982. References to GBS by each correspondent, both of whom respected Shaw. Letters span years from 1920 to 1951.

Orr, John. *Tragic Drama and Modern Society. Studies in the Social and Literary Theory of Drama from 1870 to the Present*. Totowa, New Jersey: Barnes and Noble, 1981. A number of interesting references to Shaw and his plays: Shaw's *Quintessence* diminished the significance of the tragic dimension of Ibsen's drama to misrepresent "it as a didactic condemnation of all forms of moral and political idealism. Shaw's Ibsen, largely conceived in Shaw's own image, ends up as an apostle of reform and commonsense, a Fabian of the fjords." "Despite the efforts of his most fervent supporters, Shaw amongst them, Ibsen was never given a true theatrical voice in the English theatre. As a serious dramatist, Shaw proved unable to fill the vacuum. The Edwardian age thus saw the English stage divided in tripartite fashion between a truncated Ibsen, a satirical Shaw, and a rather stiff and old-fashioned Galsworthy." On *Heartbreak*: "His idiosyncratic attempt to present Chekhovian themes to the English theatre audience for the first time." "Shaw was too literal and too sensational in bombing the upper classes out of existence, and too insubstantial in making the parasites of his eccentric 'ship' no better than caricatures. The problem was not merely thematic. He had failed to find a suitable form for serious drama, and any tragedy of contemporary life then became impossible." On *Saint Joan*: "The fact that in the one play where he really confronted the issues head on, he resorted to historical drama, meant that his dramatic work lost much in the process. Joan was a fascinating historical figure in her own right—which explains the attractiveness of the play for modern audiences—but direct references to Shaw's own life and times which the play might evoke invariably take second place."

Richards, David. *Played Out. The Jean Seberg Story*. New York: Random House, 1981. Seberg's experience during the European and American premières of *Saint Joan*, the film version in which she played the lead, is substantially analyzed. It was a critical failure as well as a commercial one. "'Two films in her career are the key to Jean,' says Dennis Berry. 'They are *St. Joan* and *Lilith*.' *St. Joan*, he believes, called upon all her intrinsic idealism, although she was too young at the time to express it adequately on the screen. 'In the late sixties she tried to become St. Joan in real life,' Berry says. 'And her crusading led her into total despair.'" Seberg spent much of the final year of her life in mental institutions.

Shoben, Edward Joseph, Jr. *Lionel Trilling*. New York: Ungar, 1981. Only a few references, but one is important because it recalls Trilling's admiration for GBS: "In the 'heartbreak' of Bernard Shaw's *Heartbreak House*, he found 'the beginning of new courage, and I can think of no more useful political job for the literary man today than, by the representation of despair, to cauterize the exposed soft tissue of too-easy hope.'"

Silver. Arnold. *Bernard Shaw. The Darker Side*. Stanford: Stanford University Press, 1982. Reviewed in this volume.

Slade, Joseph W. "The Porn Market and Porn Formulas: The Feature Film of the Seventies" in *Movies as Artifacts. Cultural Criticism of Popular Film*. Edited by Michael T. Marsden, et al. Chicago: Nelson-Hall, 1982. Radley Metzger's pornographic film *The Opening of Misty Beethoven* (1975) is a "rip-off" of Shaw's *Pygmalion* and its "success is at least partly a function of the congruence between Shaw's plot line and an ancient porn formula in which an older male educates a young girl into sexual knowingness."

Sprinchorn, Evert. *Strindberg As Dramatist*. New Haven and London: Yale University Press, 1982. Sprinchorn observes that Shaw and Strindberg were both vitalists. "Both believed that the vital spirit, however erratic its actions might appear, represented, in contrast to Schopenhauer's indifferent and directionless world will, a beneficent will striving to perfect itself by overcoming matter." For GBS it would be intellect that would triumph. For Strindberg it would be spirit. Moreover, neither believed in the devil, especially as evidenced in the history of man. "If the ultimate purpose of the social movements of history was beyond Tolstoy's comprehension, Strindberg and Shaw understood that these social movements had led to the increased power and improved welfare of the people."

Tennant, Roger. *Joseph Conrad*. New York: Atheneum, 1981. Four references including Conrad's delight with Shaw's praise of his play *One Day More*: "On the other hand the celebrated 'man of the hour' G.B. Shaw, was ecstatic and enthusiastic. 'Dramatist,' says he."

Thompson, Lawrence, and Winnick, R. H. *Robert Frost, A Biography*. Condensed by Edward Connery Lathem. One interesting reference: Frost read aloud to and delighted Sidney Cox, 22-year-old Plymouth highschool teacher, newly discovered favorites such as Synge's *Playboy of the Western World* and Shaw's *Arms and the Man*.

Thurman, Judith. *Isak Dinesen. The Life of a Storyteller*. New York: St. Martin's, 1982. Dinesen believed with Shaw, whom she was reading in autumn of 1923, that the middle classes of the late nineteenth century confused love and marriage. Later she met GBS.

Tydeman, John. See Lewis, Peter, above.

Valency, Maurice. *The Cart and the Trumpet. The Plays of George Bernard Shaw*. New York: Schocken, 1983. A paperback reprint of one of the better critical studies of Shaw.

Vitelli, James R. *Randolph Bourne*. Boston: Twayne, 1981. Bourne much preferred Shaw to Chesterton, having read and swallowed Shaw's works whole. He felt the preface to *Getting Married* might be the "profoundest and wisest word on the matter ever written." He hoped we could overthrow "the evil tentacles of English civilization in America and work the feminine into our spirit and life . . . the personal, the non-official, the spirit that Tolstoi preaches in *Resurrection* and Shaw in his best plays. . . ."

Walker, Alexander. *Peter Sellers. The Authorized Biography*. New York: Macmillan, 1981. Contains a substantial account of the circumstances and results of casting Sophia Loren along with Sellers in Shaw's *Millionairess* in the film version. It led to Sellers's major fame. Includes a photo of Loren and Sellers in *Millionairess*.

Wallace, Amy; Wallechinsky, David; and Wallace, Irving. *The Book of Lists #3*. New York: Morrow, 1983. Shaw is named in four categories among "Non-Nazis who admired Hitler," "Notable Marriage Proposals" (to Annie Besant), "Chronic Headache Sufferers," and "Gone with the Wind, sort of: Ashes of 19 Famous People—and 1 Dog."

Webb, Beatrice. *The Diary of Beatrice Webb*. Volume One, 1873–1892. Edited by Norman and Jeanne MacKenzie. Cambridge: The Belknap Press of Harvard University Press, 1982. Seven references to GBS in the body of the volume. Shaw would not meet Beatrice Potter until 1890.

Weintraub, Rodelle. See Kosok, Heinz, above.

Weintraub, Stanley. *The Unexpected Shaw. Biographical Approaches to G.B.S. and His Work*. New York: Frederick Ungar, 1983. Reviewed in this volume.

————. See also Kosok, Heinz, above.

————, ed. *Modern British Dramatists, 1900–1945. Dictionary of Literary Biography*, volume 10. Detroit: Gale, 1982. In addition to a lengthy essay on Shaw himself (part 2, pp. 129–48), including dates of all first performances and both primary and secondary bibliographies and illustrations from productions, this two-book volume offers equivalent although less extensive treatment of about seventy GBS contemporaries, including Pinero, Jones, Barker, Archer, Hankin, Bridie, Coward, Galsworthy, Barrie, and Maugham. Many of these essays also include Shavian references. Appendices include Shaw's views on stage censorship extracted from the *Blanco Posnet* preface and references to Shaw in essays on the theater in Ireland and on the theater during the two world wars.

————. *British Dramatists since World War II. Dictionary of Literary Biography*, volume 13. Detroit: Gale, 1983. The two-book volume includes essays on disciples, contemporaries and successors of Shaw, with references to him in biographies of such playwrights as Benn Levy, Terence Rattigan, Tom Stoppard, John Bowen, Ronald Duncan, Nigel Dennis and John Whiting, and others. Appendices to part 2 include Martin Quinn's "The National Theatre and the Royal Shakespeare Companies: the National Companies" (pp. 619–35), which details the involvements of Shaw, Barker, and Archer in getting a national theater concept translated into reality.

————. *The Playwright and the Pirate. Bernard Shaw and Frank Harris: A Correspondence*. University Park: The Pennsylvania State University Press, 1982; Gerrard's Cross: Colin Smythe, Ltd., 1983. Reviewed in this volume.

Wintle, Justin, ed., *Makers of Nineteenth Century Culture, 1800–1914*. London & Boston: Routledge & Kegan Paul, 1982. Curiously, Shaw is not represented by a biographical essay (he will be in a 20th century volume) although he became active as critic and polemicist in 1876, and was a national figure by the 1890s. Still, he turns up in many essays àbout others, including some misleading references, as in the Edison essay, where it appears that Shaw worked personally on Thomas Edison's "London company staff" rather than briefly for a firm using Edison's name. The W. S. Gilbert biography calls Shaw "a life-long admirer"—although nothing could be further from the truth.

Woolf, Virginia. *The Diary of Virginia Woolf*. Volume IV, 1931–1935. Edited by Anne Olivier Bell; assisted by Andrew McNeillie. New York and London: Harcourt, Brace, Jovanovich, 1982. Ten references to GBS.

III. Periodicals

Amalric, Jean-Claude. Review of *Shaw and Religion, Shaw, The Annual of Bernard Shaw Studies*, edited by Charles A. Berst, the first issue of the *Shaw* annual. *Victorian Studies*, XXVI, no. 1 (Autumn 1982), 107–8.

Barker, Chris. "Shaw on Music," a review of *Shaw's Music*, edited by Dan H. Laurence. *The Cambridge Quarterly*, XI, no. 1 (1982), 265–75. A substantial essay that agrees with the opinion that Shaw's music criticism is the most brilliant ever written.

Bertolini, J. A. "Shaw's Ironic View of Caesar." *Twentieth Century Literature*, XXVII, no. 4 (Winter 1981) 331–42. Not seen.

Bradford, Sarah, "Sale of autograph letters and MSS [at Christie's]," *TLS*, March 11, 1983, p. 252. A half-page largely on the sale, on February 23, 1983, of Mrs. Patrick Campbell's letters to Shaw (for £7,560, to Christopher Wood), including some withheld from publication in the Alan Dent edition (1952) by her descendants because she came off badly in her second marriage, to George Cornwallis-West—the younger man whom she married after finally spurning Shaw's passion. That infatuation—Shaw was 58 when it ended—is further documented in the letters.

Brain, Richard. "Arms and the Ideal Society," a review of the Lyttleton Theatre production of *Major Barbara. TLS* (November 19, 1982), p. 1271.

Carpenter, Charles A. "Shaw" in "Modern Drama Studies: An Annual Bibliography." *Modern Drama*, XXV, no. 2 (June 1982), 247–48. Twenty-seven entries, plus three cross-referenced items, including items not listed in *Shaw* checklists, from 1978 to 1981.

Chisholm, Shirley. In "Parting Words, Mostly Somber." *Time* (June 21, 1982), p. 82. In a baccalaureate speech at Spellman College in Atlanta: "For far too many females, home is still—as George Bernard Shaw noted—'the girl's prison and the woman's workhouse.' . . ."

Czarnecki, M. "A Festival in Search of a Foundation." *Macleans*, (June 7, 1982), pp. 62–63. Wonders whether Shaw's plays are good enough to support a "Shaw Festival." Has no encouraging answer.

DeVine, Lawrence. "Gambling Shaw Director Girding for Critics." *Detroit Free Press* (Sunday; May 16, 1982), p. 4G. A sample of American reaction to the continuing controversy, critical and economic, surrounding the Shaw Festival in Canada.

"George Bernard Shaw" in the 1981–1982 Annual Review number of *Journal of Modern Literature*, IX, nos. 3/4 (December 1982), 531–32. Eleven selected entries, plus nine additional citations through the index, representing years from 1978 to 1981.

Grene, Nicholas. "Dramatist at Work," a careful and extensive review of *Bernard Shaw: Early Texts: Play Manuscripts in Facsimile. TLS* (July 16, 1982), p. 768.

Hobson, Harold. "Drunk with Rhetoric," a review of the Theatre Royal, Haymarket, production of *Man and Superman. TLS* (December 3, 1982), p. 1337.

Holroyd, Michael. "St. Christopher and the Dear Childe," a review of Mary Hyde's edition of the Bernard Shaw/Alfred Douglas correspondence. *TLS* (December 31, 1982), p. 1438.

———. "Subtle Feeling for a Brass Band," a review of Theatre Royal, Haymarket, production of *Captain Brassbound's Conversion. TLS* (June 25, 1982), p. 692.

———. "Chivalrous Shaw and Horrible Harris," a review of Stanley Weintraub's *The Playwright and the Pirate, The Sunday Times* [of London], 13 March 1983, p. 44. An essay on the mismatched pair and on the writing of Shavian biographies, with no perceptible critical comment on the edition.

Hyde, H. Montgomery. "Shaw and His Disciple," a review of Mary Hyde's edition of the Bernard Shaw/Alfred Douglas correspondence. *Books and Bookmen*, CCCXXVI (November 1982), 19–21.

Klein, Alfonso. Review of Gordon N. Bergquist's *The Pen and the Sword: War and Peace in the Prose and Plays of Bernard Shaw. Anglia, Zeitschrift für Englische Philologie*, Band 100, Heft 3/4 (1982), 546–48.

Lipman, Samuel. "Pshaw!" *The American Scholar*, LI, no. 4 (Autumn 1982), 513–20. A pianist and a music critic for *Commentary* writes an account of Bernard Shaw as music critic, noting that the recent publication of *Shaw's Music*, edited by Dan Laurence, among other works, makes the task easier to do than before. Samples from Lipman: "He was not, on the most tolerant of assessments, a trained musician. It hardly mattered; there were, after all, established music critics entrenched in English concert life who knew all about music. Shaw knew something much more valuable: he knew what he liked." One must wonder "what there is in Shaw's record to justify the nearly universal assessment of him as the finest music critic in the English language. This strong judgment, which has been widely held for many years, has now been reinforced by the enthusiastic reception given to the present edition both here and in England."

Morgan, Kenneth. "Purpose before Pleasure." *TLS* (July 23, 1982), p. 883. This review of

Ian Britain's Fabianism and Culture (see "Books and Pamphlets" above) is decorated with a photo of Beatrice and Sidney Webb and GBS from the *Illustrated Dictionary of British History*, edited by Arthur Marwick.

Myer, Valerie Grosvenor. "*Peregrine Pickle* and *Pygmalion*." *Notes and Queries*, XXVIII (October 1981), 430–31. Shaw admits his debt to Henry Sweet in *Pygmalion*, but not to Smollet's *Peregrine* (1751). All the key incidents of *Pygmalion* parallel those in Smollet's novel. "It cannot be coincidence that both Eliza and Peregrine's beggar girl are married off with wedding presents of £500."

Tobias, Richard C. "Shaw" in "Victorian Bibliography for 1981." *Victorian Studies*, XXV, no. 4 (Summer 1982), 603. Eighteen entries and cross-references.

Weales, Gerald. Review of Bernard Dukore's *Money and Politics in Ibsen, Shaw and Brecht. Modern Drama*, XXV, no. 4 (December 1982), 578–80.

———. Review of *Collected Screenplays of Bernard Shaw*, Bernard Dukore, ed., *The Georgia Review*, XXXVI, no. 4 (Winter 1982), 923–26.

Woodfield, James. Review of J. L. Wisenthal's, editor, *Shaw and Ibsen: Bernard Shaw's The Quintessence of Ibsenism and Related Writings. English Studies in Canada*, VIII, no. 4 (December 1982), 517–20.

The Independent Shavian. XX, no. 1 (1982). Journal of the Bernard Shaw Society. Includes "Bernard Shaw on the Jews" by Bernard Shaw, "Shavian Word From the Nation's Capital," "Why Not Another Why Not?" "Reds," "The World Betterer: Shav Versus Shav" by Richard Nickson, "When Else?" "The Right of Controversy," "Milestones or No?" "A Corker," "Shavian Foresight," "American Shaw Festival," "Society Activities," "Déjà Vu," "You Never Can Tell," "News About Our Members," and "Our Cover."

The Independent Shavian. XX, nos. 2/3 (1982). Journal of the Bernard Shaw Society. Includes "The Atom Bomb" by Bernard Shaw, "Throwing Atomic Bombs" by Bernard Shaw, "'Creation, not Destruction'," "Moot Question," "The Science of Wishful Thinking," "The Art of Realist Thinking," "A Devilish Addendum," "Shaw and the Bomb" by Richard Nickson, "On Books and Bookshops" by Bernard Shaw, "Too True to Be . . . Juliet," "Imitatio Shavi," "G.B.S. as a Member of Parliament," "Shaw Cornered," "Shaw on Spiritualism, Creationism, and Contraception," "Shavings-on-the-Lake," "Shaw and Wilder Again" by Richard H. Goldstone, "The Good Side of Cathleen Nesbitt," "Shaw's Purity of Diction," "Wells and Shaw," "Book Review" [of the first issue of the *Shaw* annual] by Fort Manno, "Shaw Among the Artists," "Book Review" [of Elizabeth Langford's *Eminent Victorian Women*] by Lillian Wachtel, "News About Our Members," "Society Activities," and "Our Cover."

IV. Dissertations

Al-Abdullah, Mufeed Faleh. *The Legacy of Prospero in Twentieth Century British and American Drama* (Indiana University 1981). *DAI*, 43 (July 1982), 172–A. "This dissertation examines the dramatic archetype [Prospero] of Shakespeare's *The Tempest*, testing it in Philip Barry's *Hotel Universe*, T. S. Eliot's *The Cocktail Party*, Bernard Shaw's *Heartbreak House*, William Saroyan's *The Time of Your Life* and Eugene O'Neill's *The Iceman Cometh*." In Shaw's and Saroyan's plays "the redeemer shows a limited success in the consummation of his healing mission."

Coskren, Robert Patrick. *Resonances of Wagner's Ring in the Plays of Bernard Shaw* (Pennsylvania State University 1981). *DAI*, 42 (April 1982), 4456–A. "Traces *Ring* elements in the plays of Bernard Shaw. These are taken to be emblematic of the larger influence, primarily psychological, of the German upon the British dramatist." The human scene tended to present itself to GBS in Wagnerian analogues. Shows *Ring* elements in *Widower's Houses, Candida, Man of Destiny, Major Barbara, Methuselah, Saint Joan, Apple Cart* and *Heartbreak House.*

Day, Arthur R. *The Shaw Festival at Niagara-on-the-Lake in Ontario, Canada, 1962–1981: A History* (Bowling Green State University 1982). *DAI*, 43 (January 1983), 2157–A. Includes 1) how the Festival's founders overcame the first problems of limited facilities and "less than full support"; 2) a *first* documented study of the Festival; 3) an attempt to fit it into the context of other studies of histories of theatres such as Arena Stage in Washington, D.C., the Alley Theatre in Houston, and the Stratford Shakespeare Festival Theatre in Stratford, Ontario; and 4) a discussion of the theatre/community relations in a summer resort town of about 3000 residents. The study makes substantial use of minutes of the Shaw Festival Board and the Niagara-on-the-Lake town council, and personal interviews.

Kershner, William Robert. *The Theatre as a Social Institution: A Study of Harley Granville-Barker's Theories of Theatrical Art* (University of Southern California 1981). *DAI*, 42 (April 1982), 4203–A. Deals in part with the relationship of Shaw and Granville-Barker, especially in matters surrounding the Court Theatre successes that brought world fame to both.

Kiser, Edmond Lawrence. *The "Inspirational" System of Philip Moeller, Theatre Guild Director* (Wayne State University 1981). *DAI*, 42 (May 1982), 4650–A. Moeller's system: "extensive experience plus thorough pre-rehearsal preparation equals inspired directing." "O'Neill, Elmer Rice, S.N. Behrman, Maxwell Anderson and others . . . [let Moeller] revise their scripts as he directed them; furthermore, even George Bernard Shaw allowed Moeller to direct two of his world premières."

Luter, Gary Sheldon. *Sexual Reform on the American Stage in the Progressive Era, 1900–1915* (University of Florida 1981). *DAI*, 43 (July 1982), 18–A. Notices, among other things, that "productions of Clyde Fitch's *Sapho* (1900), Shaw's *Mrs Warren's Profession* (1905) and Eugene Walter's *The Easiest Way* (1909), which argued against the sexual double standard, were censored and suppressed by outraged anti-vice crusaders."

Marcus, Maury Hal. *Freedom and Tyranny in the Theatre of Late Franco Spain* (Southern Illinois University 1981). *DAI*, 42 (April 1982), 4203–A. "Spain's politically aware playwrights . . . used portrayals of historical conflicts to present opposition to current authoritarian practices. . . ." Among major Western dramatists, Euripides, Aristophanes, Shakespeare, Shaw, Brecht, Anouilh, Sartre and Miller followed this practice.

Taub, Michael. *The Martyr as Tragic Heroine: The Joan of Arc Theme in the Theater of Schiller, Shaw, Anouilh and Brecht* (University of North Carolina, Chapel Hill 1982). *DAI*, 43 (November 1982), 1536–A. "Explores the tragic aspects" of the plays of these writers with Max Scheler's "theory of the tragic."

Vincent, Judith. *George Bernard Shaw, Novelist: The Right Man in the Wrong Place?* (University of East Anglia, Norwich, England 1981). Abstract provided by author for following excerpts and summary: "In choosing to write novels, Shaw had not lost his way. . . . Shaw attempted to challenge the assumptions which he considered underpinned the novel of the 1880s, and that his own fiction demonstrates a distinctly Shavian theory of fiction as well as attacking the weaknesses and inadequacies of the contemporary novel." Chapter I explains why Shaw started with novels rather than plays, and outlines his theory of fiction. Chapter II explains how the novels weren't successful. The remaining five chapters are devoted each to the five GBS novels: The presentation of character in *Immaturity*; the critique of conventional portrayals of love, marriage, and the heroine in *The Irrational Knot*; Shaw's theory of art in *Love Among the Artists*; a satirical attack on the conventions of the popular novel in *Cashel Byron's Profession*; and the problem of Shaw as a propagandist in *An Unsocial Socialist.*

V. Recordings

Gandhi. Directed by Richard Attenborough. Los Angeles: Columbia Pictures, 1982. Academy Award nominee for Best Picture, selects Bernard Shaw as one of three or four British personages to remember having been met by Gandhi when Gandhi went to England. GBS is not seen, but named in the film by the voice of a newsreel narrator.

Contributors

Jean-Claude Amalric is Director of the Centre d'Études et de Recherches Victoriennes et Édouardiennes at the Université Paul Valéry, Montpellier, France, and the editor of its journal, *Cahiers Victoriens & Édouardiens*.

Karl Beckson is Professor of English at Brooklyn College of the City University of New York. An authority on Wilde and the 1890s, he is author of a biography of Henry Harland, editor of the memoirs of Arthur Symons, and editor of the *Critical Heritage* volume, *Oscar Wilde*.

Charles A. Berst is Professor of English at the University of California, Los Angeles, author of *Bernard Shaw and the Art of Drama* and editor of *Shaw and Religion (Shaw, I, 1981)*.

Marianne Bosch teaches English and German language and literature at a private school in Baden-Baden, Federal Republic of Germany. Her M.A. at Albert Ludwigs University in Freiburg involved a thesis on Shaw.

Ray Bradbury is the author of a recent collection of verse as well as the novelist of *The Martian Chronicles* and *Fahrenheit 451*.

Constance Cummings made her Broadway debut in 1928 and her London debut in 1934. She has appeared in Shakespeare and Shaw, has acted in *Who's Afraid of Virginia Woolf?* and narrated *Peter and the Wolf*.

Richard F. Dietrich is Professor of English at the University of South Florida and author of a book on Shaw, *Portrait of the Artist as a Young Superman*.

Bernard F. Dukore is Professor of Drama and Theatre at the University of Hawaii, author of *Bernard Shaw, Playwright*, and *Bernard Shaw, Director* as well as editor of *The Collected Screenplays of Bernard Shaw*.

Daniel Leary, Professor of English at the City College of the City University of New York, is the author of many critical articles on Shaw and editor of *Shaw's Plays in Performance* (*Shaw*, 3, 1983).

Frederick P. W. McDowell is author of books on Forster and other 20th century masters, and is working on a book on Shaw, about whom he has been writing critical essays since the early 1950s. He is Professor of English at the University of Iowa.

W. R. Martin is Professor of English at the University of Waterloo, Ontario, Canada. He has published on other moderns but this is his first essay on Shaw.

The late Lisë Pedersen was Professor of English at McNeese State University, Lake Charles, Louisiana. An earlier essay by her on the Shakespearean element in Shaw appeared in *Fabian Feminist: Bernard Shaw and Woman*.

John R. Pfeiffer, Bibliographer of *Shaw*, is also noted as a bibliographer of science fiction. He is Professor of English at Central Michigan University, Mount Pleasant, Michigan.

Martin Quinn, Foreign Service information officer with the United States Information Agency, has been assigned to the American Embassy in Ryadh, Saudi Arabia. His biographical essay on William Archer recently appeared in *Modern British Dramatists 1900–1945*.

Alfred Turco, Jr. is Associate Professor of English at Wesleyan University, Middletown, Connecticut, and author of *Shaw's Moral Vision: The Self and Salvation*.

Stanley Weintraub, General Editor of *Shaw* and editor of this volume, is Research Professor and Director of the Institute for the Arts and Humanistic Studies at The Pennsylvania State University, University Park. He is the author or editor of a number of books on Shaw, including two reviewed in this volume.

Sam A. Yorks is Professor of English at Portland State University in Oregon and author of *The Evolution of Bernard Shaw*.